FORTIES FASHION

Gants d'Alexandrine,
parapluie "Abri de Greéné
Sac et écharpe de Henry a la Pensée
Gants d'Alexandrine
Sac de Dubost
Gants de Aris
Sac cachemire de Duvelleroy
Gants de Nicolet
Sac parapluie de Jac
Gants Perrin
Sac de Dal
Gants d He
Ascott
Jean Hervey
Joseph Casale
Gillet
Georgette
Marc
Léandre

JONATHAN WALFORD

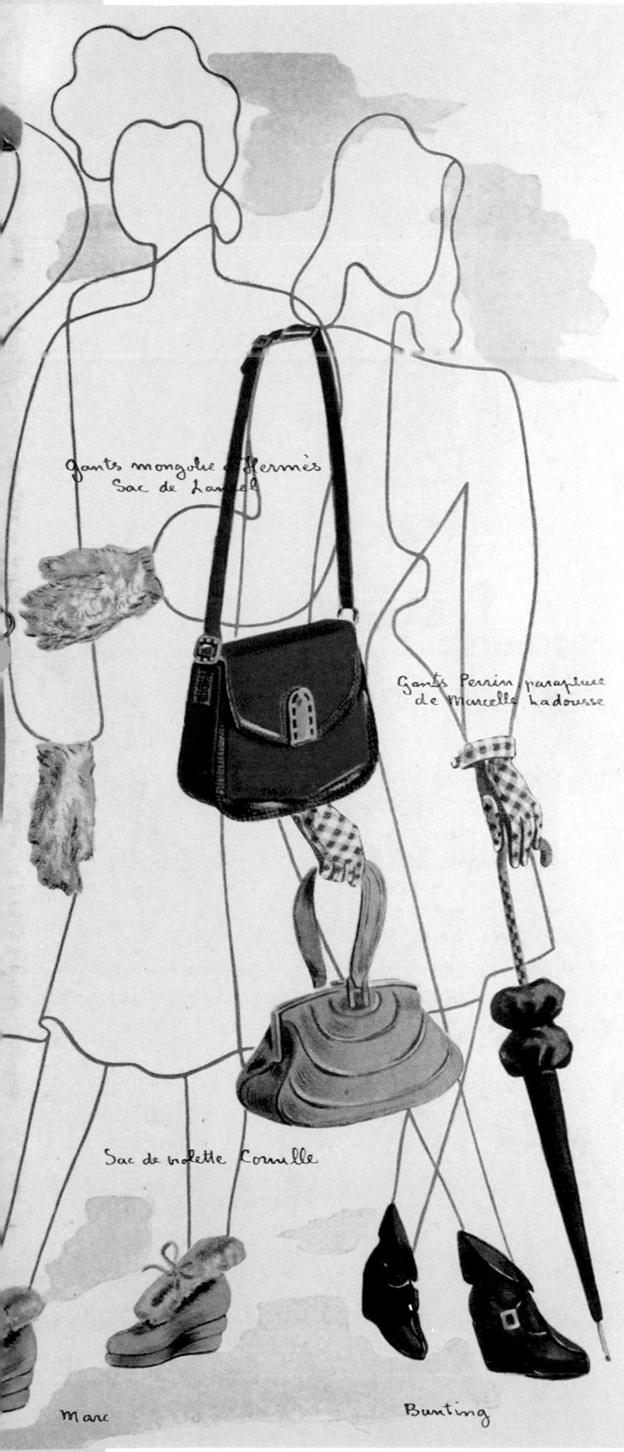

FORTIES FASHION

FROM SIREN SUITS TO THE NEW LOOK

With 250 illustrations, 196 in color

Thames & Hudson

To Ann

On the cover:

For captions to the illustrations on pp. 1–4, see pp. 46, 166 and 181.

First published in 2008 in hardcover in the United States of America by
Thames & Hudson Inc., 500 Fifth Avenue,
New York, New York 10110

thamesandhudsonusa.com

First paperback edition 2011

Library of Congress Catalog Card Number 2008900999

ISBN 978-0-500-28897-9

Printed and bound in China by Everbest Printing Co. Ltd

CONTENTS

INTRODUCTION 6

DRESSING THE NATION
Preparing the home front for conflict 10

KANGAROO POCKETS AND SIREN SUITS
Dress, patriotism, and propaganda in the first year of war 24

RATIONING, UTILITY, AND AUSTERITY
The British way to winning the war in fashion 36

INDEPENDENCE AND LIMITATIONS
The rise of the American designer under wartime restrictions 58

ZOOTS AND ZAZOUS *Anti-fashion in a time of crisis* 82

BEAUTY ON DUTY
The war effort and the pursuit of novelty and beauty 90

MAKING DO *Creative solutions for dire shortages* 108

PACIFIC FRONTS
Japan, Australia, New Zealand, and Canada 132

OCCUPATION COUTURE *Paris ignores the war* 142

PIECES OF RESISTANCE
New regimes and everyday apparel 158

FASHION AMONG THE RUINS *The German home front* 168

NEW LOOKS *Rebuilding fashion in the post-war world* 180

Acknowledgments 204
Bibliography 204
Index 206

INTRODUCTION

The war started only days after the final autumn 1939 couture fashion show had been held in Paris. Innovations included a proliferation of tweed suits that could take a woman from mid-morning to late afternoon functions. Hemlines hovered at about 15 inches (38 centimetres) from the ground, and most skirts showed an A-line silhouette, sometimes with a small bustle or peplum. Jackets were narrowly tailored at the waist. For evening, waists were even tighter, sometimes corseted, creating an hourglass figure in a full-skirted evening gown with sweetheart neckline, worn with coloured gloves or a tiny muff.

In the first Paris collections after Britain and France declared war on Germany on 3 September 1939, practical clothes for the domestic market were still designed with an eye for beauty. In Paris and London utilitarian capes with large pockets and hoods, trousers and zipper-fronted jumpsuits appeared, as suitable and smart attire for bomb shelters. Turbans showed up as fashionable and efficient coverings that protected the hair from grime and accidents at industrial plants, where many women took up occupations building armaments. The beginning of war did not mean the end of glamour: the skirts of bouffant evening gowns slimmed down and long-sleeved evening dresses to combat chilly interiors were shown with matching jewelled jackets or cardigans.

It might seem irreverent to consider fashion in the context of a war that resulted in so many civilian deaths. But the experience of war ranged dramatically according to who and where you were. Obviously fashion was of no concern to those living under desperate affliction or confinement – but where hope existed, so did fashion. Survival and victory were priorities, but for most civilians life still went on between the air raids. The influences of World War II upon dress go well beyond the introduction of the Eisenhower jacket or

Women wearing dresses made to resemble Allied flags – American, French, British and Russian – celebrate the liberation of Paris, late August 1944.

General Montgomery's beret. Despite limits set by practical considerations, material shortages and government restrictions, aesthetic and desirable suits and dresses were created for the duration. All fashion during the war, from the humblest of everyday clothing to the most elite couture, was to some degree affected by military strategy. Wartime propaganda was unrelenting in letting it be known that every yard of fabric saved might mean a quicker route to victory. However, although resources and technology may have been key to winning the war, the value of a tube of lipstick as a morale booster was well understood.

Shortages of leather, silk and wool became dire in 1941, and clothing rationing was introduced in Britain and France, now cut off from the rest of the fashion-conscious world. American designers took the lead and showed less fitted clothes, using harem drapery, deep-cut armholes, and dolman sleeves. Shoes with wooden platform soles and oilcloth uppers compensated for the lack of leather footwear in France and Germany. When the United States entered the war in December 1941, there were already precedents for governments, not designers, to decide on how many yards of rayon were allowed per garment and how many buttons a dress or coat might have.

In Britain, fashion underwent near nationalization under the Utility scheme in 1942, as styles were manufactured using the barest minimum of resources. American fashions were limited in spring 1942 by a government decree that froze the silhouette through a long list of do's and don'ts for manufacturers. The long evening gown all but disappeared for lack of occasion, and was even outlawed in Australia and France in 1943. Millinery was the only source of novelty, as skimpier silhouettes became prevalent and women were encouraged to make over old clothes. In France, although the hemline was raised to about 18 inches (46 centimetres) off the ground, the silhouette defined by Parisian couturiers was far from skimpy, using full skirts and sleeves, and towering headdresses. As the war turned in favour of the Allies, shortages became dire in Germany, and procuring any new clothing became impossible.

When Paris was liberated at the end of the summer in 1944 the city immediately made plans to recover its place as the fashion capital of the world. The couture industry had survived, but in order to export clothes it needed to adapt its extravagant silhouette to meet legal fabric allowances abroad. In the first year after the war, Paris recycled ideas used under the occupation, including draped skirts with panniers, peplums and pockets. The female form reappeared with a strong bosom, low, square neckline, narrow waist, and full round hips. Hemlines slipped back down to 15 inches (38 centimetres) from the ground and full-skirted evening gowns re-emerged. For daywear, loose fitting batwing and dolman sleeves became popular for dresses and suits. And with the war over, a sense of humour returned in brightly coloured novelty prints.

However, Paris did not immediately regain its fashion dominion. America had its own designers now and a strong partiality for homegrown casual chic. Eastern Europe was being politically and culturally separated from the West, and rationing and restrictions of fabric usage would remain in effect in Britain for several more years. Then, in early 1947, Christian Dior's 'New Look' heralded a renaissance in French couture. The old-fashioned, full-skirted, soft-shouldered, hourglass-shaped dresses and suits picked up where fashion had left off before the war but with an exuberant confidence that occurred at just the right moment. Feminine luxury and elegance became the symbol of post-war prosperity and defined the silhouette for the coming decade.

DRESSING THE NATION

Preparing the home front for conflict

Since 1922 Mussolini had sought to unify the Italian people, who traditionally identified themselves by region or city – Neapolitans, Sicilians, Romans, etc. – rather than by nationality. He looked to historic commonalities to build an Italian identity, and used the Roman Empire and the Renaissance, symbols of the country's glorious past, to create a modern, strong, self-sufficient Italy, purged of foreign influence. When Hitler came to power in Germany in January 1933, the National Socialists used Italy as a model for the New Order. In the United States, President Franklin D. Roosevelt even modelled some of his New Deal on Mussolini's ideas. In return, Mussolini borrowed the idea of the Boy Scout movement as an effective way to instill Fascist values in the nation's youth through sporting and social activities. Uniforms adopted by youth groups in Italy and later in Germany symbolized classless unity and national community, while preparing boys and girls for future service to their country.

Fascist theory did not accept the role of the modern emancipated woman that had emerged in the years following the Great War. Women would earn an honoured place as wives and mothers of the nation by returning to their pre-emancipation roles. The Nazi ideal of the Aryan beauty was a youthful, healthy, tanned, physically fit and fertile woman with a natural look. Blonde hair and blue eyes were an asset, but they were not enough: vices had to be avoided, including the use of alcohol, cigarettes and cosmetics. A good German woman was a smart consumer who bought only German products and avoided

The National Socialist ideal: a 'Black Forest maiden', on the cover of *Frauen-Warte*, a Nazi party propaganda magazine for the German woman. (The ideal was still being promoted in the dark days of the war: this issue was published in June 1943.)

LEFT AND BELOW **Elements of folk wear were commonly used as inspiration for fashion in the late 1930s and early 1940s. These illustrations appeared in two German magazines: the French-named *Panorama de la Mode* (available in Germany and Hungary), July 1941, and *Neuer Modenspiegel*, c. 1941.**

wasting money on selfish trifles like cosmetics to paint herself up like a French coquette or American Hollywood vamp. Mussolini was less adamant. An article appeared in Mussolini's newspaper, *Popolo d'Italia*, that quoted the dictator's response to the Nazi regime's disdain for lipstick and rouge: 'Any power whatsoever is destined to fail before fashion.' Mussolini was correct. While sales of sunlamps and blonde hair dye increased in Germany (Eva Braun's own blonde hair was straight from a bottle), cosmetic sales showed no sign of slowing.

The posters issued by Propaganda Chief Joseph Goebbels regularly featured blonde Nordic beauties, usually wearing dirndls, the *Trachtenkleidung* (folk costume) of the region centred on Munich, where the Nazi party had arisen. The scrubbed-faced fair maiden in a dirndl may have been the fascist feminine ideal, but chic German women derisively called her 'Gretchen'.

Despite the Nazis' endless Gretchen images on propaganda posters, the wives of the Nazi elite stuck to designer clothing and French cosmetics. Magda Goebbels and Emmy Göring were both obsessed with fashion and ignored Nazi ideology, buying clothes from Jewish couturiers and stores until 1938. In the autumn of 1939,

OPPOSITE **Black loden wool suit with pewter buttons and red scroll stitching and binding, from Munich in Bavaria, c. 1938–40.**

Emmy Göring appeared at the opera wearing a brocade evening dress with a train reported to be 12 feet (3.6 metres) long. A foreign diplomat recognized the material for the gown as having come from the draperies of the Belvedere Palace in Warsaw. The less ostentatious but more chic Frau Goebbels appeared on the covers of Germany's fashion magazines, always in full make-up. Unwilling to risk losing the support of women on the home front, the Nazis continued to allow German magazines to feature French fashions and cosmetics – until war began.

European regional dress had been disappearing at an accelerated pace since the late nineteenth century. Most women had ceased wearing folk dress for its impracticality and out of a desire for modernity. City women associated traditional costume with backward, rural ways, charming for regional festivals and marketplaces but hardly chic and cosmopolitan. Now both Italy and Germany looked to regional dress for styles that reflected their nation's heritage. The dirndl may have originated in the Alps, but Nazi propaganda encouraged its revival as German national dress. In Italy, the 'Ente nazionale artigianato e piccole industrie' (National Body for Crafts and Small Industries) was created to preserve and promote traditional embroideries, lace and straw work. Elements of regional costume occasionally appeared in Italian high fashion; but that convincing women to adopt folk dress for everyday wear was a foolish prospect is something the Italian Fascists seemed to understand better than the German Nazis.

In 1935, French *Vogue* featured the *bonnet du fascio,* a hat that resembled the fez worn by the Italian Fascist militia. *Vogue* suggested wearing it with a deep green suit trimmed with astrakhan, leaving the jacket open to reveal a black shirt. However, Italian Fascism's influence on haute couture was brief. References to Germanic folk dress first appeared in French fashions in the spring of 1936. Elements of Alpine style, as it was often called, could be found in embroidered floral bands, scrolling stitch-work, and two-tone loden wool suits. In 1922 the Austrian clothier Josef Lanz had opened a business offering Alpine clothing in Salzburg; he emigrated to the United States in 1936 and opened a shop in New York, which the blonde Hollywood star Marlene Dietrich frequented, thus popularizing Germanic folk dress in the United States (she

RIGHT A print rayon dress by Lanz of Austria, from his New York shop, *c.* 1938–41.

herself had left Germany and refused to return due to the political situation). Other fashion leaders, the Duke and Duchess of Windsor, adopted *Trachtenkleidung* during their honeymoon in the Alps in the summer of 1937. Mainstream fashions for autumn 1938 and spring 1939 often included dirndl-inspired dresses and puffed-sleeved suits worn with peaked-crown hats.

By the end of the 1930s Alpine/Bavarian folk dress was perceived by some to show an affinity for Nazi ideology. In Czechoslovakia, traditional Bohemian and Moravian influences in dress appeared as early as 1936. Elsewhere, embroidery patterns were sought from a variety of other cultures far beyond the Alps. In the United States, President Roosevelt's 'Good Neighbour' policy, created in the early 1930s to improve relations with Latin America, resulted in Mexican, Central and South American themes in dress, especially Mexican prints and Guatemalan woven patterns; Hawaiian themes were included in the 'south of the border' group. American clothing designers and manufacturers also looked closer to home for inspiration, using pioneer, cowboy, and Indian themes.

Historically, Italy had been the centre of fashion during the Renaissance, but France had slowly usurped the position during the seventeenth and eighteenth centuries, although Italy remained an important centre for textile production. Before the Fascists came to power in 1922, Mariano Fortuny and Monaci Gallenga had already brought international prestige to Italian design, textiles and workmanship by creating clothes inspired by the Renaissance. Yet despite their success, fabric from Como and Florence was still being sold to Parisian designers, who sent it back in finished garments for sale at high prices to Italian women.

For the Italians to succeed in competing with the French, the apparel industry had to work together. There was a strong division in the country between the technologically advanced north and the traditional agrarian south, and as most of the textile industries were in the north, Turin was chosen as the fashion capital in 1932. Italian and German fashion houses, like the fashion industries in other countries, were in the habit of either copying French models or making clothes according to French modes to please their clientele. French

OPPOSITE AND ABOVE **Three plates of Czech folklore-inspired clothes in keeping with high fashion trends, from *Svéráz*, published in 1940 by the Association of Czech Fashion.**

Leuchtend starke Farben gehören unter den durchsichtig blauen Himmel Italiens. Alles Grelle, Intensive schwinde in der südlichen Sonne, alle Töne werden in Licht aufgelöst. Die Tagesjacke zum schwarzen Rock mit einfachstem Schnitt wirkt allein durch das helle Gelb, das Material ist schmiegsame Lamawolle. Zum schwarzen Kleid ein Mantel in bläulichem Rot mit weiten Glocken, durch schwarze Bänder um Hals und Hüften eingehalten. Modelle: Fercioni, Mailand. Zeichnung: Ley Else Haertter.

OPPOSITE Italian fashions by Fercioni of Milan, illustrated in the German magazine *Elegante Welt*, 31 March 1939.

RIGHT American white cotton dress with Mexican-style embroidery and striped sash belt, *c.* 1940.

fashions, even if not chic or smart, were considered chic and smart by virtue of being French. Most wealthy women were in the habit of travelling to Paris to buy their couture clothes. Margarita Sarfatti, the lover of Mussolini, often went to Paris to buy couture – although she usually frequented the atelier of Italian-born Elsa Schiaparelli. Propaganda slogans – 'The Italian woman must follow Italian fashion' and 'Dress in an Italian manner' – promoted the economic importance of supporting domestic industry. In 1932 Mussolini founded a government institution that became known as the 'Ente nazionale della moda' (National Fashion Body) to build up the fashion industry so it could compete in the foreign market and create a distinctive Italian style.

Likewise, in 1933, the 'Deutsches Modeamt' (German Fashion Bureau), soon renamed the 'Deutsches Mode-Institut' (German Fashion Institute), was founded to promote German fashion, free of foreign influence, through exhibitions and fashion shows. Magda Goebbels was appointed the Fashion Institute's first honorary president; however, after she had declared that she intended to make German women stylish and intelligent, not 'the Gretchen type', she was relieved of her office by her husband. The motivation for these organizations was primarily economic. German fashion and textile industries were suffering from high unemployment. If German fashion could offer couture-quality design at ready-to-wear prices, it would be able to compete with French fashion. The Deutsches Mode-Institut correctly anticipated the direction prêt-à-porter would take – combining high fashion design with mass production – but that trend would only take off in the 1950s with the development of boutique lines.

In 1930, Parisian designer Elsa Schiaparelli used rayon for the first time in haute couture: working with the French company Colcombet, she explored new materials and blends of natural and man-made fibres to create unique new textures, weights and weaves; and her shiny, crinkly ribbons of cellophane and rhodophane (cellophane woven into cloth) were particular favourites. (She was also influential in the adoption of the slide fastener, or zipper, in 1935; by 1939, when the war started, it had just become a standard garment closure, but then metal shortages required manufacturers to revert to older methods.)

Despite Schiaparelli's promotion of rayon, France had not been a large manufacturer of the fabric, as most couturiers relied upon traditional and natural luxury materials. The development of industries specializing in the manufacture of man-made materials offered opportunities for both Germany and Italy to compete with the French for dominance of the fashion industry. By 1929, Italy was the second largest producer of rayon in the world: rayon was made for domestic use, while Italy's more lucrative silk production was exported for profit. When the League of Nations imposed sanctions on Italy for invading Abyssinia (Ethiopia) in 1935, imports of raw materials ceased and many export markets were closed to Italian products. Without imports of coniferous wood pulp, rayon production decreased and funding for research into developing other man-made textiles increased. A native plant called *canna gentile* was found to be an excellent substitute, and rayon production resumed.

Before the National Socialists came to power, Germany had been importing the majority of the raw materials needed for its textile industry. National Socialism promoted traditional culture, but when it came to anything technological modern developments were of great interest. One of the earliest National Socialist directives was to decrease Germany's dependence on foreign imports and to increase its exports. For the development of German textiles, I. G. Farben had been involved in the early experimental production of man-made materials, and increased its contribution as efforts accelerated towards making the country self-sufficient.

Germany's use of substitute materials extended back to the First World War, when British blockades forced Germans to look to unconventional sources such as paper to clothe civilians. A chemist by the name of Todtenhaupt developed a wool-like substitute made from casein, the protein found in milk, but the war ended before any commercial application of the fibre was launched. An Italian engineer, Antonio Ferretti, improved the process in 1935 and called the imitation wool 'Lanital'. The dyeable, mothproof product was intended to revolutionize the wool industry, but low tensile strength, especially when wet, was a problem. Nevertheless, rights of production were sold to Germany, Belgium, France, Britain, and the United States (where it was made

›Bemberg‹
Lavabel
Wollen Sie »Bemberg«-Lavabel tragen, dürfen Sie nicht nur »Lavabel« verlangen. Nein, wer »Lavabel« sagt, muß erst »Bemberg« sagen.
Am Kantenstempel »Bemberg«-Lavabel erkennt man die Güte und Echtheit.

Advertisement for Bemberg rayon in the German magazine *Elegante Welt*, 31 March 1939.

under the name 'Aralac'). Italy alone produced 5,000 tons (over 5,000 tonnes) of Lanital in 1938.

By 1937, Germany was leading the way in recycling existing fur, cotton, linen, wool, and even rayon garments. Two years later experimental fibres were being made from potato peels, cornhusks, soybeans, and the wastewater from margarine production. To make natural materials such as cotton and wool go further, higher percentages of synthetics were blended in, decreasing the quality. German army privates were sometimes jokingly referred to as 'Men from Mars' because their bodies took on a greenish hue from the dye that bled from their high-synthetic-fibre-content uniforms.

In 1938, Italy, Germany and Japan were the leading manufacturers of man-made textiles. In that same year, I. G. Farben, through a process similar to that used for nylon (see p. 109), developed a fibre called Perlon. It was never used for civilian purposes: instead it went immediately to making parachutes, and bristles for brushes to clean machinery and weapons. Without Perlon, Germany would have had to rely on its domestic silk industry and on imports. Germany had once been home to an important sericulture, but in 1806 Napoleon had his army destroy Germany's mulberry trees – the food of silkworms – so that French silks would dominate the market. Following the National Socialist assumption of power, mulberry trees were planted wherever possible, and by 1939 German sericulture was once again established.

The fight to free fashion from French influence included the expulsion of French fashion vocabulary. Mussolini had words and expressions of foreign origin removed from the Italian language. This profoundly affected the fashion industry, whose language included numerous French words and phrases, and to fill the void, an Italian dictionary of fashion was published in 1936. Similarly, the National Socialists purged German of foreign terminology. Words with French roots were replaced with Germanic designations: 'haute couture' became 'Hauptmode', and 'chic' was spelled 'schick'; 'Konfektion' was considered to have too Jewish a flavour for ready-to-wear, which became 'Bekleidung' (apparel) after October 1936.

Deutsche, verteidigt Euch
gegen die jüdische
Greuelpropaganda,
kauft
nur bei Deutschen!
Germans defend
yourselves against jewish
atrocity propaganda
buy only at German shops!
Deutsche!
Wehrt Euch!
Kauft nicht bei Juden!

In August 1933 the first Deutsches Mode-Institut fashion shows in Berlin were held a week before the French shows – to attract buyers first, and to prove that the German collections were uninfluenced by French styles. By 1937 the Institute was following the Nuremberg race laws: Jewish designers and manufacturers were no longer welcome, eliminating some of the best talent and skill in the country. Every rung of the clothing industry ladder, from textile manufacturing to fashion-magazine publishing, had a long history of Jewish involvement. Shortly after the first government-sanctioned boycott of Jewish businesses on 3 March 1933, Georg Riegel, a clothier in the ready-to-wear industry, invited colleagues to establish a thoroughly German association: within a year it was registered as the 'Arbeitsgemeinschaft deutscher–arischer Fabrikanten der Bekleidungsindustrie' (Association of German–Aryan Clothing Manufacturers), known by the acronym 'Adefa'. Around two hundred member firms placed Adefa labels in their clothing, starting a campaign for people to buy only Aryan products, with the intention of purging the German clothing industry of Jewish ownership, workmanship, or influence.

To further Adefa's goals, an additional organization was founded by many of the same members in January 1938. The 'Arbeitsgemeinschaft deutscher Unternehmer der Spinnstoff-, Bekleidungs- and Lederwirtschaft' (Association of German Firms in the Weaving, Clothing, and Leather Trades), or Adebe, was founded to further the cause in the textile and leather industries, as well as the retail and wholesale trades. The Ministry for the Economy temporarily banned this new organization, on the grounds that it might interfere with the economy, especially as German clothing exports were dropping, but Nazi ideology overrode economic interests and the ban was lifted. By 1 April 1938, Adefa had more than six hundred member firms that now displayed signs in their shop windows stating: 'Ware aus arischer Hand' (Made by Aryan hands). This statement also appeared on the labels which were now required in every garment made by an Adefa member.

OPPOSITE AND ABOVE **The first National-Socialist-organized boycott of Jewish businesses, on 3 March 1933, was a test to see what the international reaction would be to State-organized anti-Semitism. Posters fixed to the windows of both shops instruct shoppers: 'Germans! Be on your guard! Don't buy from Jews!'.**

The actions of *Kristallnacht* on 9 November 1938 – the 'Night of Broken Glass', a pogrom against Jewish businesses and synagogues throughout Germany and parts of Austria that resulted in the streets being covered in shards of glass from smashed windows – and the 'Ordinance on the Exclusion of Jews from German Economic Life' that followed on 12 November, compelling Jews to sell all their enterprises, furthered Adefa's aims. Berlin's oldest department store, 'Nathan Israel', had been in business since 1815 but was forced to close its doors. Magda Goebbels, who realized her favourite Jewish couturiers would have to close, remarked, 'Elegance will now disappear from Berlin along with the Jews.' On 15 August 1939, the director of Adefa declared that the goal of Aryanizing the German garment industry had been achieved, and that the organization was dissolved.

OPPOSITE AND ABOVE **A pale gold coat and the 'Adefa' label within it, c. 1938–39. The letters of the acronym – for 'Arbeitsgemeinschaft deutscher–arischer Fabrikanten der Bekleidungsindustrie' (Association of German–Aryan Clothing Manufacturers) – form an eagle. The label guaranteed that the garment was made by Aryan hands.**

The Paris fashions for autumn 1939 showed an overall trend for broader shoulders, smaller waists, and shorter and fuller skirts. But the headline-grabbing reintroduction of corsets and bustles infuriated the political leaders in charge of Germany's fashion industry. With days to go until the start of war, Dr Robert Ley, the Labour Front leader, attacked Paris fashions in German journals, warning that chic, slim figures do not fit into German life and that German men do not like to see their wives in a new dress every few months. *Time* magazine reported his tirade on 21 August 1939: 'to abandon a dress when it is used up and not when it becomes unfashionable ... is in accordance with the present economic policy.' *Das Schwarze Korps*, the official organ of the SS, added:

> Other nations elect ... beauty queens, but Germany honors women with many children and therewith honors a beauty that is uninfluenced by any fashions ... All this is no fulmination against lipstick, powder and silk stockings; quite the contrary ... Every woman should be beautiful; every woman should have the opportunity to accentuate her natural charms ... so that she can not only carry out her duties, but also bring pleasure into the life of the working and fighting man.

It was clear that fashion was politics and politics were leading to war.

KANGAROO POCKETS AND SIREN SUITS

Dress, patriotism, and propaganda in the first year of war

American purple velvet afternoon suit with matching velvet peaked hat, *c.* autumn 1939.

The summer of 1939 had been the most glamorous in Paris in almost a decade. The Depression was now a memory, and tourists were filling the capital. Chic spring woollen suits, made popular by Queen Elizabeth during her tour of North America in May, were displaced in mid-summer by floral print crepe dresses and wide-brimmed hats. Beachside slacks and shorts were inching further into town for recreational bicycling, and playsuits worn with matching overskirts made summer activity wear instantly acceptable for street wear.

Reporters and buyers from around the world had arrived by the start of August for the autumn collections. They had heard rumours that there would be a hint of nineteenth-century elegance from many designers. The Eiffel Tower, considered an eyesore by many Parisians when built, was now being celebrated as an architectural icon on its fiftieth birthday, and Schiaparelli, inspired by the fashions of 1889, made bustled evening gowns in commemoration. Puffed sleeves inspired by the 'Belle Époque' (the decades around 1900), less inflated than when introduced in 1938, continued to be popular, and wide sweeping evening skirts were taking over from close-fitting bias-cut gowns. Perky little hats trimmed with veil and flowers, some with peaked crowns, and huge cart-wheel hats, some tying under the chin, were throwbacks to *fin-de-siècle* millinery glamour. After an absence of twenty-five years, corseted waists also returned to fashion. In crinolined evening gowns, corseted waists seemed more in keeping with the Empress Eugénie's Paris of 1860 than a modern woman's wardrobe. The French magazine *Marianne* reported on the autumn/winter styles in their August 1939 issue: 'this winter's very extravagant fashion calls for a certain dignity and an enormous amount of style ... Learn to handle a fan gracefully and to wrap your stole round you.' The Victorian coquette was in vogue.

LEFT Canadian crepe afternoon dress, *c.* 1939–40.

BELOW Canadian print cotton playsuit with overdress, *c.* 1939.

American navy and cream plaid jacket with matching hat, *c.* 1939. Tailored suits and sports clothes offered a practical element to dressing for most daytime occasions and one that would become more important during the war.

As elegance flowed in afternoon and evening clothes, daytime clothes were practical, almost uniform-like at times, with *air du temps* manifestations of militarism apparent in some suits and hats. Chanel showed frogging, shoulder braid and tassels on boleros and jackets, and many designers offered a prophetic glimpse of military-style hats.

In the days leading up to the declaration of war on 3 September 1939, the windows of Paris and London's public buildings were taped, monuments were sandbagged, and kerbs were painted white to help vehicles and pedestrians find their way in the dark. Cellars were converted to bomb shelters and windows were painted, covered in tarpaper, or draped in black-out cloth to hide any light during the air raids that would soon come. In France general mobilization resulted in five million men being called up, most of whom would be posted along the Maginot Line to forestall an invasion coming from Germany, directly across the border. As in London, Parisian children were evacuated to the countryside, and many Parisians themselves left the city: by all accounts most fled overdressed in their best apparel, looking more like guests at a summer reception than refugees fleeing an imminent invasion. Most however returned within weeks, after the initial fear of bombardment and invasion had passed.

In France, the quick movement to create an army left the home front depleted of a workforce. Women filled the gap as best they could, but an early autumn frost in 1939 resulted in heavy crop losses. Women's war work was vital for the country, and city streets were soon filled with women dressed in aprons and smocks with scarves tied into cowls about their heads as they travelled to work in factories. In Britain, invasion was not an immediate threat, and the country could afford a more orderly approach to organizing its citizens and increasing its army. An aerial attack, however, was a definite possibility.

OPPOSITE French illustration of evening dresses by Balenciaga, September 1939. In the autumn of 1939, fashion began taking on elements of style not seen since the nineteenth century. Some designers were showing corsets, others were suggesting bustles; evening dresses with full crinoline skirts and puffy sleeves or bare shoulders were blatant revivals of Victorian gowns. Crinoline skirts and nipped waists would subside for the duration of the war, but come back into vogue by 1947.

Gold lamé evening gown with mink-trimmed trained jacket, labelled 'Mme Desmarias – Montreal'. This dress was worn to a dinner given in May 1939 in honour of the visiting King George VI and Queen Elizabeth, the first reigning British monarchs to visit North America. The inevitability of war had prompted the royal tour, to remind Canadians of their historic ties to the motherland, as well as to align isolationist American sympathies with Britain.

King George was a shy man, but his wife, who had served as a nurse during the First World War, had an innate ability to radiate regal confidence. The royal family refused to evacuate London during the war, preferring to share with fellow Britons the experience of heading to bomb shelters during air raids, which damaged Buckingham Palace nine times. After consultation with her dressmaker, Norman Hartnell, the Queen decided not to wear black to visit bombed areas of London. Black was too obviously associated with death. Instead, inspired by lilac, a semi-mourning colour, gentle dusty pastel tones were chosen to suggest hope. She always dressed her best during these visits, with gloves and hat, maintaining that people dressed well to visit her, so she would do likewise. Looking regal at all times, she nevertheless always carried her gas mask, and observed wartime style limitations. Her clothes were cut down for the royal princesses, and older outfits were restyled. Hitler was well aware of how much of an asset the Queen was to the British war effort, prompting him to remark that she was 'the most dangerous woman in Europe'.

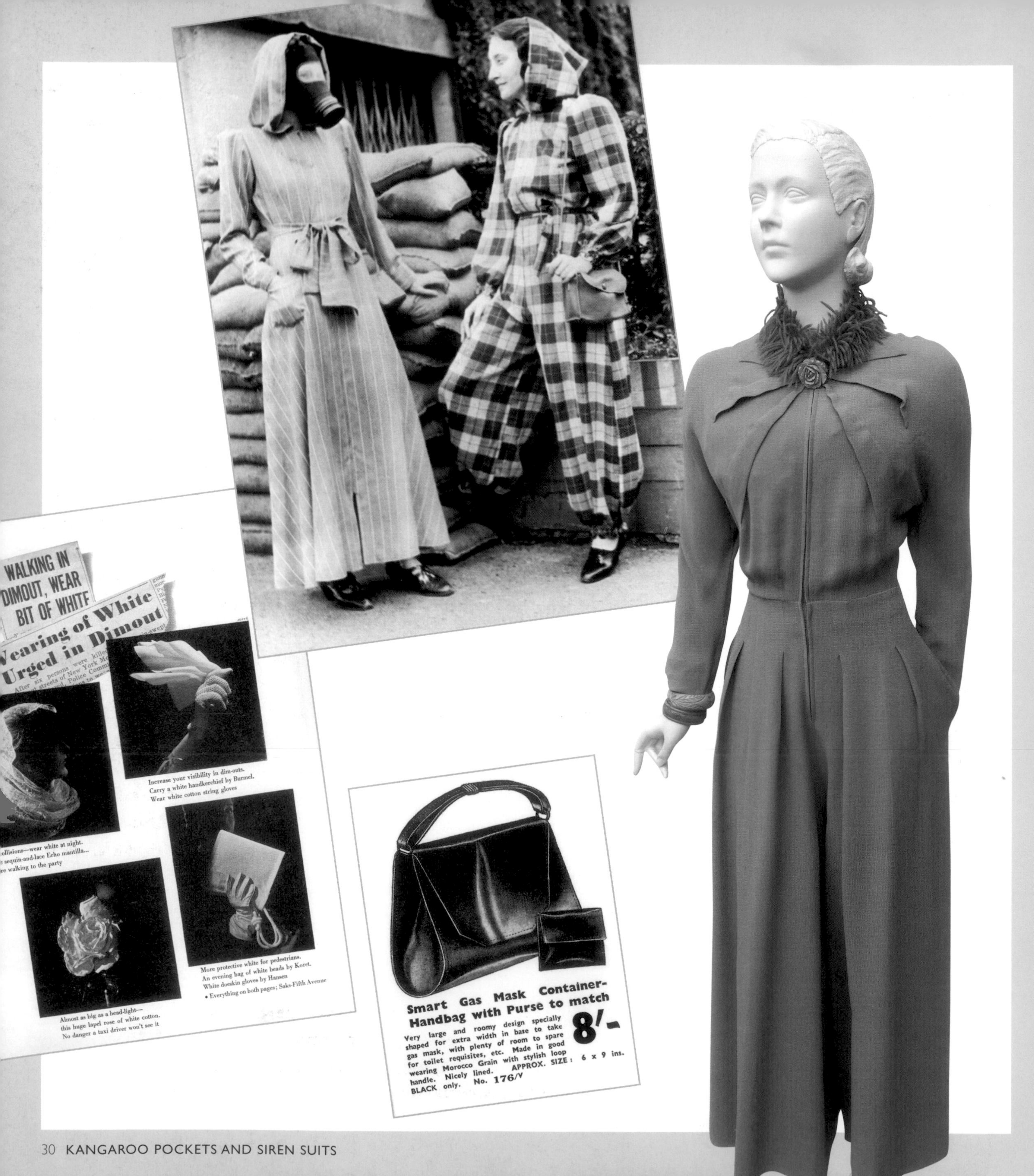
WALKING IN
DIMOUT, WEAR
BIT OF WHITE
Wearing of White
Urged in Dimout
Increase your visibility in dim-outs.
Carry a white handkerchief by Burmel.
Wear white cotton string gloves
ollisions—wear white at night.
sequin-and-lace Echo mantilla...
re walking to the party
More protective white for pedestrians.
An evening bag of white beads by Koret.
White doeskin gloves by Hansen
• Everything on both pages; Saks-Fifth Avenue
Almost as big as a head-light—
this huge lapel rose of white cotton.
No danger a taxi driver won't see it
Smart Gas Mask Container-
Handbag with Purse to match
8/-
Very large and roomy design specially shaped for extra width in base to take gas mask, with plenty of room to spare for toilet requisites, etc. Made in good wearing Morocco Grain with stylish loop handle. Nicely lined. APPROX. SIZE: 6 x 9 ins.
BLACK only. No. 176/V

OPPOSITE

ABOVE English designs for a siren suit and a hooded coat, intended for air raids, autumn 1939.

BELOW LEFT A page from American *Vogue*, 15 February 1943, advising readers to wear white during blackouts.

BELOW An English advertisement for a handbag that could accommodate a gas mask, *c.* 1940.

RIGHT An American zippered-front gold wool jumpsuit modelled on the siren suit, *c.* 1940.

RIGHT French air-raid-shelter suits.

BELOW French clothing for emergencies, autumn 1939: a reversible wool 'air-raid warning outfit' by Robert Piguet, of which the cape could also be used as a blanket.

"SAUTE-EN-CAVE"

Tenue d'alerte en lainage réversible. La cape indépendante peut servir de couverture.

Air warning outfit, in reversible woollen. The separable cape may be used as a blanket.

ROBERT PIGUET.

"FAVORI"

Gas masks had been distributed in Germany in 1937 and Britain in 1938. There was never a law requiring citizens to carry them, but as the war dragged on, British citizens became notoriously careless. A joke even did the rounds that suggested the only Londoners carrying gas masks were German spies. The most common British civilian mask was issued in a cardboard box through which a string was threaded to carry it over the shoulder. Shortly after war was declared, commercially made gas mask cases, ranging from oilcloth slipcases to leather handbags with compartments for the respirator, went on sale. The *Daily Mirror* reported in September 1939 that a new hairstyle had been created in the West End of London called the 'Gas Mask Curl': it consisted of clusters of curls on either side of the head with a centre part, perfect for accommodating the main strap of the gas mask.

By October, fashion's response to the crisis began to appear in store windows: siren suits (to be worn when the sirens sounded) were zipper-fronted one-piece jumpsuits that could be worn over pyjamas or nightgowns. Alternatively, hooded capes and coats were offered that could be easily slipped on for a quick run to the air raid shelter. Fashion historian Charles Cunnington, who worked as a doctor in London during the war, remarked on siren suits in his autobiography: 'They say a good deal of attention is paid to the cut so that it may give the wearer an attractive appearance, so necessary of course when she is about to be blown into fragments, in which case her charm will abruptly cease.' Cunnington continued, less ironically: 'A new fashion is a walking stick marked with black and white rings for use at night and called a "kerb-finder."'

Cunnington also noted how daily fashions were responding to the new circumstances:

> The wearing of trousers by women is the most significant fashion so far. Our domestic appears in a smart pair of dark blue with an embroidered jumper. I delighted her by suggesting she should wear this for daily work. Evidently she had had longings in this direction

A coat with 'kangaroo' pockets by Schiaparelli, autumn 1939.

> but feared it would not be allowed. In London trousers are said to be more commonly worn than skirts by young women. How quickly we accustom ourselves to new conditions!

However, the adoption of overalls and trousers for practicality provoked indignation from some. British *Vogue* reported in their first wartime issue of 20 September 1939: 'We deplore the crop of young women who take war as an excuse for ... parading about in slacks. Slack, we think, is the word.' In December 1939, they ran an advertisement for 'Aristoc' stockings with the caption: 'If she's taken to wearing trousers and you don't like them – give her some Aristoc. She'll soon be raising the national morale by showing her shapely legs once more.'

Parisian couturiers worked on their winter collections to offer designs that were better adapted to the new circumstances, with practicality being of prime concern. British *Vogue* reported in December 1939 on chic Parisian wartime clothing, such as pyjamas by Molyneux, and suits by Schiaparelli with large pouch pockets that some dubbed 'kangaroo' pockets for their size and usefulness. Schiaparelli recalled in her autobiography, *A Shocking Life*:

> We built up a collection in three weeks hoping for some response. This was the 'cash and carry' collection with huge pockets everywhere so that a woman, obliged to leave home in a hurry or to go on duty without a bag, could pack all that was necessary to her. She could thus retain the freedom of her hands and yet manage to look feminine.

Ostentatious jewelry and eccentric hats were frivolities that now seemed out of place. Practical wardrobes consisting of roomy coats, plenty of fur, tailored tweeds, knitwear and hooded jersey dresses worn with solid laced walking shoes were *de rigueur*. On 20 December 1939 in *Marianne* magazine Maggy Rouff referred to the change from pre-war fashions: 'Born in peacetime, created for carefree days, our gowns have retired for a deep and unexpected sleep ...' However, practicality did not rule out novelty: umbrellas with flashlights in the handles, and luminous white jewelry and footwear for blackouts, provided whimsy. The Soviet invasion of Finland on 30 November 1939 was also a source of inspiration for some designers, who took decorative elements from Finnish emblems and traditional clothing for high fashion styles. British designers were also working on finding the right shade of purple for women's garments that complemented army khaki (German designers had already discovered how well red worked with Nazi brown).

Some foreign fashion journalists returned to Paris for the winter shows; Carmel Snow, editor in chief of *Harper's Bazaar*, wanted to see for herself what the effects of war would be upon style. Now the audiences busied themselves knitting army scarves and gloves while the mannequins paraded by. This time the collection was openly inspired by militarism and patriotism. Colours were called 'Aeroplane Grey', 'Maginot Blue' and 'French Soil Beige'. Garment models were similarly named: pyjamas were called 'Alerte', an evening gown was reportedly named 'Leave', and a suit by Piguet was dubbed 'Service Secret'. Jeanne Lanvin showed practical day dresses, while most of her business turned to making uniforms. Molyneux and other designers used uniforms as an inspiration for making epaulette-decorated militaristic suits. *Harper's Bazaar* reported in their November 1939 issue: 'The French have decreed that fashion shall go on, even in the dark, anxious nights. Though no one wears full dress, everyone makes an effort to be as elegant as possible, not only for the morale of their friends, but to keep up France's greatest industry, on which so many workers depend.'

After the initial panic of September 1939, cinemas and theatres reopened in Paris, but semi-formal cocktail dresses in dark colours with subtle embellishment and understated jewelry now seemed the appropriate attire. It was well known that Germany was already rationing clothing in November 1939 – a sign, it was thought, of an ill-equipped enemy who would not be able to sustain an offence in Western Europe. But shortages would plague the French clothing industry soon enough, as pre-war contracts for leather, furs, silk and wool became more difficult to fill. With the fear of gas attacks past, gas mask bags began doubling as handbags (old leather bags were already being cut apart to repair shoes).

A jacket with gathered front pockets, by Alix, spring 1940. The atelier Alix had been in operation since 1934 but was sold soon after war broke out. The designer behind Alix, Germaine Krebs, reopened in 1942 under the new name of Madame Grès (see p. 153).

For winter's chill, however, warmth was more important than novelty. In February 1940 *Fourrures* magazine extolled the virtues of fur-lined military jackets that were finding their way into fashion: 'Patrols and trench life have brought into general use those waterproof jackets called Canadiennes that are lined with sheepskin, lambskin or some other fur. A belt with a buckle draws them in at the waist. A wide fur band at the neck frames the face and protects the chest against damp and cold.'

Eve Curie, daughter of Pierre and Marie Curie, the discoverers of radium, and biographer of her mother, was appointed by the French Information Minister as head of the feminine section of the Commissariat of Information. In early 1940 she went on a two-month lecture tour of the United States with a wartime wardrobe designed by Schiaparelli that included a lambskin-lined oilcloth coat with huge 'kangaroo' pockets. Her lectures on 'French Women and the War' enlightened Americans on the role of women war workers and impressed on them how important the luxury fashion trade was for France. *Time* magazine quoted her in the 12 February 1940 issue:

> We produce a billion francs worth of silk exports alone every year, four hundred millions in perfumes, four hundred and fifty millions in jewelry, and six hundred millions in exports of dresses and hats. Luxury trades are not luxuries but necessities in French commercial life. To eliminate our so-called luxury trades would be not only a temporary loss for France but a loss forever and for everyone.

At stake were over twenty thousand jobs in the couture industry of Paris alone, as well as much-needed foreign cash. Lucien François, editor of *Votre Beauté*, wrote in May 1940 that Parisian women had a duty to continue to be elegant. 'Every woman in Paris is a living propaganda poster . . . the universal function of the Parisian woman is to remain a coquette.' In the first months of the war Parisian women had forgotten they were on the world stage of style.

Couturiers created an explosion of colourful print dresses for the spring 1940 collections, including floral printed pinafores with large straw hats decorated with nosegays – a huge departure from the dark sombre styles of the winter. There was still an underlying practicality to the clothes intended for the domestic market. French women no longer changed for each activity several times a day, and clothes were created that could be worn for several functions. An afternoon dress could be matched up with an embroidered jacket for dinner or a plain jacket for town wear. The most elegant and sophisticated designs created in silk were intended primarily for overseas sales to the United States and South America. Britain too focused on exports of fashion to North and South America for foreign cash, to the point where the best textiles and clothes never saw British shops, especially after Paris was occupied and cut off from delineating fashion outside of France.

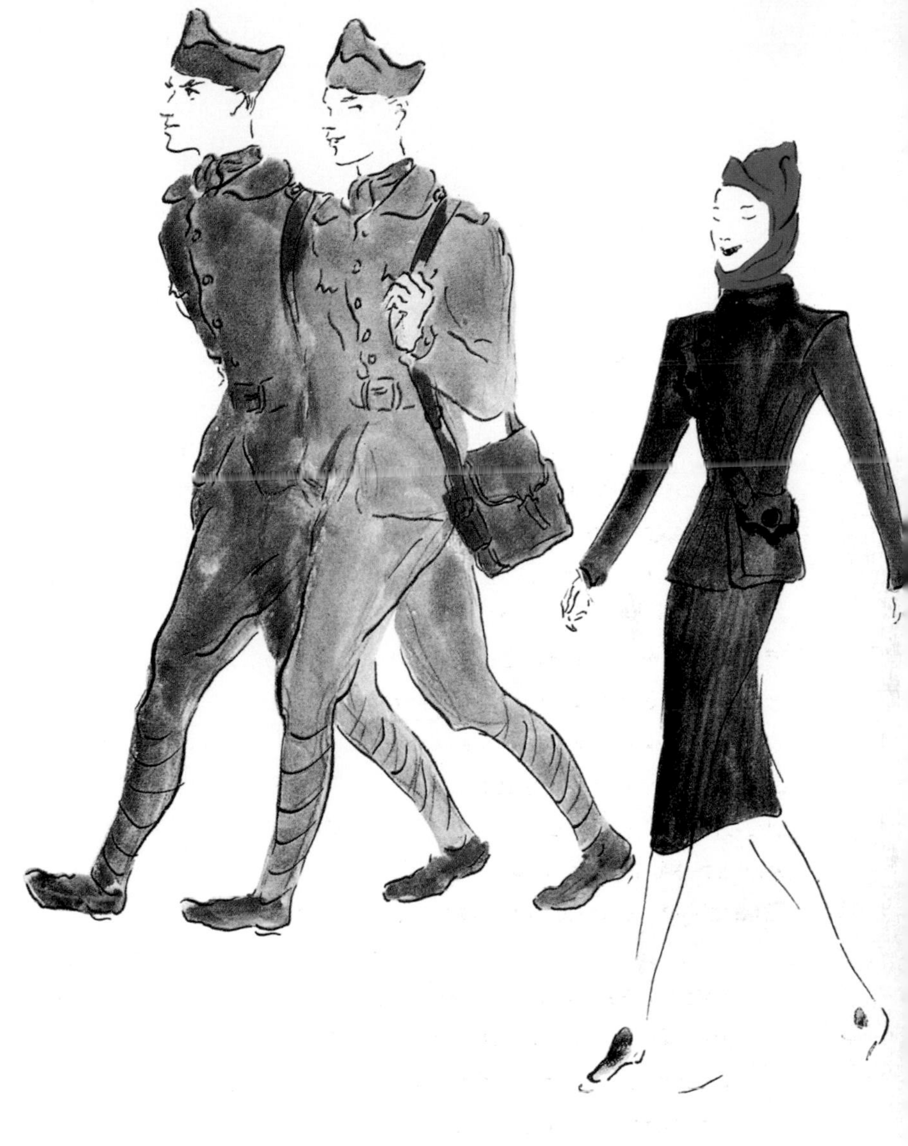

ABOVE **A Schiaparelli suit with pocket imitating a shoulder-sling bag, from *Harper's Bazaar*, February 1940.**

On 10 May 1940 the German invasion began, when the frontiers of Holland and Belgium were overrun. Refugees from the north herded into Paris during the following weeks and the majority of Parisians once again fled south ahead of the advancing army to Bordeaux and Marseilles, or even further, to Portugal, if they had the permits. Those who had fled the capital when war was declared the previous September took more care in packing than they had done the first time. *L'Action française* advised on 4 June: 'If you are going away to some provincial refuge . . . take with you things that cannot easily be replaced. Ladies, abandon your sundress rather than your plain clothes. Do not forget to equip yourself with a pair of sensible shoes in case of storms, leave a hat rather than a book or a cherished photograph.'

RATIONING, UTILITY, AND AUSTERITY

The British way to winning the war in fashion

Anticipating the coming conflict, Britain had been stockpiling many essential goods by negotiating surplus shipping contracts as early as 1938, including the entire Australian sheep clip of 1940. Before the fall of France in June 1940, rationing of British civilian supplies had been minimal; but imports did not meet civilian demand, and supplies were dwindling. The national resources would need to be thriftily managed to ensure a secure supply of food, fuel, and clothing for every citizen.

A National Registration of the British population was held on 29 September 1939. Any temptation to withhold one's name, to avoid being called up in the armed forces, was eliminated by registration also being essential to procure an identity card and ration book. The identity card was issued during October 1939 by members of the Women's Voluntary Service (WVS), which had been founded in May 1938 to aid civilians during the upcoming conflict. At first, retailers were required to ration whatever items were in short supply, but complaints quickly came in from the public, who felt they had been shortchanged. Beginning in January 1940, food was the first resource to be rationed. Gradually, items were added as supplies were monitored to ensure that fair shares of a balanced diet were maintained for all. The diet was boring, but it provided enough protein and nutrients, and even the occasional treat, to keep Britons nourished for the duration.

For civilian clothing, the problem was tackled in three ways – rationing, Utility, and Austerity. Together, these methods would literally shape British fashions not only for the war but for several years following victory.

In a British menswear shop, c. 1941. Once rationing had been introduced, to avoid coupon crime the Board of Trade required all clothing retailers to display a notice declaring it illegal to offer or accept loose clothing coupons.

RATIONING

By 1941 the supply and distribution of civilian clothing was beginning to falter. Factories had been requisitioned and civilian workers withdrawn for essential wartime work, depleting the clothing industry's skilled labour force. Raw materials were also becoming scarcer; a ban on silk for civilian clothing, including stockings, came into effect in January 1941. A memorandum to the War Cabinet from the President of the Board of Trade identified problems arising:

> supplies of new material for civilian clothing have been drastically curtailed; the amounts of cotton and wool available are not more than about 25 percent of the pre-war normal. Hitherto consumers have been drawing on the large stocks held by traders and have not felt the full impact of the severe cut in supplies. Stocks are now giving out and shortages are beginning to appear. These shortages will increase rapidly, and I fear that unless either supplies are increased, or the distribution of the existing supplies is equalized (which means rationing), some part of the population will have to go short of clothing in the autumn and winter; there will be panic buying and shop queues, prices will rise and the shops will be cleared by the better-to-do, leaving yet smaller supplies or none at all for the poorer classes.

On 1 June 1941 a rationing plan was introduced that had been developed by the Board of Trade earlier that year. A coupon system meant that both cash and coupons were required for the purchase of each item of clothing. Different types of garments required varying amounts of coupons, depending on how much fabric and labour were needed for production. Alfred Maizels, one of the members of the Board that developed the ration scheme, admitted that they had based it on the German rationing plan of November 1939 (see p. 173), of which a copy had been supplied to them by British Intelligence. The system gave as much freedom of choice as possible. Heavily taxed luxury items such as hats, lace, and fur coats were considered inessential and left off the ration. Second-hand articles presented too many administrative difficulties,

Coupon values for men

Unlined cape or mackintosh	9
Raincoat or overcoat	16
Jacket or blazer	13
Waistcoat or cardigan	5
Wool trousers	8
Corduroy trousers	5
Overalls or dungarees (denim)	6
Dressing gown	8
Pyjamas or nightshirt	8
Wool shirt or combination (one piece undergarment)	8
Shirt or combination, not wool	5
Socks	3
Collar or tie or two handkerchiefs	1
Scarf or pair of gloves	2
Slippers or rubber galoshes	4
Pair of boots or shoes	7

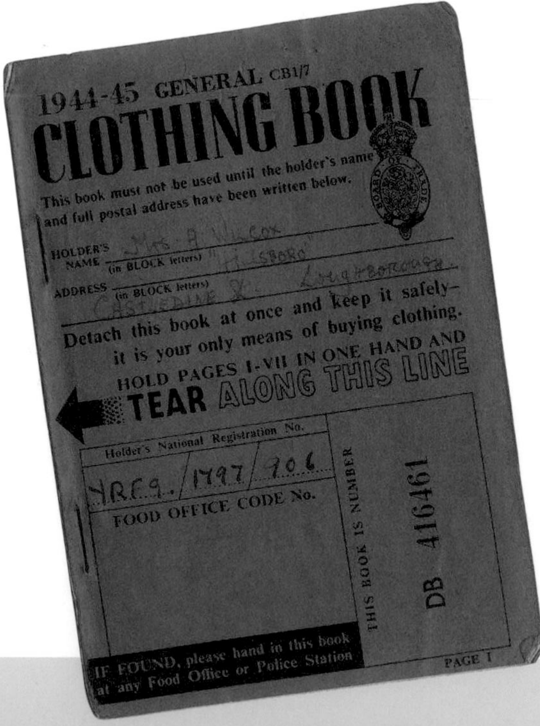
1944-45 GENERAL CB1/7
CLOTHING BOOK
This book must not be used until the holder's name and full postal address have been written below.
HOLDER'S NAME (in BLOCK letters)
ADDRESS (in BLOCK letters)
Detach this book at once and keep it safely—it is your only means of buying clothing.
HOLD PAGES I-VII IN ONE HAND AND TEAR ALONG THIS LINE
Holder's National Registration No.
FOOD OFFICE CODE No.
THIS BOOK IS NUMBER
DB 416461
IF FOUND, please hand in this book at any Food Office or Police Station
PAGE I

so they too were left off the ration. For those with the time and needle skills, making clothes at home saved money and coupons. Wool cloth could be purchased with 3 coupons per yard for 36-inch widths (91 x 92 centimetres); cotton cloth of the same dimensions required only 2 coupons. Although knitting wool required 1 coupon to acquire 2 ounces (57 grammes), all sewing and mending threads, braids and ribbons 3 inches (7.5 centimetres) or less in width were off ration. To help home economy, clothing for children under the age of four was coupon-free, as were boiler suits (coveralls), sanitary towels, clogs, braces (suspenders) and garters, and boot and shoe laces. Purchasing clothes from abroad to supplement the ration was not allowed. British residents could not order clothing from family or friends in Ireland, which was neutral and did not adopt a clothing rationing plan until 9 June 1942. Those caught doing so were fined.

OPPOSITE AND BELOW **The cover and interior, with coupons, of the British 1944–45 clothing rationing book.**

Coupon values for women

Lined coat over 28 inches [71 cm] in length	14
Jacket or short coat	11
Wool dress	11
Non-wool dress	7
Blouse, cardigan or jumper	5
Skirt or divided skirt (culottes)	7
Overalls or dungarees	6
Apron or pinafore	3
Pyjamas	8
Nightdress	6
Slip, petticoat or combination undergarment	4
Corset	3
Stockings	2
Ankle socks	1
Pair of slippers, boots or shoes	5

Printing millions of ration books in advance of launching clothing rationing would have tipped off the public – as was later proven when printers of Australia's clothing ration books leaked information, setting off a panic buying spree. The initial allowance of 66 coupons per adult per year was made up of 26 coupons at the back of the already distributed food coupon books, marked to be used for margarine (so as not to raise suspicion), and 40 coupons on a green card that was printed and distributed shortly after the introduction of clothing rationing. Period statistics from Mass Observation (an organization that monitored the everyday lives of ordinary British citizens from 1937 until the early 1950s) show that men adapted better to rationing than women, but overall the majority felt rationing was fair because of the equality of sacrifice across the classes.

Coupon crimes were not uncommon. Incidents of stolen and forged coupon books, double registrations, coupon swapping, replacements of 'lost' ration books, and a black-market trade in unused coupons were rife. The going rate for purchasing clothing coupons on the black market was around a crown (2*s*. 6*d*., one-eighth of a pound). Many poorer Britons exchanged their clothing coupons for clothes from a black-market middleman in the second-hand clothing business. Clothing coupon fraud was easier and more common than food coupon fraud because shopping for clothes did not require the coupon holder to register with a specific shop. In February 1942 a large-scale printing operation was uncovered where almost 100,000 forged clothing coupons were seized. Coupon crime was not uniquely a British problem: wherever there was a rationing system in place, coupon crime occurred.

On 1 June 1942 the 1942–43 ration book was issued with only 60 coupons. These were supposed to last until 31 July 1943, but in March of that

A **Canadian suit made from imported British kilt quality wool, *c*. 1940–41. Export fashions and textiles continued to showcase the luxury of English woollens and tailoring: it was imperative to keep money coming in from trading partners.**

year it was announced that they would have to last until 31 August. Preparing the public for a reduction to what would be 48 coupons per year, Hugh Dalton, the President of the Board of Trade, announced in mid-1942:

> The people of this country can congratulate themselves on the results of clothes rationing. In the first twelve months more than a quarter of a million tons of shipping space were saved in textiles alone. Nearly four hundred thousand men and women had been released from making cloth and clothing for civilians, and have gone into the Services or on to war production, while the workers that are left can be confident that they are making only the necessaries of wartime life. The increasing strain of war on our supplies has made inevitable a cut in the clothing ration. But the cut is least for those whose needs are greatest, the children and the Industrial workers. Any sacrifice of comfort or appearance which clothes rationing may bring to any of us will, I am sure, be cheerfully borne, in order that victory may come sooner. Many patriotic people have returned unused coupons to the Board of Trade, thus helping our war effort by saving precious shipping space, material and labour. I hope that many more will do the same.

Unlike military uniforms, workplace clothing and footwear were generally not provided by the employer, and employees had to surrender coupons for their purchase. Household linens were included in the rationing scheme in 1942, effectively reducing the number of coupons available for clothing. Baby clothes were added to the scheme by August 1941, but expectant mothers were issued with 50, and later 60, coupons to purchase the baby's layette (many complained that the coupons were insufficient to purchase the necessary number of diapers). There was no special consideration for maternity clothing. The Board of Trade suggested that most clothes in the mother's wardrobe could be altered; on the other hand, if maternity garments were purchased,

Advertisement for British Viyella wool in the Canadian *National Home Monthly*, January 1945.

Advertisement in the Canadian magazine *National Home Monthly*, June 1944, for Gor-Ray skirts – 'made in Shakespeare's country, but banned to women living in the United Kingdom'.

this saved wear on clothes that could be worn again after the child was born. Children's clothes required fewer points, and after 1941 supplementary coupons were issued to compensate for the fact that children outgrew clothes, particularly shoes. The lack of well-fitting children's shoes, and the fear that this might lead to foot deformities, was noted in the Home Intelligence Weekly Morale Report for 7 September 1943: 'Shoes are responsible for more parental worries and grey hairs than all the air raids.' Alleviating some of this anxiety, the WVS opened clothing exchanges where good quality children's clothes could be swapped for larger sizes without the need for any money or ration coupons.

To celebrate victory in Europe on 8 May 1945, red, white and blue bunting was available without coupons for one month, but it was not until 15 March 1949 that clothing rationing was finally discontinued.

UTILITY

Rationing had proved useful in limiting the amount of cloth and clothing made, but it did not address distribution, cost or quality. The system worked better for the wealthy customer, who with 7 coupons and more money could afford a well-made dress, whereas a poorer client had to surrender the same number of coupons for a cheap dress that fell apart after a dozen wearings. Wealthier women also had larger wardrobes and stockpiles of undergarments and linens that they could rely on for the duration. Working-class women had less to begin with, and now they had to deal with the rising price of clothing, which more than doubled between September 1939 and May 1941. To make matters worse, prices continued to rise after the introduction of rationing, to compensate for the drop in expenditure. Woolworth's abandoned their company's motto, 'Nothing over 6*d*.' or 'Nix over six' because few items could be found to retail for less than sixpence.

With hopes of controlling clothing price inflation in 1941, the Board of Trade fixed maximum prices based on cost plus 5 per cent, and appointed inspectors to regulate the trade. Unfortunately, a smaller workforce combined with the regulated profit margin resulted in few affordable good quality garments. Stopping short of nationalizing the British clothing industry and creating standardized civilian battledress (a topic that was seriously discussed at the highest levels of government in 1940), the Board of Trade sought to consolidate manufacturing by reducing the number of factories making civilian clothing.

Before November 1941, the private sector oversaw quality control from raw materials through the manufacture of cloth to the final production of clothing. There was a chasm in quality between cheap and expensive clothing, and the Board of Trade initially focused on setting specifications for the weight and weave of fabrics. Reducing the vast range available to a select few helped to concentrate efforts on the production of textiles that would wear and clean well. The system of making clothes out of such cloths and selling them at a regulated price without purchase tax became known as the Utility Clothing Scheme. The term was unfortunate, as it conjured up visions of dowdy serviceable clothes: in fact, the Utility scheme actually improved the overall quality of ready-to-wear clothing in Britain.

The Utility Apparel Order came into force in the first week of February 1942. The Board specified that all garments were to be marked using a 'CC41' label, which stood for 'Controlled Commodity 1941'. Commercial artist Reginald Shipp designed the stylized mark during the planning stages for Utility dress – hence the 1941 date. With its modern design, most people thought it resembled two wheels of cheese.

Incentives were offered. Manufacturers of Utility clothing received a higher quota of material, and the Ministry of Labour also promised that no further workers would be withdrawn from any firm where Utility clothing comprised 75 per cent of the output. In 1942, 50 per cent of all clothes produced came under the Utility scheme; by the war's end that had increased to 85 per cent. *The Times* reported on 4 February 1942: 'Short of clothing everyone in a sort of "battle-dress," the scheme is believed to be the only way of effectively controlling prices.' Price controls were set, with a sliding price to accommodate the location of retailers (London's West End shops had higher rents). Although Utility garments were cheaper, and tax-exempt, the public reaction was not entirely positive at first. The bulk of complaints came from customers of higher-end clothes who saw Utility clothing as substandard.

Navy rayon handbags, one printed with wreaths surrounding the Roman numeral VI, for King George VI, and the other with landmarks of London. The selvedges bear the message: '10% of all fabric sales donated to British American Ambulance Corps'. These patriotic British prints were advertised in the June–July 1941 book of Vogue Patterns, together with others including 'Royal Ribbons', 'Victory Palms', and 'The Lion Fights'; all were available in a range of colours.

In April 1942, a new move was made to produce Utility clothing by leading designers. It was the outgrowth of earlier actions by the Board of Trade. Wanting to seize the opportunity of promoting British exports after the fall of France, in the autumn of 1940 the Board had commissioned British designers to create a collection of clothes for the South American market. It was a success, and in the spring of 1941 the Board decided to organize a similar venture, this time for the North American market. That scheme was dropped when the pressure to obtain exports to the United States lessened after the Anglo–American Lend-Lease agreement came into effect in March 1941. However, the bringing together of London designers to create those collections prompted Alison Settle, editor of British *Vogue*, to suggest to the Board of Trade and London's Fashion Group (made up of society ladies and working women in the fashion industry) to organize the Incorporated Society of London Fashion Designers. What came to be known as Inc. Soc. was founded in January 1942. Its purpose was to band together London's designers, not unlike Paris's haute couture syndicate, to coordinate shows, develop standards of workmanship, represent collective interests to the government and press, and protect original fashion designs. By doing these things and by collaborating with British fabric and manufacturing firms to increase the prestige of British clothes at home and abroad, the Society would develop the reputation of London as a centre of fashion. The initial designers included Norman Hartnell, Bianca Mosca (designer for Jacqmar), Digby Morton, Peter Russell, Victor Stiebel, Elspeth Champcommunal of Worth, and Hardy Amies. Edward Molyneux and Charles Creed, both of whom had been working as couturiers in Paris when war was declared but had returned to Britain in 1940, joined the Society shortly after its founding.

Black crepe and brown rayon taffeta evening dress, labelled Molyneux, London, c. 1941.

Norman Hartnell in his London office, comparing his original sketch and a fabric sample to the finished garment, worn by a model, *c.* 1943. The jewel print fabric was made to his design.

OPPOSITE Two views of a khaki green crepe evening gown, labelled Hardy Amies, *c.* 1946. Hardy Amies reopened his business after being discharged from British Intelligence, where he had served in the Belgian division. His first post-war client, in November 1945, was Eaton's department store chain in Canada, and the khaki dress seen here may have been from that first collection.

MADE IN ENGLAND
Hardy Amies
14, SAVILE ROW, W.1.

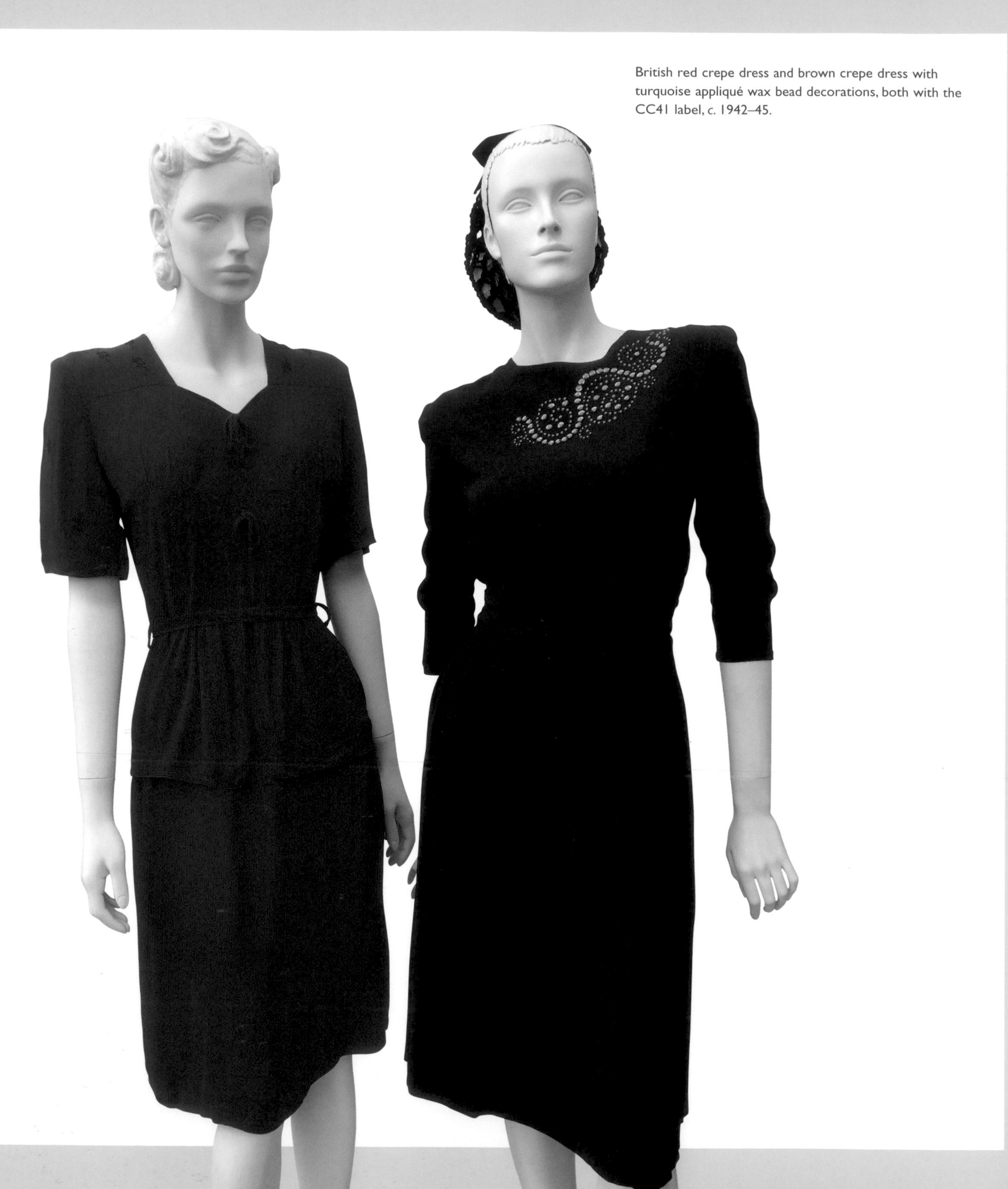

British red crepe dress and brown crepe dress with turquoise appliqué wax bead decorations, both with the CC41 label, *c.* 1942–45.

British wool tweed coat with the CC41 label, *c.* 1942–45. The hat, *c.* 1940–42, is typical of English fashion hats of the early 1940s that were made to represent mannish styles in miniature.

In May 1942 the Board of Trade commissioned Inc. Soc. to create suit, coat, and dress designs that used Utility specification cloth and conformed to all Austerity rules (of which more later); the clothes would hopefully be desirable – but not so much as to stimulate demand. To simplify the manufacturing process, each designer was to create a design using a limited amount of cloth, and the designers suggested a yardage restriction as the easiest method to limit production costs: 2¾ yards (2.5 metres) for an overcoat, 2½ yards (2.3 metres) for a suit, and 2 yards (1.8 metres) for a dress. Each designer was to submit four designs. Thirty-two of the resulting garments were shown in September 1942, modelled by war-workers who volunteered their time for the fashion parade; individual designers were not credited. Government-delineated standardized fashions had not initially been seen as a good idea; but now the fashion press and the public appreciated the attractive, well designed, good quality clothes at affordable prices. The October 1942 issue of British *Vogue* praised them for being elegantly simple and entirely wearable: 'All women have the equal chance to buy beautifully designed clothes suitable to their lives and incomes. It is a revolutionary scheme and a heartening thought. It is, in fact, an outstanding example of applied democracy'. Government-controlled design was seemingly a success, and the Utility grade was expanded the following year to include furniture.

However, balancing supplies with demand continued to be a problem, and tighter controls on distribution became necessary. When supplies of cotton cloth for Utility clothing fell short of the estimated demand in 1942, Hugh Dalton of the Board of Trade appealed to the War Ministry to cut back on the unending demand for men's underwear from the armed services, pointing out that civilians left with coupons for which there were no goods jeopardized the Utility scheme. In the early summer of 1942 the Board was given the power to direct manufacturers – all but officially nationalizing the clothing industry. The manufacture of civilian clothing was concentrated in fewer factories, so that by the end of 1942 80 per cent of all Utility garments were being produced by less than 10 per cent of the firms engaged in clothing manufacture. During 1942 many branded goods disappeared, and the only label appearing in most clothes until the end of the war was the CC41 Utility tag.

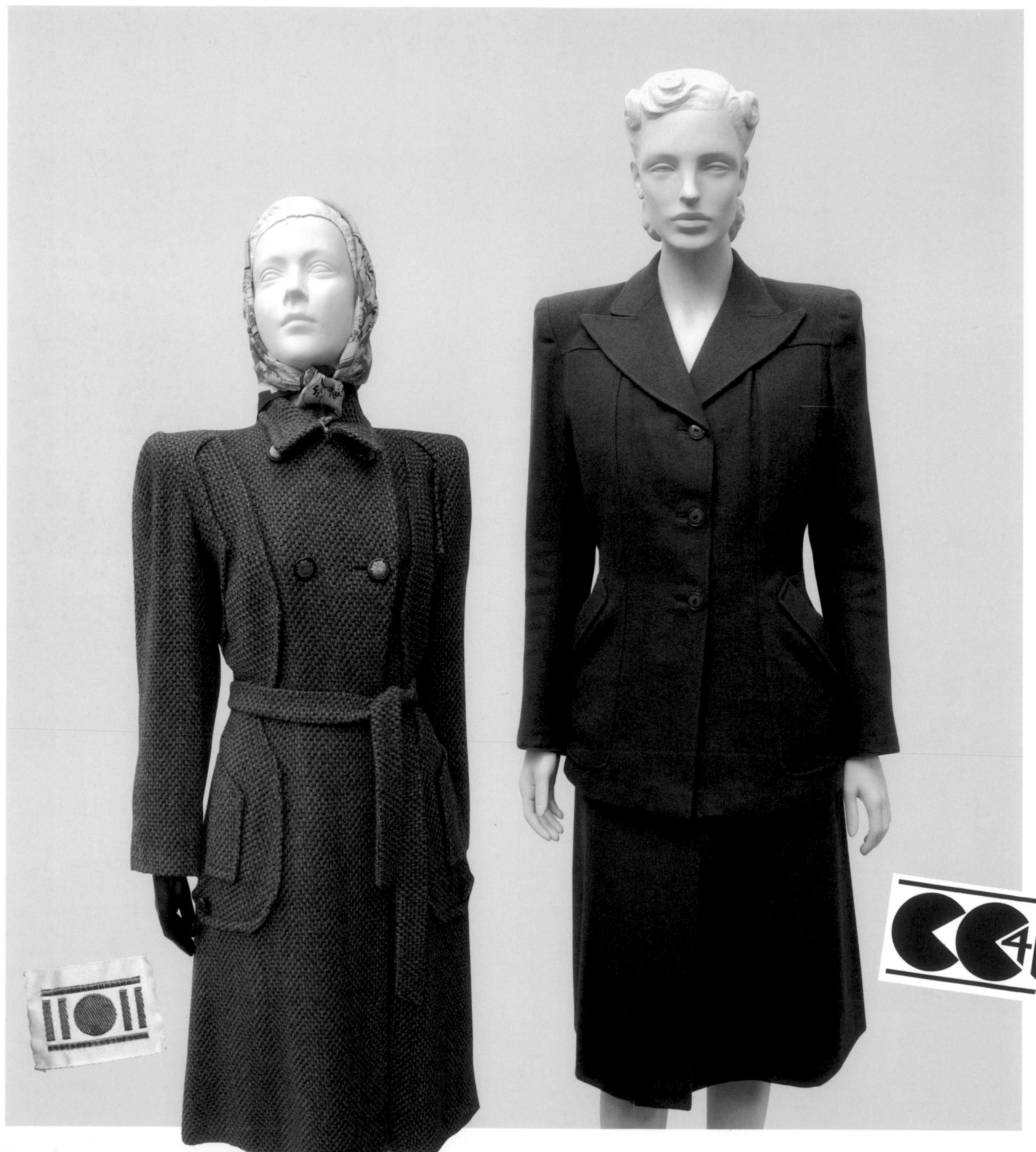

OPPOSITE

LEFT British wool tweed coat, with the 'Double Eleven' Utility label, *c.* 1945–47.

RIGHT British wool tweed suit, with the CC41 label, *c.* 1942–45.

RIGHT British hand-knit sweater, black rayon 'Montgomery' beret, and black cotton skirt made from blackout fabric, *c.* 1945. Blackout cotton was provided coupon-free, to make drapes to keep any light from escaping through windows during air raids. Although this was not officially allowed, the material was commonly used to make up skirts for bicycle riding, and some women tried bleaching it, with little success. After the war, in September 1945, it joined all other textiles in being available only with coupons. The beret was made popular in England by early 1943, when General Montgomery, famous for wearing the style, became a war hero for his military successes in North Africa.

British cotton corduroy suit with matching coat and 'Montgomery' beret, worn by an English war bride who emigrated to Canada, *c.* 1947–48. It bears the 'Double Eleven' Utility label.

Inc. Soc.'s membership increased to ten with the addition of Angele Delanghe in 1945, but it could do little until after the war, especially as Hardy Amies and Victor Stiebel were in service. In 1946, the Society worked on an exhibition of British clothes for the export market held at the Victoria and Albert Museum in London, entitled 'Britain Can Make It'; the clothes on display involved more fabric and greater detail than those for the domestic market. Post-war British clothing exports were five times greater than they had been before the war. In 1947 the Society, with altered membership, acquired the nickname 'The London Ten': Jo Mattli and Michael Sherard replaced Angele Delanghe, who had gone out of business, and Edward Molyneux, who had returned to Paris. It continued to operate throughout the 1950s, but lost influence in the 1960s and disbanded in 1970.

The Utility scheme expanded its range of textiles beginning in late 1944. A second label referred to as the 'Double Eleven' seems to have appeared around the end of the war in 1945 to identify a better quality garment, but the exact conditions of its use are currently unknown. Despite the Board of Trade's attempts never to use words like 'standardized' in descriptions of Utility garments, the British public never quite separated Utility from austerity, and Utility apparel became associated with drab, detail-less, government-standardized dress. Utility clothing continued to be made until March 1952.

British cotton/rayon blend two-piece suit printed with gingham bows, unlabelled but with original CC41 hanging tag, *c.* 1947–48.

BELOW AND OPPOSITE, LEFT Details from Jacqmar scarves, with phrases from popular radio programmes, and with Navy, Army, and Air Force motifs and the words 'Combined Operations'. The English textile-printing company Jacqmar produced some of the most memorable propaganda prints of the Second World War. The large scarves were especially popular sweetheart gifts, bought by American soldiers posted in London.

AUSTERITY

Beginning around the same time as the Utility scheme, 'Austerity' directives were issued to manufacturers that applied to all clothing, including custom work. Bespoke work and non-essential items, such as millinery, were permitted for wealthier clients, as both were subject to a 33 per cent luxury sales tax.

To define the rules, the Board of Trade created numerous committees and subcommittees to deal with various sectors of the clothing industry. These panels dictated how garments should be modified to save on cloth, labour and costs. By the end of 1941 Austerity restrictions limited jackets and coats to no more than three pockets, and dresses to two. Further restrictions were introduced on 1 May 1942 that limited the number of buttons, seams, pleats, ruching and gauging on women's dresses and blouses; all braid, embroidery and lace were banned. For men, trousers were to have legs no more than 19 inches (48 centimetres) in circumference, no turn-ups/cuffs, no elastic in waistbands, and no zip fasteners; there were to be no metal or leather buttons, no raglan sleeves, no tail coats, and no jackets and coats with pleated backs and half-belts. No boys under the age of thirteen were to have long trousers. On 1 June 1942 yet more restrictions came in: corset manufacturers were prohibited from using trimming, fancy stitching or lace, and gauging, shirring and ruching were banned on women's underwear. No form of embroidery, scalloping or trimming was allowed on infants' clothes. Double-breasted suits were banned, as were pockets on pyjamas. Skirts were limited to three buttons, six seams, two box pleats, and one pocket. No metal jewelry was to be produced.

RIGHT British housecoat, with a printed design of vegetable-seed packets and the slogan 'Dig for Victory', c. 1941–45.

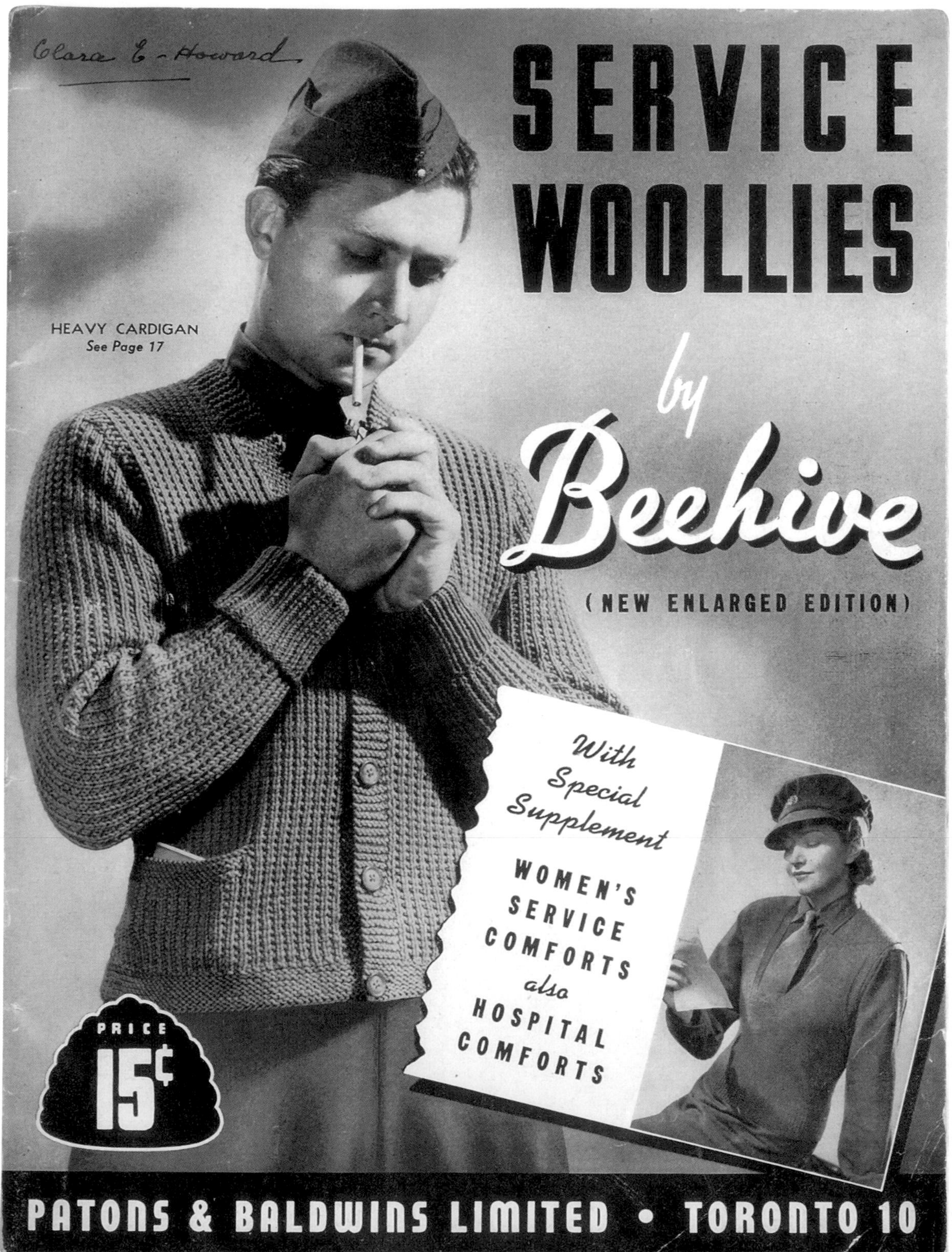
Clara E. Howard
SERVICE WOOLLIES
by Beehive
(NEW ENLARGED EDITION)
HEAVY CARDIGAN
See Page 17
With Special Supplement
WOMEN'S SERVICE COMFORTS
also
HOSPITAL COMFORTS
PRICE
15¢
PATONS & BALDWINS LIMITED • TORONTO 10

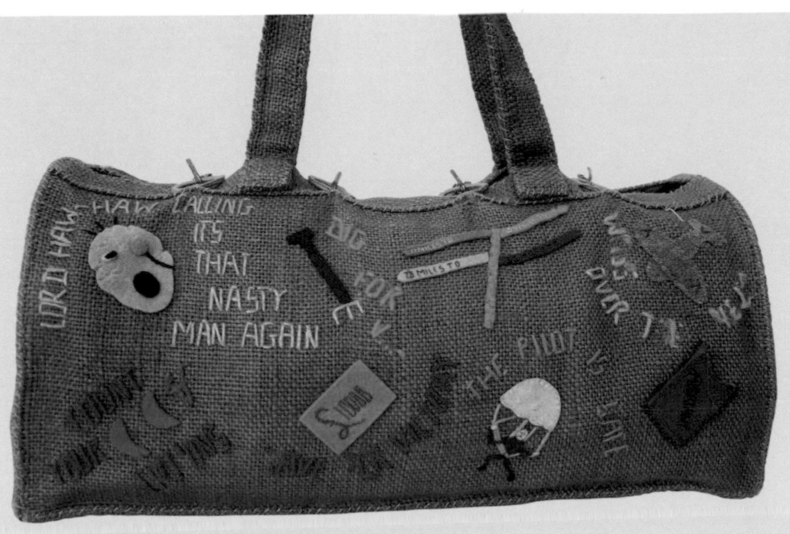

OPPOSITE A Canadian knitting book with patterns for British and Canadian servicemen and women, *c.* 1940.

BELOW American 'Bundles for Britain' brooch, *c.* 1941. Bundles for Britain was founded by the New York socialite Natalie Wales Latham: in December 1939 she started a knitting circle to make scarves, gloves and balaclava helmets for British sailors on the North Atlantic, and soon it became an official organization. In 1941 badges loosely based on the royal crest were sold for $2.50 to raise money to pay for the cost of shipping clothing and blankets, as well as medical aid, to Britain.

Although some restrictions were accepted as necessary for the war effort, not all were. Limiting men's waistcoats to two pockets, no collar or watch-chain hole, and no adjusting strap in the back brought comments of dissatisfaction from the editor of *The Times* and members of Parliament in March 1942. Some of the directives could be evaded, such as turn-ups on trousers: by simply ordering a pair too long in the leg and turning them up at home, the problem was solved.

Towards the end of the war some restrictions were lifted. With victory in sight, on 1 February 1944 trousers with turn-ups were allowed again, and restrictions on skirt pleats and buttons were removed. Double-breasted suits were allowed by the end of the war, and were often made for demobilized soldiers: they were not well liked by most of the men returning to civilian life, to whom they appeared pre-war and old-fashioned, but a new suit was a welcome change from scratchy wool service uniforms.

ABOVE LEFT AND LEFT Two views of a British green burlap duffle bag with felt appliqués and wartime phrases in yarn embroidery, *c.* 1942–45. The phrases include 'Dig for Victory' and 'Britannia Rule the Waves', and a reference to 'that nasty man' Lord Haw-Haw – the traitor William Joyce, who broadcast for Germany throughout the war. Britain and the United States were both adept at creating propaganda slogans like 'Keep it Under Your Hat', 'Make Do and Mend', 'Remember Pearl Harbor', 'Is This Trip Necessary?', and 'Loose Lips Sink Ships'. Home front propaganda typically sought to instil unity and loyalty by building morale and encouraging everyone to do their bit, even if it meant sacrifice, to become victorious over the enemy.

INDEPENDENCE AND LIMITATIONS

The rise of the American designer under wartime restrictions

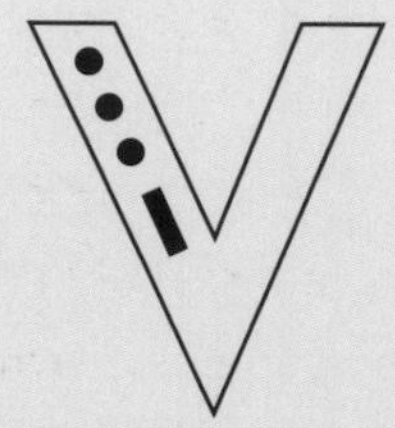

American red crepe dress with brass studs in the shape of bullets trimming the upper sleeves and yoke, *c.* 1942–45.

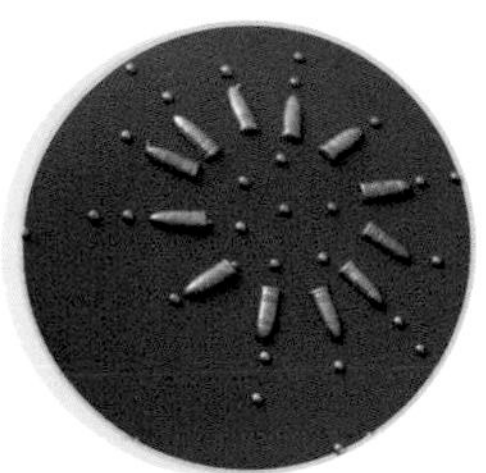

The 21 August 1939 issue of *Time* magazine reported on the Paris autumn collections, and after noting the trends for broader shoulders, higher bosoms, minute waistlines, full skirts, and eye-catching bustles, the writer quipped: 'whoever runs the world, Paris intends to go on making his wife's clothes.' The circumstances of war, however, were to prevent any European city – Paris, London, Turin, Berlin or Vienna – from playing that role.

The United States had the best access to labour and supplies to fill the vacancy. However, American fashion relied on Paris for its lead and had never attempted to be an oracle of style: mass production was its staple. (The American garment industry had undergone reform through the National Recovery Act of 1933 and the Fair Labor Standards Act of 1938, which introduced regulations aimed at eliminating sweatshops and providing a living wage to workers; the National Coat and Suit Industry Recovery Board and the Millinery Stabilization Commission, both formed in 1935, introduced consumer protection labels to industries involved in making women's and children's clothing and hats, guaranteeing that the item was made under sanitary conditions at current wages.) Labels crediting the designer were rare in American clothes, and to avoid any supposed conflict of interest between journalism and advertising, fashion reports in newspapers did not name designers – unless, of course, the designer was French. Most designers worked for manufacturers or department stores, so any credit was given to the employer rather than to the individual talent. This had gone to such ridiculous lengths that the *New York Times* failed to identify any designers when reporting on the American fashions featured in the 'World of Fashion' building at the New York World's Fair in 1939.

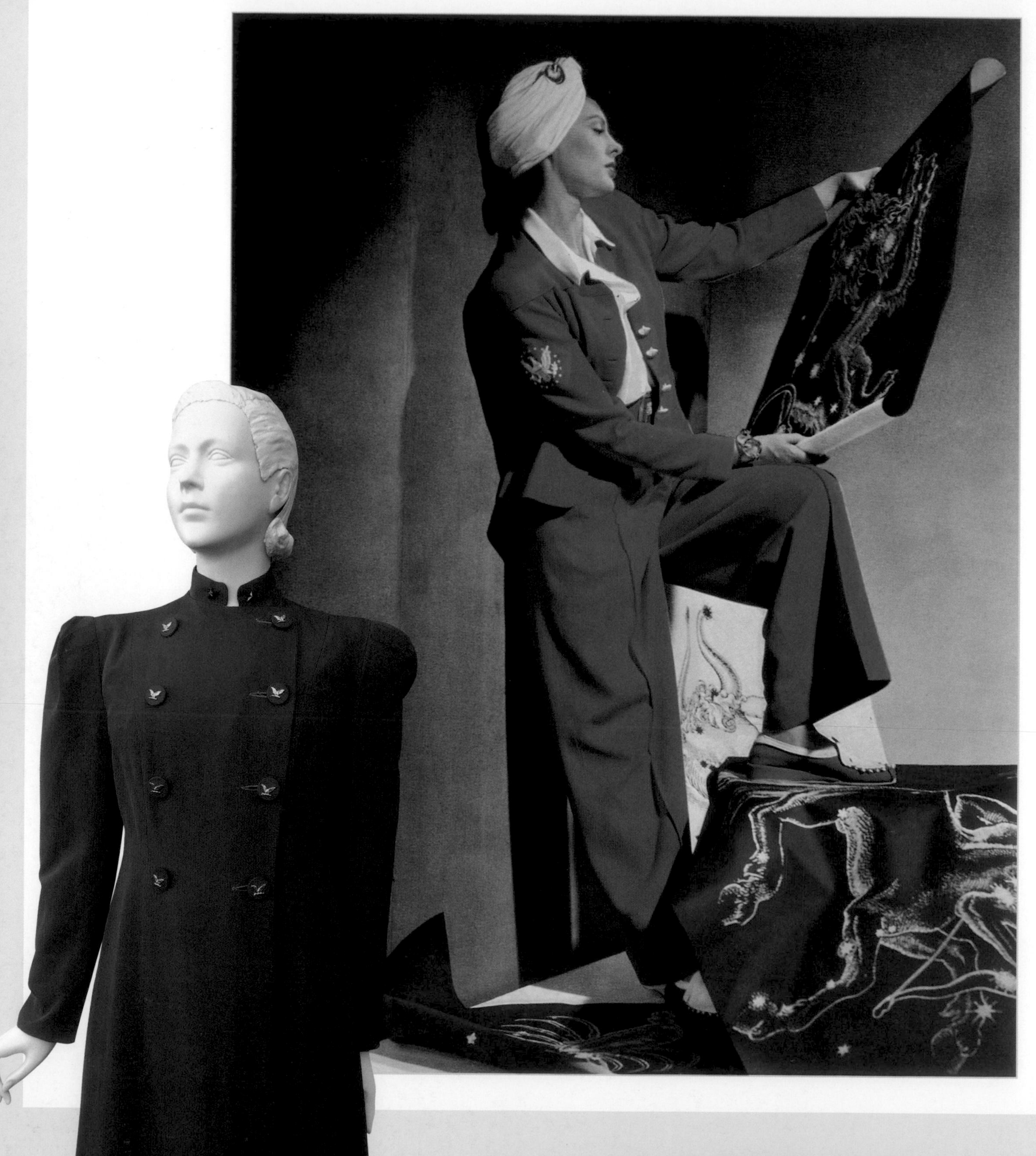

A symbiotic relationship had developed between Paris and New York in the 1920s and 1930s. By 1939, almost a third of Paris's couture was sold to the U.S. market, much of it for the express purpose of being copied or interpreted by manufacturers such as Nettie Rosenstein or Germaine Monteil. There were American couturiers who produced original garments for particular clients – notably Ethel Frankau of Bergdorf Goodman, Fira Benenson of Bonwit Teller, Sophie Gimbel of Saks Fifth Avenue, and Wilson Folmar of Jay Thorpe – but the stores within which they worked also carried models from the major Parisian ateliers for customers who preferred French clothes by named designers.

After the occupation of Paris in 1940, *Time* reported on 19 August:

> Last week, for the first time in more than two decades, some 300 U.S. dress manufacturers, designers, buyers and fashion editors failed to spend early August in Paris, France ... For the first time since they began publication, *Vogue* and *Harper's Bazaar* sent to press their all-important autumn issues without a single last-minute Paris model to rave about.

The autumn 1940 fashion shows were, however, covered by the *New York Times*. That paper also changed its editorial policy from 8 September 1940, and thereafter credited American designers' names and stores in the Sunday fashion page.

Edna Woolman Chase of *Vogue* and Carmel Snow of *Harper's Bazaar* feigned excitement over what American designers would show in their autumn 1940 collections. The look was not yet American, and the designs were mostly safe reinterpretations of the Paris midseason collections. New York Mayor Fiorello LaGuardia, however, was now tirelessly proclaiming Manhattan as the new fashion capital of the world: American fashion had its chance to pounce, and New York pounced first! Saks Fifth Avenue furthered its clothing retail

OPPOSITE

ABOVE **A trouser suit with eagle emblem based on the American seal, featured in American *Vogue*, 1 December 1940. Patriotic themes, including eagles, stars, military insignia, and lots of red, white and blue appeared in clothing well in advance of America's entry into the war in December 1941.**

BELOW **American bengaline evening coat with brass eagle appliqué buttons, *c.* 1940.**

ABOVE **Advertisement for the New York Dress Institute, 1944. The Institute, founded late in 1940, devised the label 'New York Creation' to identify members' products.**

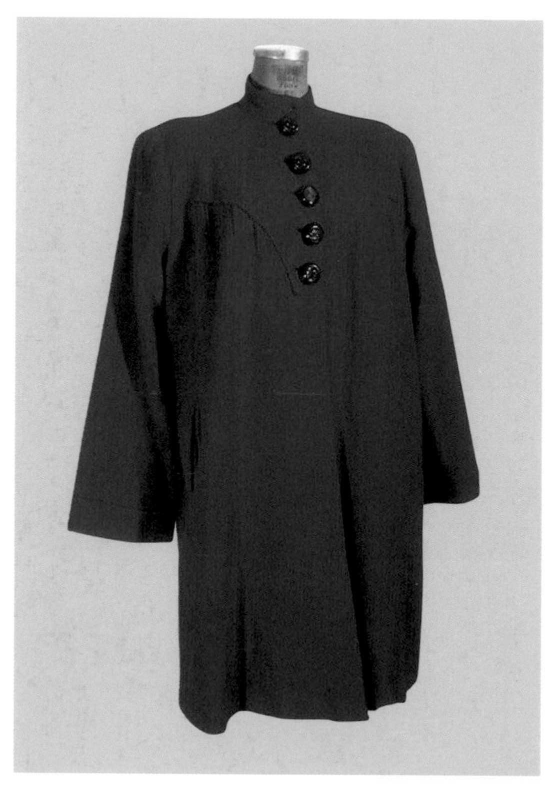

Red wool coat by Schiaparelli, manufactured in the United States, autumn 1940. Schiaparelli arrived in America for a speaking tour, only to discover that the ship carrying the couture clothes she was to use for her lectures had been sunk. The collection had to be reconstructed, which she did using the workrooms of Bonwit Teller in New York. While in the U.S., she arranged to sell her wardrobe tour designs (see opposite) to American dress manufacturers at $600 apiece, plus 7 per cent of the sales, to raise money for vitamin distribution in France. Schiaparelli once said that although France gave her inspiration, it was America that gave her approval.

empire by opening a new branch in Detroit in September 1940. The Museum of Costume Art (later known as The Metropolitan Museum of Art Costume Institute) promoted itself to supplant the vast research facilities of Paris. And the New York Dress Institute was founded, as a joint effort of the garment workers' union and local manufacturers to bolster New York's apparel industry, with a 'New York Creation' label for garments made by member manufacturers. In 1944 the Dress Institute declared: 'like the skyscrapers that dare to soar eighty stories high, New York fashions have the assurance to challenge the world . . . There is an AUTHORITY to New York fashions, because the most exciting city on earth accepts them. New York at present is "out in the lead."' The Institute's publicist, Eleanor Lambert, had created a 'Best-Dressed' list of New York socialites to help promote the makers of their clothes, and in 1943 she founded Press Week, an annual event held every year alternately at the Pierre and Plaza hotels in Manhattan. Press Week gave fashion editors from across the country a chance to see the work of American designers – particularly New York designers.

In 1942 Grover Whalen, chairman of Coty, the perfume company, created the Coty awards: fashion editors from leading newspapers and magazines in New York were to choose who they felt had been influential in the year. Fashion editor Virginia Pope reported in the *New York Times* on 8 January 1942: 'The jurors are to study fashions that make a definite contribution to New York as a fashion center'; of Grover Whalen she said, 'It has always been his pet idea to establish a fashion center in New York.'

New York's aspirations did not go unchallenged. As early as July 1940 Colonel McCormick's *Chicago Tribune* announced a $7,500 design prize with the idea of making Chicago the new Paris. Some wondered whether Hollywood's strength in anticipating fashion (clothes worn at the time of production must seem up-to-the-minute at the time of a film's release) and California's burgeoning sportswear industry made Los Angeles a natural fashion leader. Stanley Marcus, of the famous Dallas department store Neiman Marcus, was not convinced New York was the right choice: he was quoted in *Time* magazine on 25 October 1943 with the opinion that 'New York is finished as a manufacturing center. . . . They're making clothes in Kansas, Philadelphia and Texas now and they won't give it up. The day is gone when only a New York dress is a good dress.'

Line drawings of Schiaparelli's American tour wardrobe, from American *Vogue*, October 1940.

All this posturing seemed sheer nonsense to Elsa Schiaparelli, who was on a three-month speaking tour of the United States in late 1940. The most famous, probably the most influential, and certainly the most outspoken Paris designer of the time – during her tour she accepted a Neiman Marcus award for distinguished service in the field of fashion – she did not curb her words: on 30 December *Time* reported her as saying that the U.S. was too money-conscious to originate its own fashion trends and that Paris, ruled by the Nazis, still led the world of fashion: 'The Eiffel Tower is not displaced by the Empire State Building.' This roused the wrath of American apparel industry leaders, who questioned her political leanings and even her Italian heritage. Adam Gimbel, president of Saks Fifth Avenue, was quoted in *Time* as saying: 'The Paris of the old days is not the Paris under totalitarian government. Schiaparelli is either misguided – or under the influence of the Vichy Government.' (Gimbel's accusation referring to the collaborationist Vichy régime (see p. 159) didn't stand up over time: Schiaparelli, despite sage advice, returned to occupied Paris to arrange the running of her atelier and deliver vitamins bought from the sale of garments in New York, then slipped back out of France and returned to the U.S. to join her daughter Gogo until the end of the war.)

In early September 1941 the first fall collections of pure American invention were unveiled, to mixed reviews. *Time* reported on 8 September that they lacked drama: there were no headline outfits, just good, wearable, saleable clothes. Dresses were not lavishly embellished – which was not surprising, since where French embroiderers made $8 a week, American embroiderers made $50. No seductive details were noticed apart from deep armhole cuts and front peplums on short, tight skirts. American-made fabrics were featured in Howard Greer's day dresses with fishtail hemlines, Bergdorf Goodman's peg-top evening skirts, Sophie Gimbel's men's shirting cotton blouses, Jay Thorpe's Elizabethan-inspired capes and suits with high standing collars, and Milgrim's Middle-Eastern harem skirts and tunics. *Time*'s verdict was: 'On their first real test U.S. designers pass but get no A for originality.'

[Right], first: A sports dress of purple-and-green striped wool jersey, the unpressed box-pleats adjusted by a belt. Schiaparelli's new stocking-cap in plain and striped jersey

• Second: Navy-blue rayon crêpe suit, jacket lined with yellow-and-pink-striped wool jersey. There is a stocking-cap to match

• Left: Black wool suit with stone marten shawl collar and cuffs. Notice the wrap-around skirt. The amusing felt sailor has a stone marten brim

• Far left: Schiaparelli's fitted black wool afternoon coat has a new wide cape-collar and flaring mink cuffs. Notice the wrap-around skirt, the mink hat

• First: Sloping shoulders spell new Schiaparelli chic. This red wool coat is shirred from a deep yoke. Roll brim hat of black beaver

• Second: Another sloping-shoulder coat is of blue broadcloth with Persian lamb yoke; Persian lamb on gloves

• Third: Black crêpe dress for the blue coat

(Continued from page 67)

• Left: For gala evenings, black crêpe draped up in front, the shirred bodice held by wide straps

• Pyjamas for lounging after a lecture; black wool pants, pink wool jacket, bead-embroidered velvet collar. It may also be had with a black skirt

• Right: Schiaparelli is famous for her dinner-suits, such as this black crêpe one, its pockets outlined with bead-embroidered pansies. With it, a black fox busby, gloves with black fox cuffs that come together to form a muff.

• Bolero dinner-costume of royal-blue crêpe, intricately shirred at the waist

• Far left: Alaska Sealskin, Matara-brown, is the basis for a travelling-coat with a shirred back. The hat is of brown suède

• Madame Schiaparelli's wardrobe always includes a Persian lamb coat. This mandarin type swings loosely to the finger-tips

OPPOSITE

LEFT Brown wool suit and black felt hat by Adrian, the suit *c.* 1942–45, the hat *c.* 1942–43.

RIGHT Rayon and wool blend knitted two-piece suit with hook-and-eye brass front closure, probably designed by Claire McCardell, *c.* 1940.

RIGHT Grey and yellow wool skirt and jerkin vest with blouse, by Adrian, *c.* 1942–45.

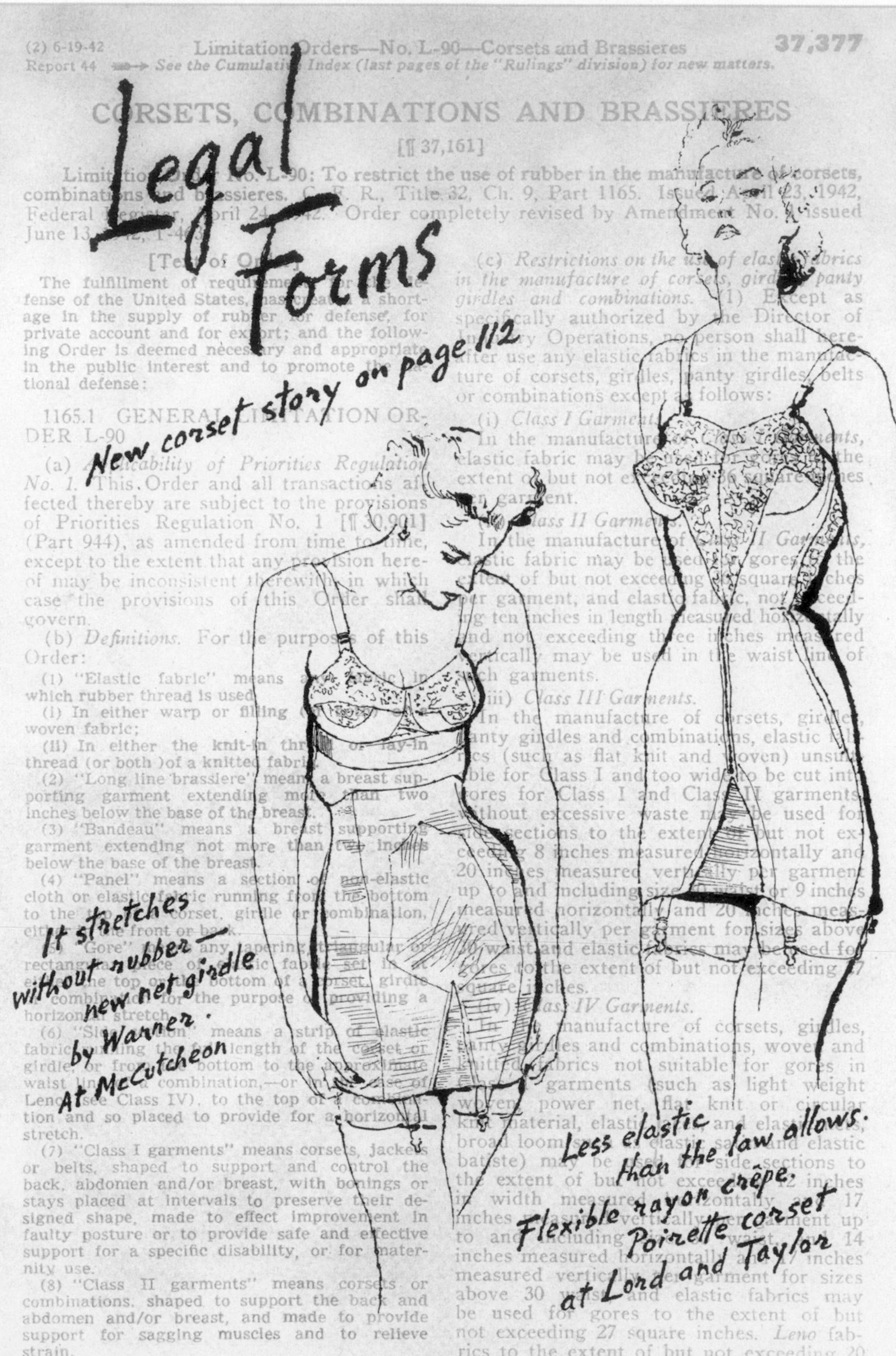

(2) 6-19-42 Limitation Orders—No. L-90—Corsets and Brassieres 37,377
Report 44 ➞ *See the Cumulative Index (last pages of the "Rulings" division) for new matters.*

Legal Forms

New corset story on page 112

CORSETS, COMBINATIONS AND BRASSIERES

[¶ 37,161]

Limitation Order No. L-90: To restrict the use of rubber in the manufacture of corsets, combinations and brassieres. C. F. R., Title 32, Ch. 9, Part 1165. Issued April 23, 1942, Federal Register, April 24, 1942. Order completely revised by Amendment No. [illegible] issued June 13, 1942, 1-4[illegible].

[Text of Order]

The fulfillment of requirements for the defense of the United States, has created a shortage in the supply of rubber for defense, for private account and for export; and the following Order is deemed necessary and appropriate in the public interest and to promote the national defense:

1165.1 GENERAL LIMITATION ORDER L-90

(a) *Applicability of Priorities Regulation No. 1.* This Order and all transactions affected thereby are subject to the provisions of Priorities Regulation No. 1 [¶ 30,901] (Part 944), as amended from time to time, except to the extent that any provision hereof may be inconsistent therewith, in which case the provisions of this Order shall govern.

(b) *Definitions.* For the purposes of this Order:

(1) "Elastic fabric" means any fabric in which rubber thread is used

(i) In either warp or filling [illegible] woven fabric;

(ii) In either the knit-in thread or lay-in thread (or both)of a knitted fabric.

(2) "Long line brassiere" means a breast supporting garment extending more than two inches below the base of the breast.

(3) "Bandeau" means a breast supporting garment extending not more than two inches below the base of the breast.

(4) "Panel" means a section of non-elastic cloth or elastic fabric running from the bottom to the top of a corset, girdle or combination, either in the front or back.

(5) "Gore" means any tapering, triangular or rectangular piece of elastic fabric set in at either the top or the bottom of a corset, girdle or combination for the purpose of providing a horizontal stretch.

(6) "Side section" means a strip of elastic fabric running the full length of the corset or girdle, or from the bottom to the approximate waist line of a combination,—or in the case of Leno (see Class IV), to the top of a combination and so placed to provide for a horizontal stretch.

(7) "Class I garments" means corsets, jackets or belts, shaped to support and control the back, abdomen and/or breast, with bonings or stays placed at intervals to preserve their designed shape, made to effect improvement in faulty posture or to provide safe and effective support for a specific disability, or for maternity use.

(8) "Class II garments" means corsets or combinations, shaped to support the back and abdomen and/or breast, and made to provide support for sagging muscles and to relieve strain.

(c) *Restrictions on the use of elastic fabrics in the manufacture of corsets, girdles, panty girdles and combinations.* (1) Except as specifically authorized by the Director of Industry Operations, no person shall hereafter use any elastic fabrics in the manufacture of corsets, girdles, panty girdles, belts or combinations except as follows:

(i) *Class I Garments.*

In the manufacture of *Class I Garments,* elastic fabric may be used for gores to the extent of but not exceeding 36 square inches per garment.

(ii) *Class II Garments.*

In the manufacture of *Class II Garments,* elastic fabric may be used for gores to the extent of but not exceeding [illegible] square inches per garment, and elastic fabric, not exceeding ten inches in length measured horizontally and not exceeding three inches measured vertically may be used in the waist line of such garments.

(iii) *Class III Garments.*

In the manufacture of corsets, girdles, panty girdles and combinations, elastic fabrics (such as flat knit and woven) unsuitable for Class I and too wide to be cut into gores for Class I and Class II garments without excessive waste may be used for side sections to the extent of but not exceeding 8 inches measured horizontally and 20 inches measured vertically per garment up to and including size 30 waist or 9 inches measured horizontally and 20 inches measured vertically per garment for sizes above 30 waist and elastic fabrics may be used for gores to the extent of but not exceeding 27 square inches.

(iv) *Class IV Garments.*

In the manufacture of corsets, girdles, panty girdles and combinations, woven and knitted fabrics not suitable for gores in Class [illegible] garments (such as light weight woven power net, flat knit or circular knit material, elastic [illegible] and elastic [illegible], broad loom [illegible] elastic satin and elastic batiste) may be used for side sections to the extent of but not exceeding 12 inches in width measured horizontally and 17 inches measured vertically per garment up to and including size [illegible] waist, and 14 inches measured horizontally and 17 inches measured vertically per garment for sizes above 30 waist, and elastic fabrics may be used for gores to the extent of but not exceeding 27 square inches. *Leno* fabrics to the extent of but not exceeding 20

It stretches
without rubber—
new net girdle
by Warner.
At McCutcheon

Less elastic
than the law allows.
Flexible rayon crêpe.
Poirette corset
at Lord and Taylor

War Law Service ¶ 37,161

OPPOSITE **New styles of foundation garments obeying Limitation Order L-90 on 'corsets, combinations and brassieres' (ghost-printed in the background), from American *Vogue*, 15 September 1942.**

Yet American design made innovative strides, free of French influence, and *Vogue* and *Harper's Bazaar* featured American designers, crediting them by name. By 1942 Hattie Carnegie, Claire McCardell and others were becoming nationally known. Although most designers worked from New York, the most influential by 1943, Gilbert Adrian, based his operations in Los Angeles.

Within months of the entry of the United States into the conflict on 8 December 1941, the government introduced rationing and price controls. For models, America could look at Britain, Canada, and even Germany, which had already had two years' experience of trying to solve the problems of shortages and inflation.

In the spring of 1942, the War Production Board (WPB) and its subsidiary, the Civilian Production Administration (CPA), issued a series of rules for the garment industry that were identified by a number preceded by the letter L, for Limitation Order. Women's clothing was covered by L-85. Stanley Marcus headed the textile division of the WPB and under his leadership the silhouette was essentially frozen by restricting fabric to its current amount, keeping seasonal changes minimal. With little or no change in style, purchases of new clothing became unnecessary, and fabric use diminished.

The WPB was anxious, if possible, to avoid coupon rationing, and L-85 restrictions put the onus on manufacturers. Rather than having small courts prosecuting individuals for petty crimes of profiteering and counterfeit, L-85 controlled manufacturers with threats of large fines and hefty jail terms if they failed to meet the regulations. The only rationed civilian clothing was leather footwear, at 3 pairs per person per year – only marginally down from a prewar average of 3.2 pairs per person per year.

Before quotas for civilian fashions were considered, all materials had to be made available for military use. Wool and cotton were domestically produced, but silk and rubber were precious. Silk had become scarce even before the U.S. entered the war: *Life* magazine reported on 11 August 1941, nearly four months before the attack on Pearl Harbor, that the last shipment was leaving Japan and that this would result in a shortage of silk for fashion use. Rubber too was mostly imported from the Far East; in fact, it was America's

Canadian silk print dress, 1940. Canadian manufacturers used American supplies of silk in the first two years of the war, before the United States entered the conflict. Silk continued to reach the United States from China and Japan until the autumn of 1941.

dependency on rubber imports that prompted the Japanese occupation of rubber-producing Malaya.

Although American rayon, wool, linen, and cotton supplies were healthy, it was better to keep reserves high by limiting their use in individual garments. Stanley Marcus actually aided the industry through his L-85 restrictions, by ensuring that American collections created without French models would continue the established mode. Fledgling American designers were forced to play safe within the parameters of established fashion: originality, which might have been beyond their ability or experience, was not encouraged. American fashions did show some progression under the restrictions, but there were no cries for novelty from the public, who understood that designers were doing the best they could under government-imposed limitations. This generally bypassed the issue of critics comparing American to Parisian designs, as had been the case with the post-occupation collections of 1940 and 1941.

Some designers were frustrated by the limitations. Chicago-born Paris couturier Mainbocher, who had fled Paris in the fall of 1939, was not used to being dictated to. He noted in his diary on 2 November 1942: 'There are too many women whose thighs cannot stand to be silhouetted and overcaressed by the too straight skirt. My responsibility will be to remember the different problems of our different clients and try to solve them within the framework of L-85.'

Fabric limitations also had the effect of ensuring maximum profitability, as manufacturers could make more garments from their material: it would be more profitable to make twenty dresses from one bolt of wool than fifteen, especially since wartime prices and wages were frozen. Colours too were subject to conservation measures. A reduction in the number of fashion colours, especially for wool, was required to conserve chemicals needed for wartime use. The Textile Colour Association of the United States released a palette for fall 1942 that included a number of shades with patriotic names such as 'Victory Gold', 'Gallant Blue', 'Valor Red', and 'Patriot Green'.

In the first edition of March 1942, L-85 regulations were intent on reducing yardage by 15 per cent in women's and girls' apparel. No more than two articles of clothing could be sold as a unit, which meant coats that matched suits could no longer be bought as ensembles, although they could be bought separately. The maximum length for a box coat was 42 inches (107 centimetres), with a hem sweep of no more than 60 inches (152 centimetres). A fitted coat could be 43 inches (109 centimetres) long and have a sweep of 72 inches (183 centimetres). A jacket could not exceed 25 inches (63 centimetres) in length. Coat sleeves could not be dolman, leg-of-mutton, or any bias cut, nor have cuffs, and coat belts could not be wider than 2 inches (5 centimetres), nor could hems. Initially, coat linings of wool or fur were not allowed, even though fur was not restricted in any other way. Skirts of day dresses could have a sweep of 78 inches (198 centimetres), and evening dresses of crepe, cotton, or velvet/velveteen could have a sweep of 144 inches (366 centimetres). Waistcoats, and cuffs or turn-ups on men's trousers, were also ruled out, and both sexes were restricted to one pocket per blouse or shirt and no patch pockets on jackets or coats. It was, however, decided that bridal and maternity fashions would not be included in the restriction, nor would theatrical costumes, or religious or judiciary robes. Summarizing some of the main points, *Fashion Digest* in the summer of 1942 printed the L-85 restrictions as 'Ode to Seventh Avenue':

> Thou shall not upon a frock drape overskirt or apron,
> Nor venture forth with any frock that has a scarf or cape on.
> Thy sweep must be within the bounds of seventy-eight inches,
> And make no gown with tucks or pleats, not even little pinches.
> Include no slip that can't be seen, nor zipper up a placket;
> And never dare to make a matching hood or jacket.
> Thou must not set into a frock such sleeves as leg-of-mutton,
> Nor trim a dress, for beauty's sake, with ornamental buttons.

American manufacturers of textiles and garments used their own publicity to promote the war effort (cf. p. 70). This Textron advertisement in 1944 encouraged readers to buy War Bonds.

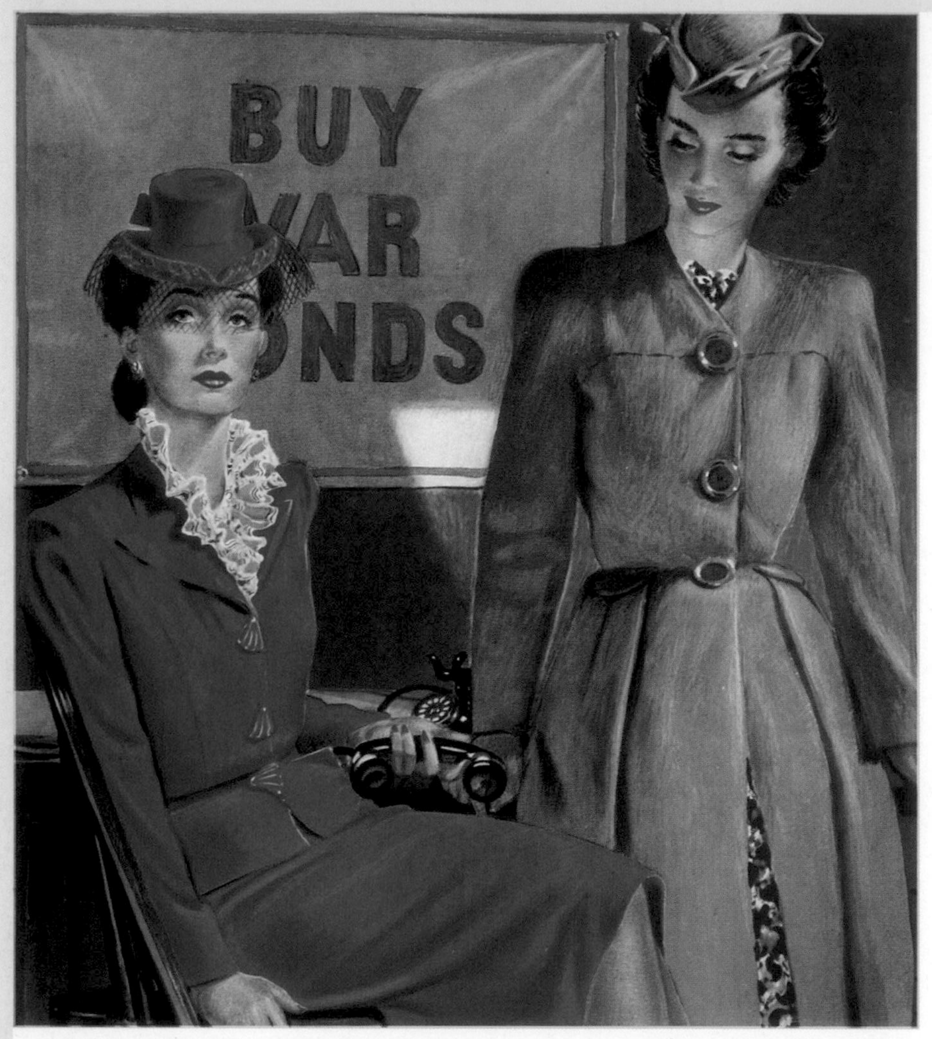

Revisions to the regulations in the summer of 1943 cut down on some materials but made others more available. Home-sewn garments had not initially been restricted, but they were now. Further changes included a reduction of the sweep of a day dress to 72 inches (183 centimetres) and a major reduction of the sweep of a crepe, cotton, or velvet/velveteen evening dress to 90 inches (229 centimetres). However, wool linings were now permitted for coats.

The restrictions, although extensive, were not dire. The long list of limitations was reasonable, and aimed at avoiding unnecessary ornamentation and excessive use of all-but-transparent materials such as netting and lace. The only civilians who found them a problem were the very tall and the portly. In the list of restrictions for 1943 (pp. 71–73) some changes from that of 1942 are signalled.

Advertisement for Hockanum Woolens, 1943. The accompanying text read: 'In all six wars in which American troops have been engaged since the founding of Hockanum Mills in 1809 . . . Hockanum Woolens of superlative quality have been supplied, as now, for the Uniforms of the Armed Forces and for Civilian Clothes on the Home Front.' While propaganda was state-operated in Germany and Italy, elsewhere it was used by businesses to sell products and retain customer loyalty. Women's magazines in Germany are usually devoid of any mention of war or rationing, whereas American magazines used every opportunity to remind women of the many sacrifices they must make during wartime.

Dresses

- The body basic hip measurement for a dress is limited to 56 inches [142 cm]
- Sleeve length for a size 16 dress is limited to 30 inches [76 cm]
- No bi-swing, vent, or Norfolk type backs
- No sleeve facings over 1½ inches [4 cm]
- No more than 2 buttons and 2 buttonholes for each cuff
- No more than 1 ruffle, not exceeding 3 inches [8 cm] in width, on each sleeve
- No more than 1 collar or revers
- No collar or ruffle over 5 inches [13 cm] wide
- No more than 2 pockets, inside or out, or any patch pocket using more than 42 square inches [270 cm^2] of material
- No more than 4 pocket flaps, limited to 18 square inches [116 cm^2] of material each
- No quilting using more than 300 square inches [1,900 cm^2] of material
- Pleating, tucking, and shirring above the waistline of a dress can use mo more than 10 per cent of the total amount of material for that part of the dress, except the entire front top of a dress may be increased by 8 inches [20 cm] of material for tucking or pleating
- The permitted 700 square inches [4,500 cm^2] for a trimming allowance on nontransparent fabrics is cut to 525 square inches (about ⅜ of a yard) [3,400 cm^2] if the hip measurement exceeds the allowable body-basic measurement listed in the order. In any case, the hip measurement can not exceed the allowable sweep. In the case of transparent fabrics, a similar provision reduces trimming allowances from 1,400 square inches [9,000 cm^2] to 1,050 square inches [6,800 cm^2] where the hip measurement is over the maximum body basic hip measure

Evening and Dinner dresses

- For evening dresses of transparent material, there is a permissible sweep of 288 inches—about 8 yards [7.3 m] of material, as compared to anywhere from 14 to 18 yards [12.8–16.5 m] consumed at present
- Swoop of taffeta, flat satin, and dresses of similar materials remains at 144 inches [366 cm]
- Since dresses shorter than ankle or floor length must conform in all respects to daytime and suit dresses, the effect is the elimination of any 'half length' dress

Maternity Dresses

- Restrictions are generally the same as those for other types of dresses, with the exception that the following sweeps are allowed: 80 inches [203 cm] for a size 16 and a junior miss size 15, and 84 inches [213 cm] for a woman's size 40
- All sizes may be made one inch [2.5 cm] longer than the lengths prescribed for daytime or suit dresses
- The full trimming allowance may be used even when the hip measurement exceeds the body basic hip measurement.

American black crepe evening dress with deep armhole cuts and peg-top skirt – two features introduced by American designers in the first collection not influenced by French couture, fall 1941.

Blouses

- If the blouse is ornamented by tucking or pleating in the front, an additional 4 inches [10 cm] of material may be used for the front width
- If there is tucking or pleating on the collar or cuffs, an additional 92 square inches [590 cm^2] of material is permitted to be used in the collar or cuffs
- If tucking or pleating is used, ruffling cannot be used and vice versa
- No more than one ruffle on each sleeve, not wider than 3 inches [7.6 cm]
- No more than one collar or revers, not wider than 5 inches [12.7 cm]
- No more than one pocket, inside or out, and no patch pocket using more than 25 square inches [160 cm^2] of material
- No more than two separate trimming bows over 2 inches [5 cm] wide
- No more than one pocket flap, limited to 15 square inches [97 cm^2] of material
- No cuffs over 3 inches [7.6 cm] wide or with more than 2 buttons and 2 buttonholes
- No bi-swing, vent, or Norfolk type back
- No hoods
- No sleeve facing over 1½ inches [3.8 cm]
- No more than 100 square inches [645 cm^2] of materials used in quilting.

Coats

- Wool linings are now permitted
- No bi-swing or Norfolk type backs
- No sleeve facings over 2 inches [5 cm]
- No more than one collar or revers (a single collar or revers of two thicknesses with an inside lining is permitted)
- No epaulets or tabs on the shoulders
- No more than two pockets, with a maximum of 64 square inches [413 cm^2] of material for any patch pocket
- No more than four flaps
- No separate or attached vestees, dickeys, gilets, or scarves
- Outside sleeve measurements limited to 30 inches [76 cm] for a size 16, in effect eliminating exaggerated types of sleeves
- Sleeve circumference is limited to 16½ inches [42 cm] for all sizes.

Jackets

- No double-breasted fronts
- Sleeve lengths limited to 30 inches [76 cm] and circumference to 14 inches [35.5 cm] in the case of a size 16
- Belts or sashes, previously banned, are now allowed if they do not exceed 2 inches [5 cm] wide
- Collar restrictions are the same as for coats, except that no collar over 5 inches [12.7 cm] wide is allowed
- No quilting
- Restrictions on shoulder epaulets or tabs on pockets and attachments are the same as those for coats, with the exception that material for patch pockets cannot exceed 42 square inches [270 cm^2]

Skirts, Skirt suits and Play suits

- Sweeps reduced from 81 inches to 78 inches [206 to 198 cm] for a misses' size 16 made in non-wool fabrics or in wool fabrics of a 9 ounce [255 g] weight or less
- Sweep on evening and dinner skirts is identical with that for evening and dinner gowns
- No culottes, reversible skirts, lined skirts, quilted skirts or skating skirts
- No separate or attached half belts, full belts, tabs, simulated belts or belt loops
- No pleating, tucking or shirring on the waistband
- No waistband over 3 inches [7.6 cm] wide
- No more than one pocket and no more than 36 square inches [230 cm^2] of material in any patch pocket
- No pocket flap

Slacks, Coveralls, Shorts, Play suits and Pants

- Restrictions on belts, pleatings and waistband are the same as for skirts
- No more than two pockets, with no patch pockets using more than 36 square inches [230 cm^2] of material
- No blouse or shirt top not conforming to the schedule on blouses.

Neckwear and related items

- No cuffs over 3 inches [7.6 cm] wide or with more than 22 buttons and 2 buttonholes
- No French cuffs
- No more than one collar or revers—except that a single collar or revers of two thicknesses is permitted
- No collar over 5 inches [12.7 cm] wide
- No more than 2 separate trimming bows
- No all-over tucking or shirring
- No quilting using more than 100 square inches [645 cm^2] of material
- No pleating, tucking or shirring which increases the front of a vestee, dickey or gilet of more than 4 inches [10 cm] of material
- If the front of the neckwear is increased, no ruffle, frill or jabot is allowed
- No more than two pin-tucks on each side of the center front of a vestee, dickey or gilet when a jabot, frill or ruffle is also used
- Shirring on lace cannot be more than half as large again as laces ¾ of an inch to 2 inches [2–5 cm] wide, and no more than twice as large as laces exceeding this width
- The following restrictions are imposed on specific types of neckwear when made or sold as independent units: Jabots cannot consume more than 480 square inches [3,100 cm^2] of material — compared to over 800 square inches [5,160 cm^2] previously. Revers cannot be more than 7 inches [18 cm] from the binding to the extreme edge, including the trim. Previously, they were upward of 9 inches [23 cm] wide. Bibs cannot be more than 9 inches [23 cm] deep, although previously they had sometimes been twice this depth. Collars of sheer materials cannot be more than two tiers of fabrics, not exceeding 5 inches [12.7 cm] in width apiece. This will eliminate the type of collar which previously had used literally any number of layers of fabrics.
- If sold as an attachment to another item of neckwear, the following restrictions are imposed: A jabot can not use more than 320 square inches [2,065 cm^2] of material. No jabot can have more than three tiers of material, 5 inches [12.7 cm] wide each. No revers can be more than 5 inches wide, including the trim. No frill or ruffle can be over 5 inches wide on either or both sides of the center front. The fullness of a ruffle or frill is limited to three times the amount of the material which it covers (3 to 1).

American handkerchief and scarves, unsigned, *c.* 1940–42. Despite the country's officially isolationist policy, American sympathies lay with the British and French. As early as the summer of 1939, President Roosevelt created a War Resources Board to mobilize business for war production. Reflecting the mood, militaristic as well as patriotic motifs were showing up in American textiles and garments by early 1940.

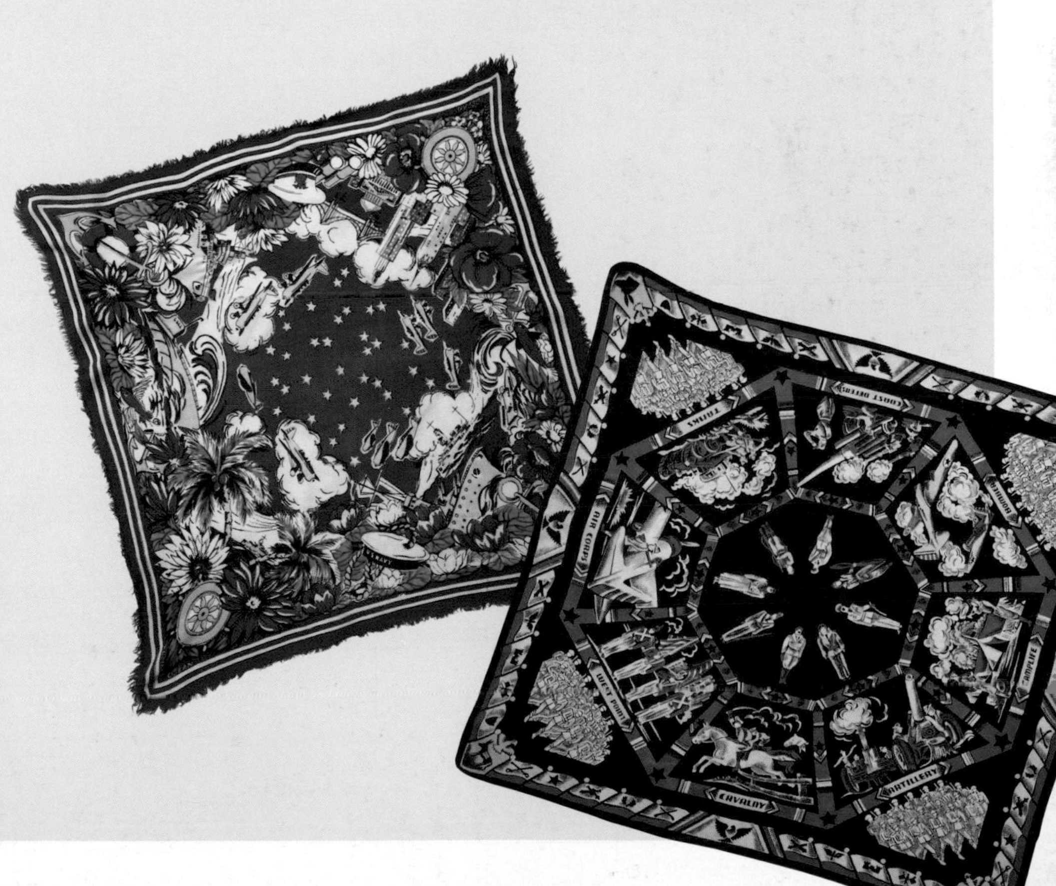

Young women wore souvenirs from boyfriends serving overseas as badges of honour. Cap badges were the most popular trinkets, despite the fact that giving them as presents contravened rules. Sweetheart brooches, incorporating the insignia of the boyfriend's regiment or brigade, were made specifically as mementos for girlfriends on the home front.

ABOVE Advertisement for antiperspirant featuring a woman wearing military insignia as brooches, in *Good Housekeeping*, October 1944.

ABOVE AND OPPOSITE, ABOVE Canadian and American wood, metal and Bakelite patriotic brooches.

American red and white print rayon suit, with celluloid heart brooch emulating a military decoration, *c.* 1942.

Militaristic inspirations showed up in some 1939 collections, but not until after war began did military-style coats, collars, braid, and hats become more commonly seen. Allusions were often not to contemporary military styles, but instead to those of the nineteenth century or earlier.

ABOVE Brown wool felt cockade-decorated kepi-inspired hat, *c.* 1941–43.

LEFT Brown wool felt and grosgrain ribbon hat inspired by historic military headgear, *c.* 1945.

Yellow wool suit with waist-length 'Eisenhower' jacket, *c.* 1944–45. General Dwight D. Eisenhower – Supreme Commander of the Allied Forces – considered the American uniform poor for combat: instead, he wanted something that would be less restrictive and more comfortable, while still looking stylish. He had his tailor modify a field jacket to his specifications, and the resulting 'Ike jacket' became standard issue for U.S. troops beginning in November 1944. Women's waist-length jackets had first appeared in 1940, but when the American army adopted the style, they took on the same name.

American *Vogue* noted in the 1 February 1943 issue that American designers had no problem meeting the requirements of L-85 and had voluntarily restrained their fabric usage even more than the law required.

Style did not immediately change following victory in Europe in May and victory in Japan in August 1945. Fall 1945 and spring 1946 collections remained under L-85 restrictions, forcing the wartime silhouette to continue. But, anticipating imminent change, American manufacturers began to push the limits of L-85 for autumn 1946 collections. *Time* magazine reported on 21 October:

> Last week thousands of hobbled U.S. dress manufacturers and retailers were hopping mad . . . Several months ago the whole industry had heard 'on reliable authority' that CPA order L-85, which was intended to conserve materials during the war, would be dropped on Nov. 12. This made sense, as the production of yard goods was rising so fast that the supply would soon be ample. Forthwith manufacturers began making dresses longer, with a greater sweep to the skirts and with pockets, matching hoods, extra-wide cuffs, sashes, and belts. But last week, just as the new dresses were going on sale, CPA dropped a cruncher: most of L-85 would stay in effect indefinitely. In fact, said CPA, there had never been any intention of dropping it. CPA also emphasized the penalty for sellers of extra-legal dresses: one year in prison or $10,000 fine, or both. What could retailers, stuck with the unsalable dresses, do? One New York syndicate alone had $1,000,000 worth on hand. Most manufacturers had refused to take the clothes back.

Canadian dirndl skirt made from American cotton yardage printed with white V shapes and the Morse code signal for the letter V – dot-dot-dot-dash – both standing for 'victory' (see p. 81), *c.* 1942–45.

BELOW American plastic buttons with aeroplanes, and American or Canadian plastic buttons with the letter V for 'victory'.

RIGHT American blue cotton culotte dress and red wool jacket with embroidered V on the breast pocket, c. 1942.

> Some stores that had illegal two-piece dresses were getting around the law by selling them as two separate garments. But most retailers have only the dubious out of snipping the illegal margins off their dresses. This would either 1) spoil the design, or 2) boost the price because of alteration cost. And the snippings would be of no use to anyone.

Retailers now faced losses in the millions because of the massive numbers of fall and winter garments manufactured in disregard of L-85. However, with wartime controls on industry falling away with each passing week, the CPA turned women's fashions back to free enterprise, killing order L-85 within a week of the appearance of the *Time* magazine report. While the full effects of the freeing of materials would not be seen until spring 1947, American fashions could now be designed as full and frilly as women wanted.

Canadian and American rhinestone and metal brooches, *c.* 1941–45.

Victor de Lavelaye, head of the Belgian Service of the BBC, first devised the idea of the 'V for Victory' campaign in a broadcast to his countrymen on 14 February 1941. Churchill popularized the symbolism with his upheld fingers in the shape of a V, and the V and the Morse code letter – three dots followed by a dash (see p. 78) – came to be found on everything from patriotic jewelry to food packaging. The tempo of the Morse signal was the same as that of the first four notes of Beethoven's Fifth Symphony, which also became a symbol of victory. Fully aware of the symbol's power, the Germans commandeered it, claiming the V stood for *Viktoria*, an old Germanic word for victory.

RIGHT Canadian brown felt turban ornamented with a symbolic V, *c.* 1942–45.

ZOOTS AND ZAZOUS

Anti-fashion in a time of crisis

American dirndl-style dresses typically worn by teenaged girls, *c.* 1940–45.

In 1934, Irving Sorger of Kline's, Inc., a department store in St Louis, Missouri, surveyed customers and found that young women wanted clothes that differed from what their mothers wore. He identified a need for what became known as the 'Junior' line, and St Louis became the American manufacturing hub of Junior ready-to-wear. In the same vein, *Mademoiselle* magazine, founded in 1935, aimed at a readership of unmarried college-age women, and the French designer Jacques Heim created a line of prêt-à-porter for young women under the name 'Heim Jeunes Filles' in 1936. The name 'Jeune Fille' was taken by Hattie Carnegie in 1941 for a new shop in New York aimed at younger customers on a budget.

In the late 1930s Mickey Rooney and Judy Garland became the first teenage screen idols. The term 'teenager' officially entered American English in 1944, and in the same year *Seventeen* magazine made its debut – the first fashion magazine aimed solely at the teenaged girl. Teenagers had become an identifiable market and American manufacturers advertised directly to them. Saddle shoes, bobby-sox, 'sloppy Joe' sweaters, kilt skirts, penny loafers, ankle bracelets, and pedal-pushers were icons of American teenage girl style. European teenage dress was not so different from adult fashions, but as American Swing music spread across Europe just before the start of the war, a subculture of youth used Swing as their anthem to dress and act in a rebellious manner.

BELOW AND OPPOSITE **American cotton evening dress with print of jitterbug dances and musical notes, and a detail of the pattern around the hem, *c.* 1943–45.**

In New York in the 1930s, a fashion evolved that became the uniform of primarily young urban Black and Hispanic males who were fascinated by jazz music. The style was identifiable by its full-legged tapered trousers and over-sized jacket with padded shoulders, all worn with a confidant swagger. These self-proclaimed 'Hepcats' dubbed the suit 'zoot' . Their girlfriends often wore similarly styled broad-shouldered long jackets with short skirts. The *New Yorker* magazine ironically quipped in 1941:

> We herewith submit a preview of men's Easter fashions from the world's least inhibited fashion centre, Harlem. Trousers will be deeply pleated with waistband just under the armpits, 30-inch [76 cm] knees, and 15-inch [38 cm] cuffs. A popular suit jacket is one that measures 36 inches [91 cm] down the back seam . . . shoulders padded out 3½ inches [9 cm] on each side, two breast pockets, and slashed side pockets. This may be worn with a white doeskin waistcoat. Shoes are pointed, the most popular leathers being light-tan calfskin and coloured suede. Hats may be worn in the porkpie shape or with crowns 6 inches [15 cm] high. Colours, as always, are limited only by spectrum.

The Zoot style was at the height of its popularity during the war and was even the subject of a 1942 song, 'A Zoot Suit', with the refrain, 'I want a zoot suit with a reet pleat, with a drape shape and a stuff cuff.'

A variation of the zoot suit style was worn by Parisian youths. The suits had shorter trousers, which exposed white or brightly coloured socks and platform shoes; a gaudy tie with a tight knot, thin moustache, quiff of hair, and tightly rolled umbrella completed the look of the French 'Zazous'. Their name seems to have originated in the Cab Calloway hit, 'Zaz Zuh Zaz'. The female version usually consisted of a short pleated skirt, broad-shouldered sweater, striped stockings, heavy-soled flat shoes, excessive make-up, and long curled hair, usually platinum blonde. Zazou style was at its most popular on the left bank of Paris in 1941, when France was largely under German occupation. Despite German disapproval of the style for its decadent American influence and disregard of clothing rationing, Zazous were unwilling to act as if there was a war on. Although Zazous were usually teenagers showing a predictable contempt for established order, the collaborationist press attacked them as idlers and associated them with black marketeers and degenerates. In July 1942, the collaborationist youth group Jeunesse Populaire began to persecute them, effectively curtailing the movement. Those who continued to follow Zazou culture openly usually ended up in labour camps.

The German Swing Kids were the counterpart of American Hepcats and French Zazous. The National Socialists denounced American jazz as degenerate in 1933, but the more melodic style of Swing found popularity in the mid-1930s. After the 1936 Berlin Olympics, however, National Socialism increasingly isolated the German people from international influence, and Swing was officially banned in 1938 as a potential menace to German youth. Underground clubs of teenaged Swing dancers then sprang up in major cities across Germany. To Swing Kids, National Socialism was a repressive regime to be ignored or defied. They dressed to identify themselves and intentionally used Swing slang, English phrases, and Yiddish in their speech. Hallmarks included haircuts and clothes that contravened the short pants and shaved temples of the Hitler Youth. Male Swing Kids favoured a look that combined the styles

worn by the British Foreign Secretary Anthony Eden and American Hollywood gangsters. A double-breasted suit with wide lapels, tight waist, and full-cut legs with cuffs/turn-ups was the basic uniform of a Swing Kid. A long overcoat and umbrella completed his look. Rationing made finding clothes a problem, but one solution was to take large-size single-breasted suits and alter them into double-breasted styles. There was some variance in the distinctive features of Swing Kid attire from city to city – something Nazi authorities documented in order to identify and suppress the movement. Swing girls typically chose overly dramatic make-up and wore their hair long, loose and curly, ignoring the 'Gretchen' braids worn by National Socialist girls. They favored shortish skirts or alternatively long trousers, and often combined parts of girls' youth group uniforms with civilian clothing. Hamburg Swing Club girls were reported as having a penchant for white-rimmed sunglasses.

Despite the open condemnation of Swing music and its followers, the teenage obsession did not abate. As late as 1944, a report from the Reichsjustizministerium (Ministry of Justice) lamented:

> One of the most . . . dangerous groups within the Reich is the so-called Swing Youth . . . These cliques begin their activities out of a selfish impulse to amuse themselves but rapidly deteriorate into anti-social criminal gangs. Even before the war, boys and girls from the elite social set in Hamburg would get together dressed

A group of affluent teenagers pose for a *Life* magazine cameraman. The boys are wearing modified zoot suits; the girls wear modest versions of the style, with long jackets and knee-length skirts.

in notorious baggy or loose clothing and become entranced under the spell of English music and English dance. The Flottbecker Clique (Swing Kids from Hamburg) organized private dance parties attended by 500–600 teenagers during the winter of 1939–40 . . . The Authorities rightfully banned such house dances, but the cliques were addicted to the English beat and continued to organize unlawful jamborees full of sexual mischief . . . They do not appreciate the success of our forces in the field, and even disparage the ultimate sacrifice of our men in uniform . . . Clique members show off by dressing audaciously in British-style clothing . . . Their mistaken ideals of individual freedom lead them openly to oppose the Hitler Youth.

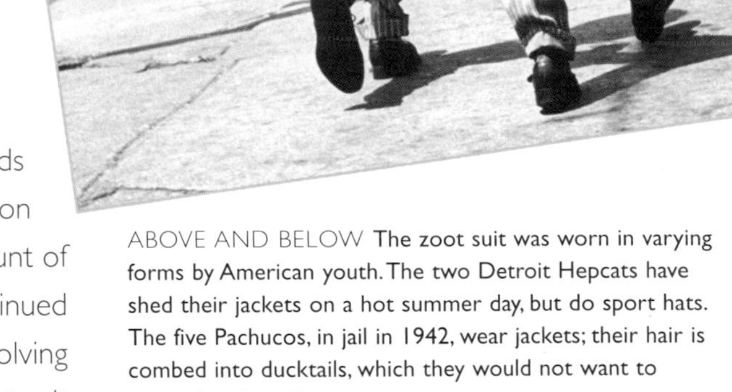

In America, where the style had begun, attitudes changed towards zoot suits shortly after the country entered the war. The War Production Board initiated clothing restrictions in March 1942 that limited the amount of wool in men's suits. The zoot suit became technically illegal, and its continued use was considered unpatriotic. A sensational murder trial in 1942 involving rival Mexican–American (Pachuco) gangs in Los Angeles associated zoot-suit wearers in the public mind with anti-social behaviour and delinquency. Pachuco style was slightly different from the New York zoot suit style: they rarely wore ties, and especially not hats, which would have hidden the slicked-back ducktail flip of hair at the nape of the neck. Their girlfriends were known for wearing skirts above the knee, jackets nearly as long as the skirt, and shoes with knee socks or majorette boots with tassels. Girls' hair was worn very high in a pompadour, usually combed over a pillow or rat at the front, with artificial or fresh flowers at the side.

In the first week of June 1943, hostility between servicemen and Pachuco youths escalated into a week-long street fight in Los Angeles, which became

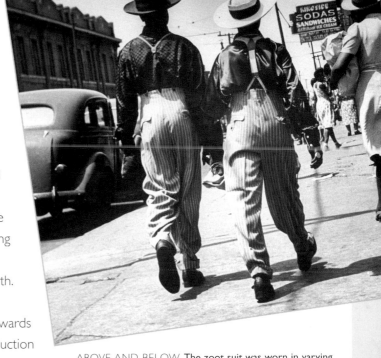

ABOVE AND BELOW **The zoot suit was worn in varying forms by American youth. The two Detroit Hepcats have shed their jackets on a hot summer day, but do sport hats. The five Pachucos, in jail in 1942, wear jackets; their hair is combed into ducktails, which they would not want to conceal under a hat.**

OPPOSITE **The Will Mastin Trio, c. late 1940s, Sammy Davis Junior, in the centre, wears an extreme version of the zoot suit for his vaudeville routine, while his father (left) and Will Mastin (right) dress in suits exemplary of the late 1940s fashion for looser fitting jackets and fuller trousers.**

known as the 'Zoot Suit Riots'. Tensions had subsided by late July, just when the film *Stormy Weather* was released which featured Cab Calloway in an extreme, almost cartoon-like, zoot suit in the finale.

However, the association of zoot suit wearers and rebellion persisted. Minor clashes in Montreal between Canadian military personnel and 'Zooters' escalated into a series of brawls, the worst of which occurred in the three days before D-Day on 6 June 1944. Based less on race and more on politics (Quebec had not shown support for conscription), zoot suits were seen as the uniform of draft dodgers – the antithesis of the military uniform. Zooters caught by marauding servicemen were routinely stripped of their outfits – including some youths who were mistaken as Zooters for wearing pre-war suits. The *Guardian* newspaper in Montreal wrote on 15 June that zoot suits were a 'symbol of insolence and army evasion, frivolity in time of war'.

With the conclusion of war, the zoot suit lost its association with delinquency or draft dodging, as de-regulated men's suits in 1946 saw fuller trousers and longer, wider jackets come back into fashion. A new suit of clothes was a standard allotment that came with a discharge from service. Suits for the demobilized (or 'demob' as they were called in Britain) looked exactly the same as suits had before the war. There had been no discernable progression in men's civilian styles: the only modifications that occurred during the war were to meet government regulations, such as the banning of pocket flaps, waistcoats/vests, and trouser turn-ups/cuffs. Now a movement towards more relaxed clothes that had begun before the war picked up speed: open-collar and short-sleeve knit shirts, ascot ties, casual shorts and trousers, and loafers and sandals all became staples of men's wardrobes.

ABOVE **A discharged GI looking at civilian suits, summer 1945.**

BEAUTY ON DUTY

The war effort and the pursuit of novelty and beauty

The movie star Mary Pickford posing with employees during her visit to the General Engineering Company munitions factory at Scarborough, Ontario, Canada, 5 June 1943.

More than any preceding conflict, World War II relied upon industrial production. From the outset the Allied nations asked women to play active roles in the industrial workforce, while maintaining morale by keeping up a feminine appearance. Almost exactly the opposite was requested of women in Germany and Japan, who were urged to remain wives and mothers but deny themselves luxuries like beauty products for the greater good of the nation; eventually, however, as labour shortages became critical towards the end of the war, they were required to take on industrial war work. In Germany they were even conscripted to work, as defeat became imminent.

The 'call-up' in Britain in March 1942 for single women and widows aged between twenty and thirty was the first time any country had conscripted women for wartime service. Many had already voluntarily joined the services or taken up war work, to ensure that they would remain close to home or be in an occupation they wanted rather than munitions work – generally considered the most dangerous job for women during the war. In July 1943 all women between the ages of thirty-one and fifty were required to register for war work. By then nearly 90 per cent of single women and 80 per cent of married women were already employed in some form of essential voluntary or paid war work, ranging from the forces and industry to running child-care centres and canteens.

Women in factories often wore shapeless jumpsuits and kept their hair pinned up under a scarf tied about their head into a turban. The scarf turban became an identifiable element of the female industrial worker's uniform

everywhere. In the United States 'Rosie the Riveter' was the icon of Working Ordnance Women (WOW), and her turban-wearing image became a symbol of patriotism used to encourage women to take on wartime jobs. Cosmetics became the only feminine reinforcement in many workplaces. Fortunately for women in munitions factories, cosmetics were recommended, especially face creams, to protect their skin from toxic chemicals. British munitions workers were even given special allowances for face creams in August 1942.

France had no time to create military uniforms for its women before it was occupied by the Germans, but Britain had uniforms designed that were based on a fashionable militaristic walking suit of 1939. In the United States, the attractiveness of the uniform was found to sway opinion in favour of one service rather than another. Finding the right balance between conformity and femininity that would appeal to female recruits was achieved in 1942 when the civilian uniform advisor to the Navy, Mrs James Forrestal, who had also been an editor for American *Vogue*, asked American-born Paris designer Mainbocher to design uniforms for the Women Accepted for Volunteer Emergency Service (WAVES). Not surprisingly, the WAVES were considered the best-dressed American women at war. The Women's Reserve of the Coast Guard (SPARS) adopted the same uniform. The stylish uniform attracted recruits, who also recognized how easily the suit might be altered to post-service use by simply removing the insignia. Despite the attractiveness of the uniform, American *Vogue* asked readers in their 15 March 1942 issue: 'Should women wear uniforms? . . . When a soldier comes home on leave, his idea is to get away from uniforms for a while. He wants to see women looking pretty, attractively-dressed, and above all, feminine; not warlike and regimented, with Sensible Shoes and a do-or-die expression.'

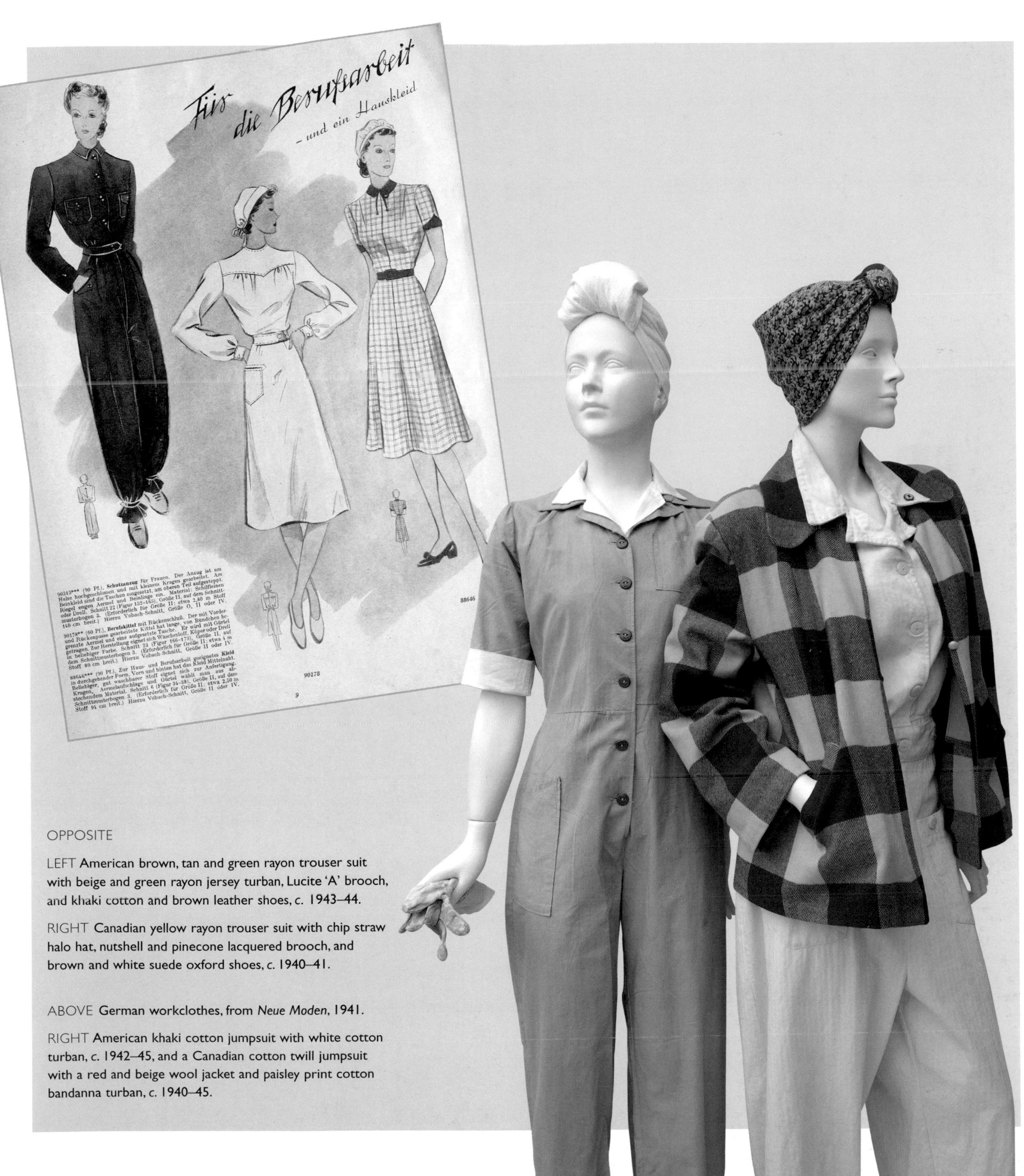

Für die Berufsarbeit

– und ein Hauskleid

90313*** (90 Pf.), **Schutzanzug** für Frauen. Der Anzug ist am Halse hochgeschlossen und mit kleinem Kragen gearbeitet. Am Beinkleid sind die Taschen eingesetzt, am oberen Teil aufgesteppt. Riegel engen Aermel und Beinlinge ein. Material: Schilfleinen oder Drell. Schnitt 22 (Figur 152–165), Größe II, auf dem Schnittmusterbogen 3. (Erforderlich für Größe II: etwa 2,80 m Stoff 140 cm breit.) Hierzu Vobach-Schnitt, Größe O, II oder IV.

90178** (60 Pf.), **Berufskittel** mit Rückenschluß. Der mit Vorder- und Rückenpasse gearbeitete Kittel hat lange, von Bündchen begrenzte Aermel und eine aufgesetzte Tasche. Er wird mit Gürtel getragen. Zur Herstellung eignet sich Waschestoff, Köper oder Drell in beliebiger Farbe. Schnitt 23 (Figur 166–173), Größe II, auf dem Schnittmusterbogen 3. (Erforderlich für Größe II: etwa 4 m Stoff 80 cm breit.) Hierzu Vobach-Schnitt, Größe II oder IV.

88646*** (90 Pf.), Zur Haus- und Berufsarbeit geeignetes **Kleid** in durchgehender Form. Vorn und hinten hat das Kleid Mittelnaht. Beliebiger, gut waschbarer Stoff eignet sich zur Anfertigung. Kragen, Aermelaufschläge und Gürtel wählt man aus abstechendem Material. Schnitt 6 (Figur 34–38), Größe II, auf dem Schnittmusterbogen 3. (Erforderlich für Größe II: etwa 2,50 m Stoff 94 cm breit.) Hierzu Vobach-Schnitt, Größe II oder IV.

88646

90178

9

OPPOSITE

LEFT American brown, tan and green rayon trouser suit with beige and green rayon jersey turban, Lucite 'A' brooch, and khaki cotton and brown leather shoes, *c.* 1943–44.

RIGHT Canadian yellow rayon trouser suit with chip straw halo hat, nutshell and pinecone lacquered brooch, and brown and white suede oxford shoes, *c.* 1940–41.

ABOVE German workclothes, from *Neue Moden*, 1941.

RIGHT American khaki cotton jumpsuit with white cotton turban, *c.* 1942–45, and a Canadian cotton twill jumpsuit with a red and beige wool jacket and paisley print cotton bandanna turban, *c.* 1940–45.

American WAVES recruitment booklet, 1943, and American WAC recruitment postcard, 1942.

For most women in wartime occupations, beauty and social convention were trumped by practical considerations. British and American government propaganda and advertisers constantly reinforced the ideals of beauty as a feminine responsibility to keep up morale. The pros and cons of ceasing the production of beauty products were debated in Britain, but all the pros did not outweigh the con of a low morale. Lipstick in particular had become so commonly used that women considered it an essential part of their morning routine. The 20 September 1939 issue of British *Vogue* worried: 'It would be an added calamity if war turned us into a nation of frights and slovens.' *Woman's Own* magazine in December 1939 went so far as to suggest complete looks for women in service, even though the use of make-up had to be authorized by the commanding officer. It was suggested that women in khaki uniforms should wear peach-tone powders; members of the Women's Royal Naval Service (WRNS) – known as 'Wrens' – should brush their hair up from the face to suit the hat; for Air Raid Precautions (ARP) wardens with their tin hats a 'bubble' perm was the best choice, and they should also use 'Auxiliary Red' lipstick and rouge, which had been created in late 1939 by the British cosmetics firm Cyclax, who made it available in service beauty kits to fit uniform pockets. Tangee connected their products with the forces by advertising lipstick using a Wren-uniformed model, with the slogan 'For Beauty on Duty'.

Eventually the lack of materials and manufacturers of cosmetics in Continental Europe meant a more natural look was inevitable. Eosin and carmine, two essential ingredients for lipstick, came from the United States, forcing French manufacturers to rely on minimal supplies of cocoa butter and beeswax. In the absence of lipstick, beetroot juice was better than nothing. Nail varnish also became hard to get, although British women found 'ladder stop' for stocking repairs worked well. The American War Production Board kept cosmetics off the list of restricted items, even though they required chemicals essential for war. The British Board of Trade also deemed cosmetics essential to female morale, and tried to keep basics such as mascara and lipstick always available.

Cosmetics pioneer Helena Rubenstein recalled in her autobiography President Roosevelt's response to her inquiry whether she could do anything to help the war effort. He had just read an account of an English woman who asked an ambulance attendant for her lipstick before being carried out on a stretcher from her blitzed London home, and assured Rubenstein: 'your war effort is to help keep up the morale of our women, and you are doing it splendidly.'

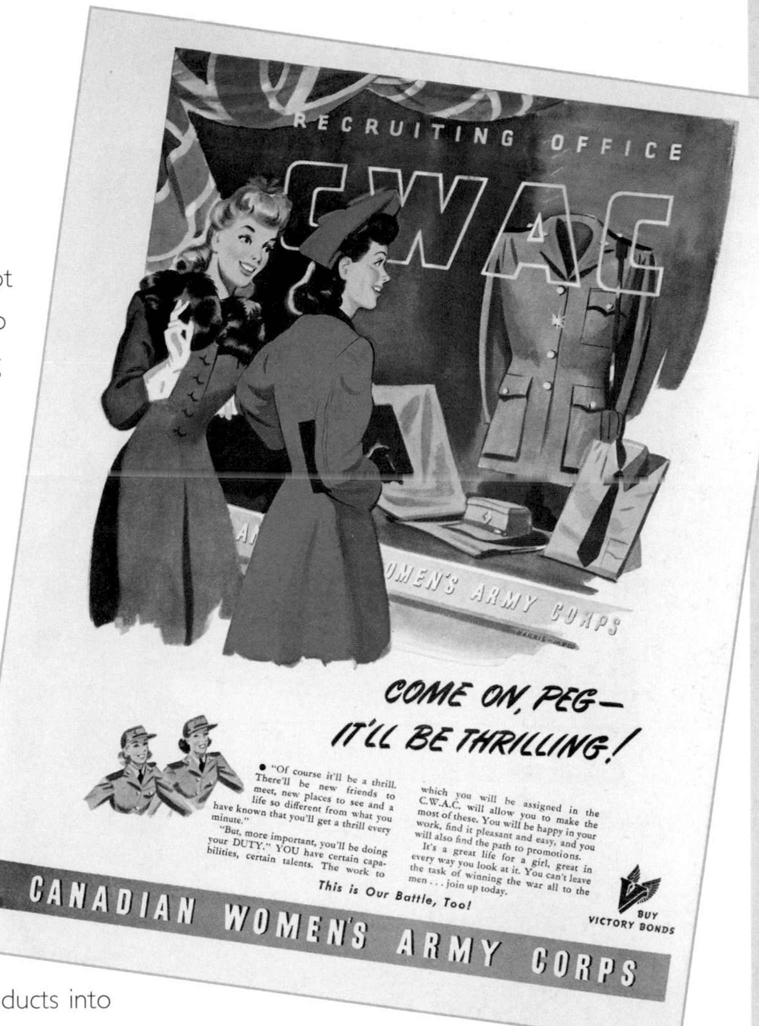

Helena Rubenstein had not yet established herself in the European market, but Elizabeth Arden had moved her products into Europe in the 1920s, just when the craze for cosmetics was becoming established, and advertisements for her products continued to appear in German fashion magazines as late as 1943, prompting an FBI investigation of her business dealings and foreign profits.

When total war was declared by Germany in February 1943, Goebbels threatened to close beauty salons, but Hitler himself intervened on this issue at the urging of Eva Braun: 'The moment one tries to lay a hand on a woman's beauty care, she becomes his enemy.' However, in secret, Hitler asked Albert Speer to stop the production of items necessary for beauty and to cease repairs to permanent-wave machines. Eventually, 'permanents' were forbidden because the chemicals were needed for the war effort.

While American women, especially younger women, often wore their hair curled and loose at the back, most younger British women were either in service or held wartime-essential occupations, and chose shorter styles for

Recruitment advertisement for the Canadian Women's Army Corps (CWAC), in *National Home Monthly*, November 1943.

BELOW An English advertisement for toilet soap, 1942. Starch and beetroot juice were classic substitutes for face powder and rouge.

ABOVE American advertisement for Tussy 'Jeep Red' lipstick, 1942.

RIGHT American advertisement for Cutex 'Alert' red nail varnish, 1943.

Paris millinery modes continued to find their way to North America via Switzerland as late as spring 1941.

BELOW Brown felt slouch brim hat, labelled 'Madame Suzy Adaptation, Paris, New York', c. 1938–40.

BOTTOM Purple felt hat with rough wool scarf trim, labelled 'Rose Valois, Paris', c. 1939–40.

easier upkeep. Snoods – netted bags that held longer hair at the back of the head – were popular for fashionable and some occupational use. On the Continent most women wore their hair longer, but pinned up. Soap and shampoo became of poorer quality and harder to get. Tricks like bathing with cologne in lukewarm bathwater or steaming hair over a bowl of boiling water while rubbing it vigorously with a clean towel to remove grease and dirt were necessary when a ration of soap per person per month was measured in a few ounces. With dyeing and permanent treatments for hair becoming impossible to obtain, the easiest solution was either to hide the hair beneath a turban or to pile it high atop the head. If you went to a professional hairdresser, you had to bring the hairpins from home. In Germany, one version of an upsweep style was known as the *Entwarnungsfrisur*, 'all-clear hairdo'. A roll at the front shaped into a V was known as the 'victory hairdo' in France.

With upsweep hairdos, hats were the best source for a bit of wartime novelty. German fashion magazines were declaring as early as 1940 'Alles ist Hut!' (The hat is everything!). By 1943 the motto had changed to 'Altes Kleid – neuer Hut' (Old dress – new hat), to reflect clothing shortages. From Berlin to New York, never had there been so much variety in millinery – from tiny doll-sized hats to wide-brimmed halo hats and from masculine fedora styles to pure feminine whimsies of flowers and feathers.

The turban had been presented as a high fashion style in 1936, and it grew in popularity until American *Vogue* declared 1940 the year of the turban. It was associated as much with exotic holidays to glamorous

Tiny 'doll' hats had been popular since the late 1930s for summer functions. In the spring of 1941, little hats appeared in Paris that looked like nests festooned with tiny stuffed birds and fabric fruit.

LEFT American Surrealist-inspired net ball of yarn with wooden knitting needles, *c.* 1941–42.

BELOW Grey wool, feather and silk doll hat by Bes Ben, Chicago, 1941.

OPPOSITE In Germany throughout the war, millinery had the fewest restrictions, least rationing and most novelty of any type of garment. These hats were illustrated in 1941.

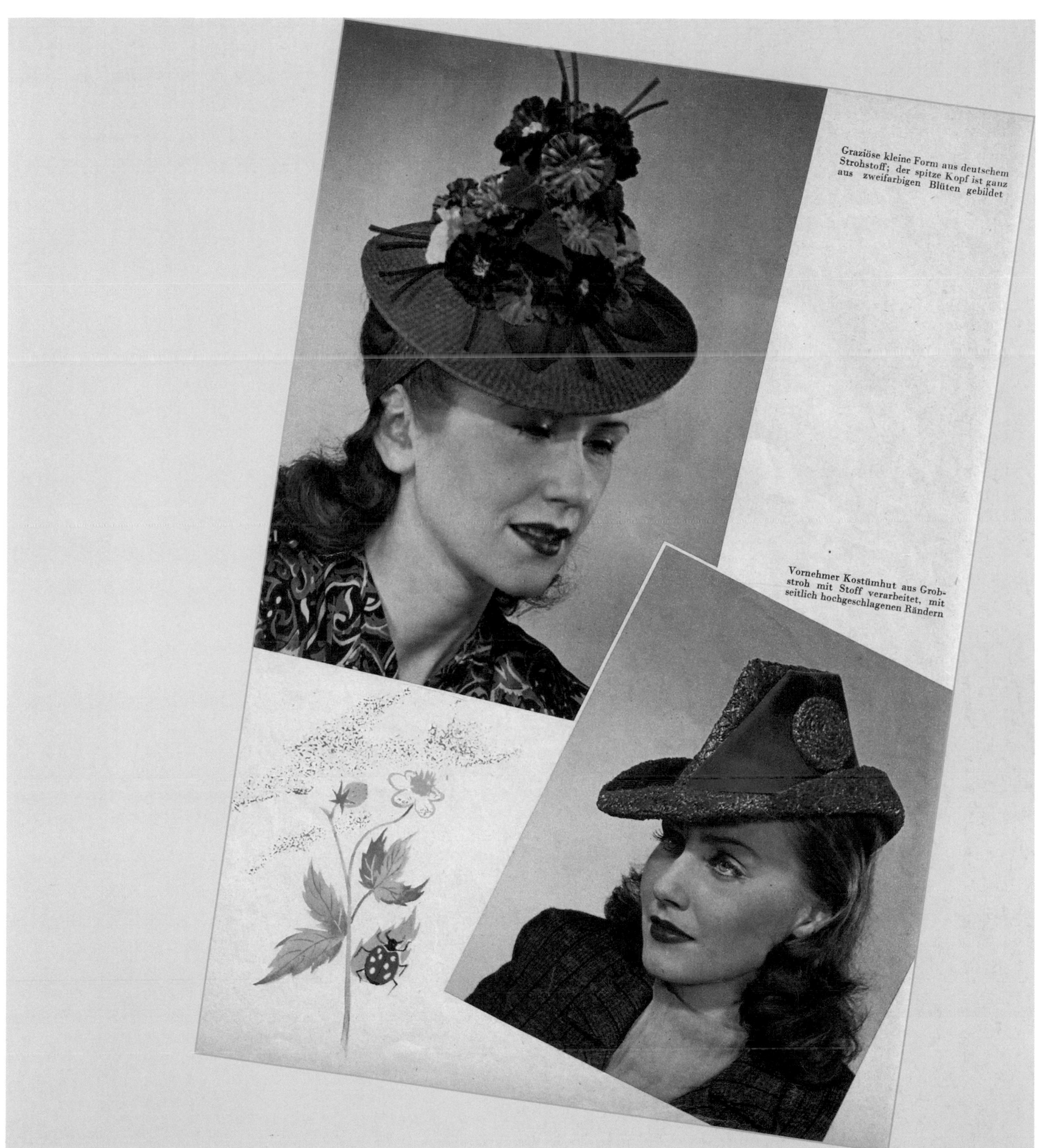
Graziöse kleine Form aus deutschem Strohstoff; der spitze Kopf ist ganz aus zweifarbigen Blüten gebildet
Vornehmer Kostümhut aus Grobstroh mit Stoff verarbeitet, mit seitlich hochgeschlagenen Rändern

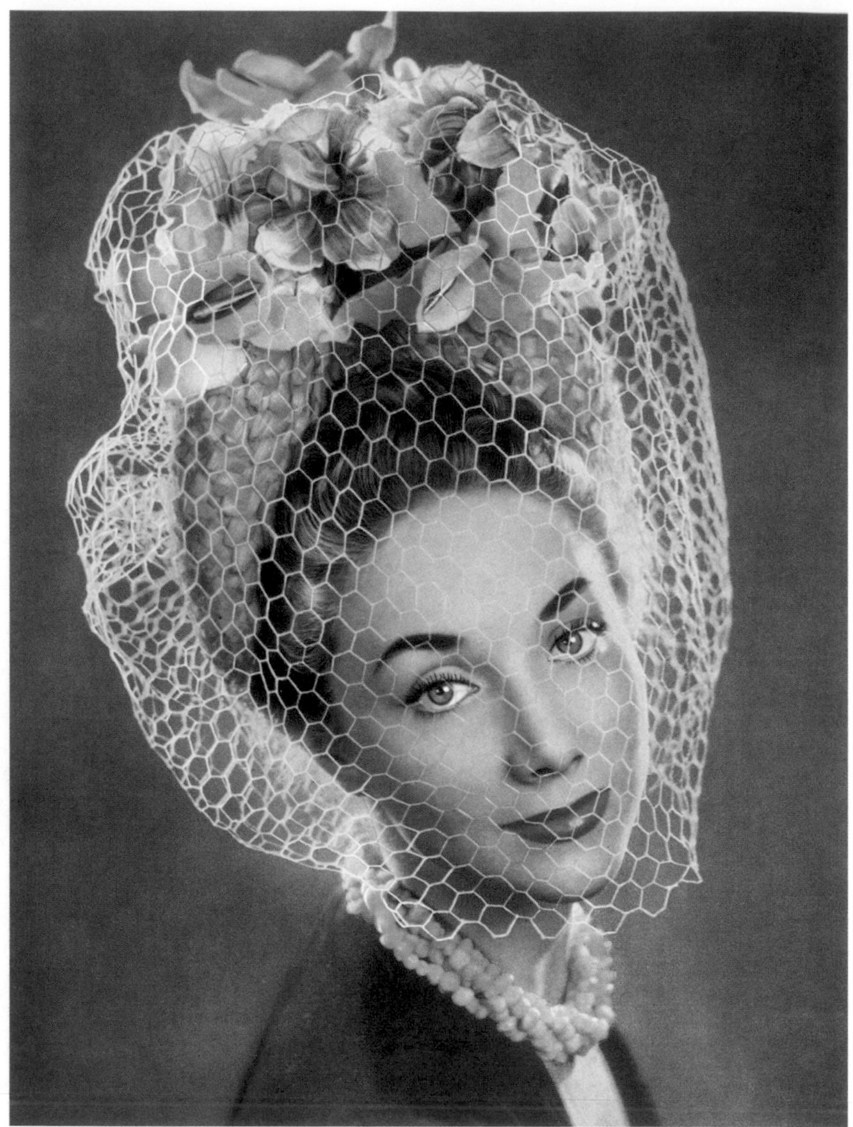

Carmen Miranda's Latin America as with hard-working Southern mammies. If nothing else, it was versatile and could be made at home or by a professional, for indoor or outdoor, daytime or evening wear. In its most basic form, a turban was a scarf or length of fabric knotted above the forehead with the ends tucked under the knot. When worn by women working in factories to keep hair clean and in place, turbans had the advantage of hiding pin-curlers, so that hair could be set in anticipation of an evening of glamour and gaiety. In Europe the turban had a practical purpose of hiding unwashed hair, especially after night-time air raids, which often left smashed water mains.

Parisian women had the most famous reputations for creative headwear. In 1942, as traditional materials became difficult to procure, Parisian milliners began creating a variety of hat styles trimmed with unusual materials ranging from crumpled paper to wood shavings. The next year hats were growing larger, taller and more ornate, and they continued to push beyond the lines of good taste in 1944. The German occupiers questioned the exaggerated hats and their squandering of material, threatening to close down every milliner's shop if necessary. Lucien Lelong, president of the Chambre Syndicale de la Haute Couture (the Paris association of couturiers), explained that the vulgar headdresses were the creations of the people, not of couturiers, and that the excessive fabric was salvaged and re-used from their wardrobes. After the liberation the hats' extravagance was again questioned, this time by the Allies, and the story changed: now they were provocative gestures of contempt at the occupier – 'les chapeaux de la Résistance'.

British women very nearly gave up fashion hats altogether. Before the war, there was a growing trend among younger women not to wear hats for sporting occasions: Mass Observation commented in 1939 that 'increasing hatlessness has gone along with churchlessness'. Hats were not rationed, but they were subject to a heavy 33 per cent tax as luxury purchases. Some thought civilian hats were

French pink and blue floral and veil-covered turban, February 1946.

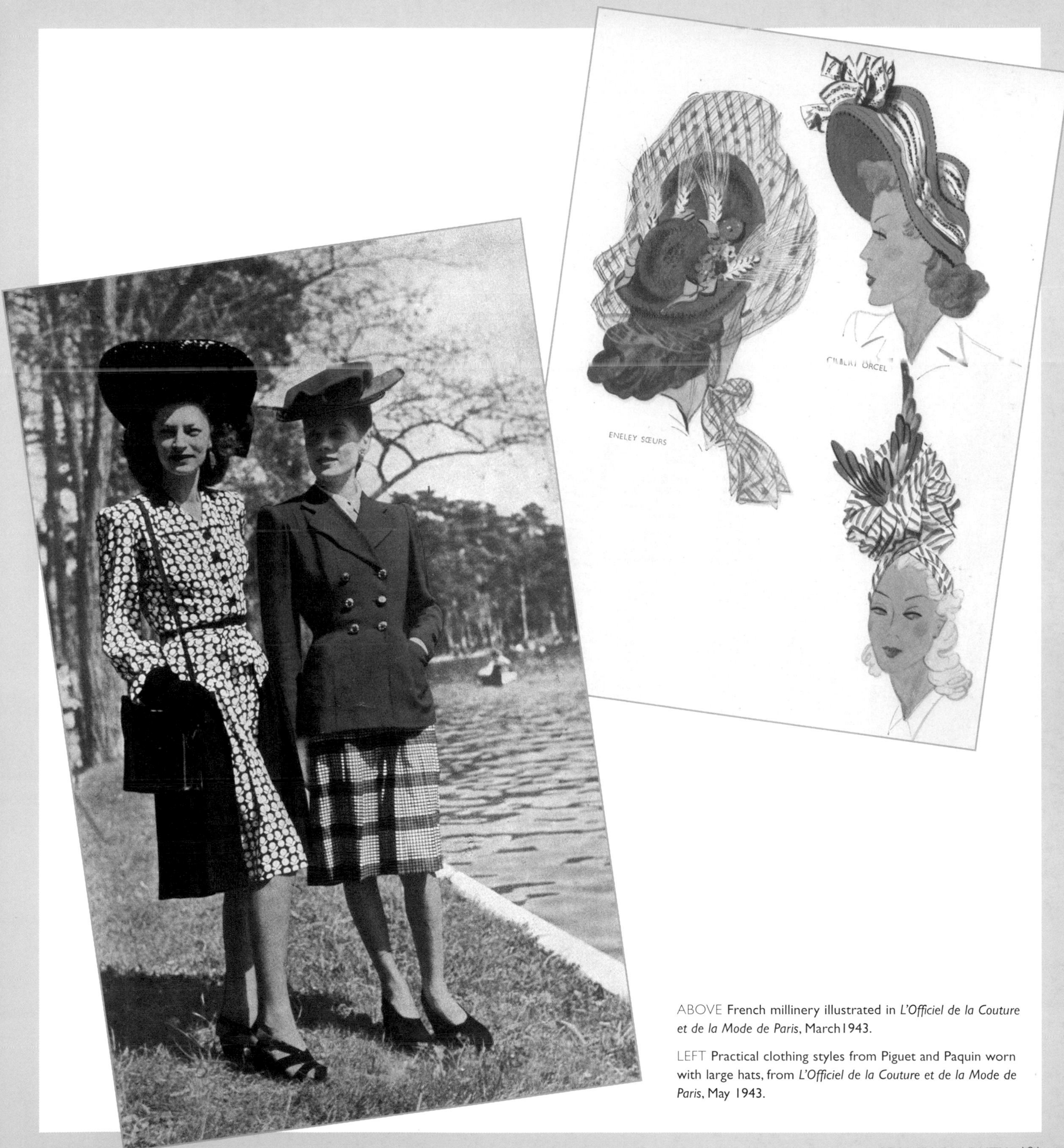

ABOVE French millinery illustrated in *L'Officiel de la Couture et de la Mode de Paris*, March1943.

LEFT Practical clothing styles from Piguet and Paquin worn with large hats, from *L'Officiel de la Couture et de la Mode de Paris*, May 1943.

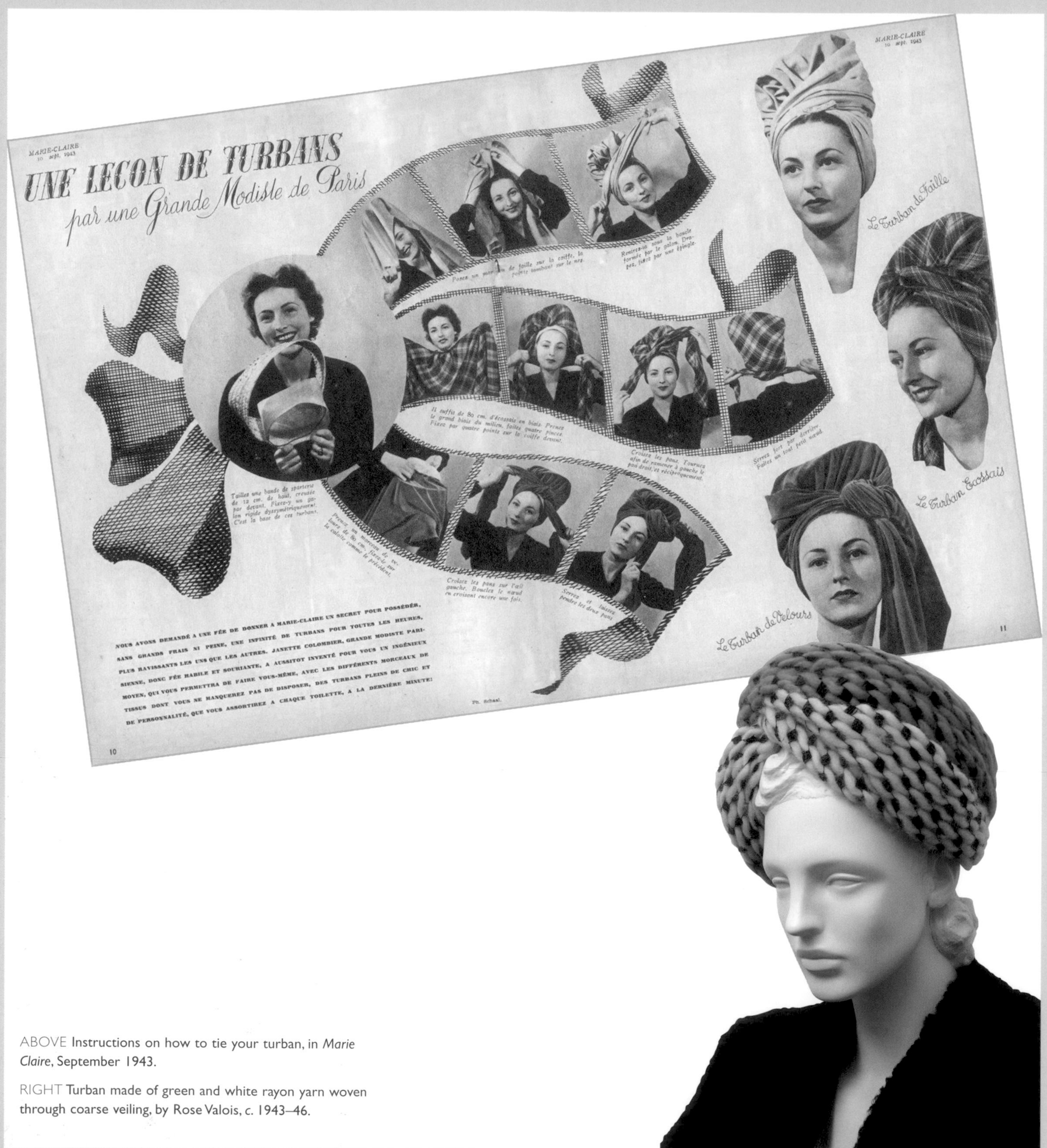

MARIE-CLAIRE 10 sept. 1943

UNE LEÇON DE TURBANS

par une Grande Modiste de Paris

NOUS AVONS DEMANDÉ A UNE FÉE DE DONNER A MARIE-CLAIRE UN SECRET POUR POSSÉDER, SANS GRANDS FRAIS NI PEINE, UNE INFINITÉ DE TURBANS POUR TOUTES LES HEURES, PLUS RAVISSANTS LES UNS QUE LES AUTRES. JANETTE COLOMBIER, GRANDE MODISTE PARISIENNE, DONC FÉE HABILE ET SOURIANTE, A AUSSITOT INVENTÉ POUR VOUS UN INGÉNIEUX MOYEN, QUI VOUS PERMETTRA DE FAIRE VOUS-MÊME, AVEC LES DIFFÉRENTS MORCEAUX DE TISSUS DONT VOUS NE MANQUEREZ PAS DE DISPOSER, DES TURBANS PLEINS DE CHIC ET DE PERSONNALITÉ, QUE VOUS ASSORTIREZ A CHAQUE TOILETTE, A LA DERNIÈRE MINUTE!

10

MARIE-CLAIRE 10 sept. 1943

11

ABOVE Instructions on how to tie your turban, in *Marie Claire*, September 1943.

RIGHT Turban made of green and white rayon yarn woven through coarse veiling, by Rose Valois, *c.* 1943–46.

unpatriotic frivolities, especially as most British women were in some form of uniform with accompanying headgear, be it a military cap or hat or an industrial turban. The civilian hat styles that did find favour were berets and miniature mannish hats, neither of which boasted frivolous feather cockades, realms of veiling, or towers of flowery drama.

The war created a new casualness in dress. Evening clothes were rarely worn in restaurants and theatres. Cecil Beaton noticed the change, commenting on guests at the Dorchester Hotel in London: 'some dress – some don't – some wear hats, some don't'. To relieve any social pressure to spend money where it could not be afforded, the Board of Trade requested the Archbishop of Canterbury, head of the Church of England, to announce that women might attend services hatless, and, more importantly, stockingless. By the middle of the war, fashion itself was out of fashion: out-of-date and worn clothes, simple hairstyles, no hats, no jewelry, and low-heeled shoes had become the new, patriotic style. British *Vogue* remarked in October 1941: 'The new look: it's a look of simplicity ... Dressiness is démodé ... The "too-good-to-be-true" look which only a personal maid can produce is absent – because the maid is absent – on munitions.'

To keep up morale, American wartime fabric restrictions did not limit wedding dress materials, although excessively full skirts and long trains were rare and silk was not available – only rayon satins, crepes, and taffetas. Wedding dresses or the materials to make them were generally not available outside North America. Tulle and lace were not rationed in most of Europe, but they were difficult to procure after pre-war stocks had been used up. In Germany, brides were even requested to donate their wedding veils for use as mosquito netting for the forces in North Africa in the spring of 1942.

Purple silk turban by Rose Valois, *c.* 1943–44.

ABOVE Beige jersey wedding dress worn by a Canadian bride in February 1942.

LEFT Pink crepe bridal dress worn by an English bride in May 1943.

ABOVE AND RIGHT Lace wedding dress worn by an English bride, Binty Mustard, when she was married on 2 October 1942 in Epsom, Surrey. The dress was off ration because it was made of lace, and as the bride was in the WAF, she was able to budget for its purchase because she did not spend money on civilian clothes.

White parachute 'silk' nylon dress, origin unknown, *c.* 1945.

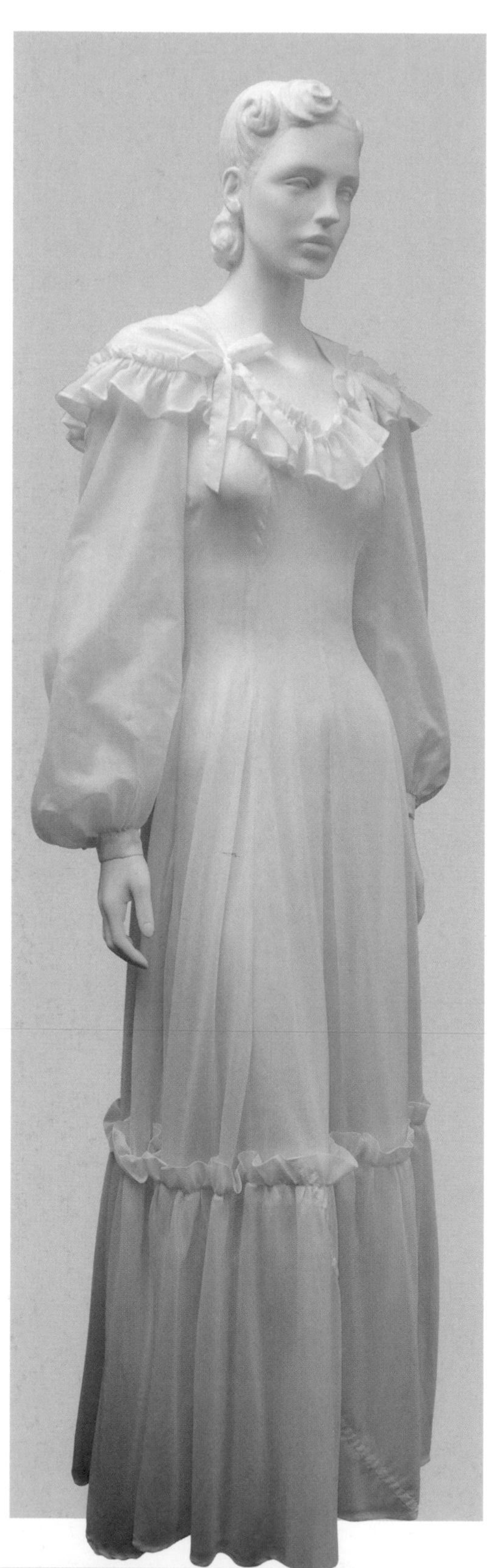

British brides unable to buy or make a wedding dress often borrowed or rented a dress or remade their mother's wedding dress. Many brides were practical and bought a new suit or day dress for the occasion; female friends and relatives often used their own coupons to buy a piece of lingerie for the trousseau. British women in uniform had no clothing coupons for civilian use and were often married in their uniforms. The lack of gold for jewelry also forced most British and Continental brides to use either an inherited ring, or a 'Utility ring' that turned the wedding finger green from its high copper content.

At the end of the war, surplus parachute 'silk' was offered to brides in Britain (Allied parachutes had in fact been made of nylon since the Americans joined the war at the end of 1941). Australian brides were also offered surplus parachute material and mosquito netting until supplies of satin and tulle became available. Using fallen parachutes while the war was still being fought was illegal in Europe: all were to be turned in to the authorities for investigation. Those most commonly found in Britain were small, heavily seamed parachutes retrieved from German landmines dropped from bombers. Parachute silk deemed surplus could be used for clothing, but only as underwear. Immediately after the liberation, French seamstresses around Normandy hastened to salvage parachutes from the D-Day landings to use for dresses and raincoats.

Holding a wedding reception could be difficult under rationing. At British weddings, it was common for guests to present the ingredients for a wedding cake, but traditional royal icing was made illegal in 1940. Throwing rice was also illegal, and confetti was unavailable. A bride with friends working in an office pool could save the paper confetti-like disks from hole punches, but many brides chose flower petals if they were available. Even an official photograph was a problem, since photographic materials were almost unobtainable; paper film instead of celluloid could be found, but the results were rarely satisfactory.

During a trip to London in 1944 Eleanor Roosevelt saw for herself the problems young British brides faced in having a wedding; to help the situation, the First Lady collected a number of wedding dresses and veils from American brides who had recently married, and sent them to Britain to be loaned to servicewomen. In spring 1945, Simpson's, a department store in Toronto, donated a blush pink satin wedding dress and two matching bridal maid ensembles to women in overseas service at the Canadian Red Cross headquarters at Corps House, London. The dress arrived on 24 May – the day before one of the women, Mary Louise Harrington, was to be married to Captain James Stewart, without a wedding dress. She inaugurated it, and before the summer was out, twenty-one different brides had worn the dress.

"I'm depending on mother's wedding dress—and you!"

a bride-to-be told her Singer Sewing Center

"I'm going to be a real war bride," this pretty and patriotic girl said, "and buy as little new as possible. I have mother's lovely wedding dress that will fit with a little altering. And some of my own clothes I'd like to fix up. Please—could you help me?"

Could we! Here are just a few of the things we did —

"WE'LL HELP YOU ALTER THAT DRESS so it fits like a dream!" we told her. And we showed her how to adjust the shoulders and take in seams, until it was exactly right. Singer now gives special help in make-over and alteration, for a small charge. (Also help in cutting and fitting, and making your own and children's clothing . . . Hom Decorations too!)

"ANY HOPE FOR THESE?" the bride asked, holding up two last year's dresses. We did a little figuring and came out with an idea. Why not combine them to make a short-skirted dinner dress? (Our Make-Over Guide booklet has dozens of other ideas for salvaging old clothes, complete with directions, for only 25¢.)

Need a Machine?

Of course you know that Singer is busy making war equipment instead of sewing machines these days. But we have a few new and reconditioned machines for sale or rent.

SINGER SEWING CENTERS

"HERE'S ANOTHER HELP — OUR NOTIONS COUNTER!" we said. We picked out the proper shoulder pads for her dress—helped her choose bindings, threads, and sewing supplies. "And if you're making your own aprons and house frocks, here are rickrack braids and trimmings for only 5¢ a yard up!" we told her.

"ANY BUTTONS YOU WANT COVERED?" we asked her next. Singer does lots of finish-up jobs—such as making buttonholes, covering buttons and buckles, hemstitching linens. All for a reasonable charge. "Well, I just hope I land near you after I'm married!" sighed the bride. "You probably will!" we said. "There are lots of Singer Sewing Centers everywhere!"

Copyright, 1943, by The Singer Manufacturing Co. All rights reserved for all countries.

SINGER SEWING MACHINE CO.

ALL SINGER FACTORIES ARE PRODUCING EQUIPMENT VITAL TO VICTORY

October, 1943—Page 59

Singer Sewing machine advertisement for remaking the bride's mother's wedding dress, and other clothing, from the Canadian magazine *National Home Monthly*, October 1943.

MAKING DO

Creative solutions for dire shortages

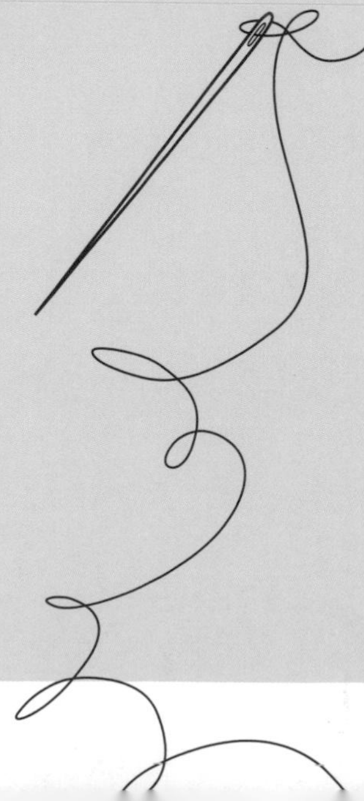

Ships of steel for even keel
Need tons and tons of corset steel.

Army trucks if they're to hurdle
Need the rubber of the girdle.

The time has come, the gods have written,
Women now must bulge for Britain.

Anonymous World War II poem

A woman dressed entirely in materials originating in the laboratory, from the *National Geographic* magazine, November 1939. 'At a New York fashion show,' the article began, 'we saw a girl clad from head to foot in artificial materials. Everything she wore was made from synthetic stuffs created by chemists. Her hat was Cellophane; her frock was rayon. She wore "Nylon" stockings and carried a patent-leather handbag and stood in imitation alligator shoes and wore "jade" bracelets and "ivory" beads; her parasol handle was from beautifully colored plastic. Even the faint hint of musk on her imitation silk handkerchief came from a synthetic perfume; on her nails there glistened a synthetic dye, and other coal-tar dyes imparted rich shades to her ensemble.'

The crucial need for petroleum, leather, rubber and silk for the war effort meant civilian use of these materials was strictly controlled. Until the commercial introduction of nylon in 1939, the United States had been dependent on Japan for 90 per cent of its silk imports, most of which was used for making ladies hosiery. DuPont announced the creation of their first all-synthetic material to the world in October 1938. 'Fiber 66' was originally to be called 'norun' – but the fiber could run, so committee meetings transformed 'norun' into 'nylon'. Nylon's lightweight, sheer qualities and high tensile strength, even when wet, were showcased at the New York World's Fair of 1939–40.

YOU'RE HOLDING BEAUTY
WHEN YOU'RE HOLDING
VINYLITE
PLASTICS
HANDBAGS AND LUGGAGE of breath-taking beauty and amazing sturdiness made from VINYLITE plastic . . . the last word in modern, exciting glamour.
No more worries about exposing your handbags and luggage to rain and sleet—*VINYLITE plastic is waterproof—does not peel, crack, or curl up.*
Drop them, handle them harshly—they show no ill-effects.
VINYLITE plastic does not fray or scuff.
Let them rest in the harsh light of the glaring sun—
VINYLITE plastic does not fade.
They clean like magic—a swish of a damp cloth and their original lustre becomes sparkling bright again!
VINYLITE plastic handbags and luggage come in ranges of colour almost unlimited in scope—designed to match and flatter your VINYLITE plastic footwear.
You will also be interested in purchasing some of the many other products made from VINYLITE plastics—footwear, umbrellas, rain apparel and household accessories.
IT'S RIGHT—IF IT'S
Vinylite
PLASTICS
CANADIAN RESINS and CHEMICALS LIMITED
MONTREAL, QUE. • TORONTO, ONT.

31

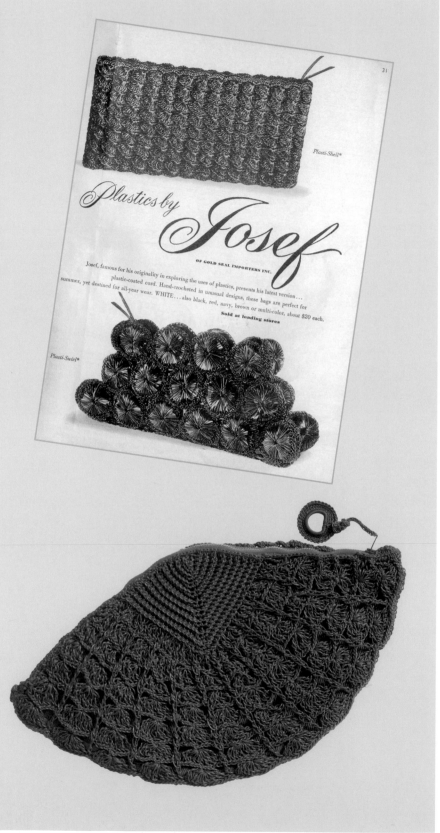

*Plasti-Shell**

Plastics by Josef

OF GOLD SEAL IMPORTERS INC.

Josef, famous for his originality in exploring the uses of plastics, presents his latest version… plastic-coated cord. Hand-crocheted in unusual designs, these bags are perfect for summer, yet destined for all-year wear. WHITE… also black, red, navy, brown or multi-color, about $20 each.

Sold at leading stores

*Plasti-Swirl**

OPPOSITE

FAR LEFT Advertisement for Vinylite, from the Canadian *National Home Monthly*, May 1946.

RIGHT, ABOVE American advertisement for plastic purses by Josef, 1944.

RIGHT, BELOW Green plastic purse, *c.* 1944–46.

Rayon, celluloid and Bakelite were already in common use when the 'World of Tomorrow' theme of the Fair showcased many new materials that would come into common use during the war. Carbide and Carbon Chemicals Corp. announced in early 1940 that its 'elastic Vinylite' was being commercially made into a variety of items ranging from shower curtains to see-through shoe uppers. Vinylite was particularly good at imitating patent leather and was supple and wore better than real patent leather. Another new material introduced in the 1930s was acrylic glass or Lucite (also known as Plexiglas or Perspex), used for making buttons, clasps, and even shoe heels and bridal crowns. Neoprene and nylon were newly perfected materials that would prove essential in the coming war effort as substitutes for rubber and silk. (Wartime developments also created the first polyester fibres, Terylene and Dacron, but neither would be put into production until the mid-1950s.) At the DuPont 'Wonder World of Chemistry' exhibition, 'Miss Chemistry' modelled entire outfits of nylon stockings, shoes with heels of Lucite, rayon underwear, cellophane hats, and other synthetic materials.

Strong, sheer and light-weight, the first nylon stockings were test-marketed in Wilmington, Delaware, on 24 October 1939, but were not put on sale to the general public until 15 May 1940. About 192 million pairs had been produced by the time the United States entered the war, but on 11 February 1942 DuPont turned over all nylon to the War Production Board. It was now to be used for parachutes, rope, tarpaulins, fishing line, and bristles for brushes.

Other than very hard to find silk stockings, there were rayon or cotton stockings, plus cotton or wool socks. It was against social convention to go bare-legged other than at home or the

American suede shoes with Lucite heels and ornaments, *c.* 1940.

seaside, so the problem was greater for women of the 1940s than can be understood from a modern perspective. Many women took to wearing trousers for war work and continued to wear them outside work, both for convenience and to preserve their precious stockings for special wear. In late 1940, after the German occupiers had purchased every available pair of silk stockings in Paris, a joke went the rounds throughout France: 'A German officer said to a saleswoman, "Now it is the Berlin women who wear silk stockings." And the Frenchwoman replied, "Yes, but when a Parisienne wears cotton stockings, cotton stockings become the style."'

As supplies of silk and even rayon stockings continued to dwindle, it became impossible to fill ration quotas. In 1941 the ration of women in New Zealand was reduced to two pairs of stockings per year; German women were rationed to five, but the chances of a German woman getting her quota were slight. The few pairs of stockings women had were prized, and specialist menders were hired who used tiny hooked needles with latches to reloop ladder runs. Women in service to whom stockings were supplied could only get a new pair for old when the old showed a certain number of darns – as many as twenty, depending on supply and the officer's prerogative.

Many younger women took to going bare-legged in summer. The Australian government went so far as

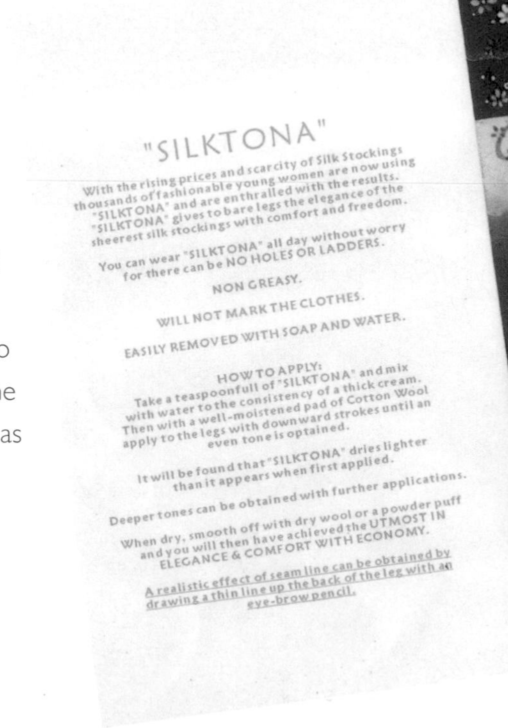

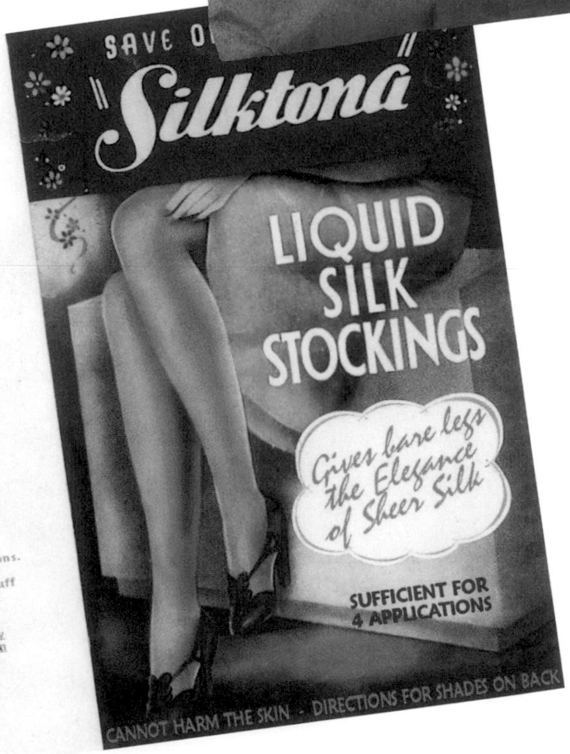

German and English packaging for leg paint.

American and Canadian advertisements for leg paint by Elizabeth Arden and Helena Rubenstein, 1944.

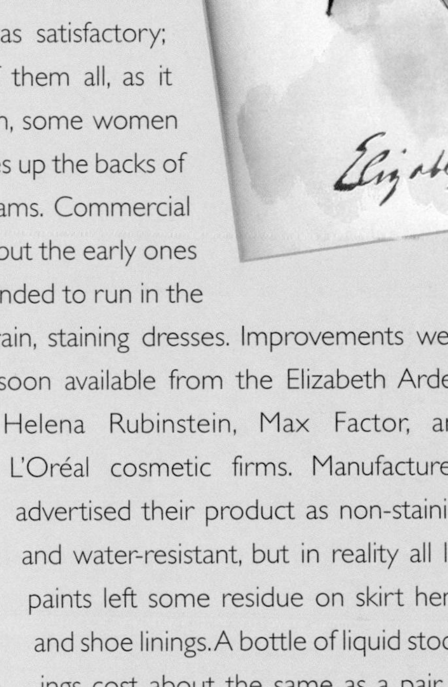

More beautiful than ever . . . in
Velva Leg Film
So easy to apply and quick to dry, Elizabeth Arden's leg make-up stays on the legs and off the clothes. Water-resistant. Clings, until deliberately washed away, with a blemish-concealing sheer textured beauty that trims the ankle—slims the leg. Be sure to wear Velva Leg Film with bathing suits or shorts, it makes your legs look sun-burnished . . . far more lovely.
Sun Beige (light)—Sun Bronze (medium)—Sun Copper (dark)
Approximately 20 pairs in a 1.00 bottle. Almost 50 pairs in the large 2.00 economy size.

to forbid employers to require women to wear stockings in the office. A bit of sun was the easiest way to improve the colour of white legs in climates like Australia, but in places like Britain the possibility of sun tanning was limited. Gravy browning, walnut juice, tea, iodine, and brown shoe polish were all tried, but none was satisfactory; gravy browning was the worst of them all, as it attracted flies. To add to the illusion, some women used an eyebrow pencil to draw lines up the backs of their legs to resemble stocking seams. Commercial leg paints appeared on the market, but the early ones were difficult to apply evenly and tended to run in the rain, staining dresses. Improvements were soon available from the Elizabeth Arden, Helena Rubinstein, Max Factor, and L'Oréal cosmetic firms. Manufacturers advertised their product as non-staining and water-resistant, but in reality all leg paints left some residue on skirt hems and shoe linings. A bottle of liquid stockings cost about the same as a pair of rayon stockings but offered the equivalent of several pairs, since care and luck were needed for real stockings to last more than a few occasions.

"Take Summer in Your Stride"
WITH
"AQUACADE" LEG LOTION
by
Helena Rubinstein
"AQUACADE" LEG LOTION
helena rubinstein
So satin-smooth! So uniformly lovely! The golden-beige beauty of Helena Rubinstein's cosmetic stocking sensation —Aquacade Leg Lotion—is something that must be seen to be believed. Economical to use, supremely natural in appearance, Aquacade Leg Lotion spreads evenly and easily, conceals small flaws and blemishes, remains impervious to rain and water splashes. 1.00
helena rubinstein
126 BLOOR STREET WEST, TORONTO

The Italian shoe designer Salvatore Ferragamo worked around shortages by designing footwear using substitute materials. Beginning in 1936, cork and wood wedge and platform soles were paired up with a variety of upper materials, including twisted and woven cellophane and raffia. In his revival of tall platform shoes, not seen since late Renaissance Venice, Ferragamo was influenced by the Fascist glorification of Italy's history. He was equally influenced by the Italian Futurists. Predating the rise of Fascism but fitting in perfectly with the concern for Italian identity and nationalist ideals, the Futurist movement sought inspiration from the vibrant green, white and red colours of the Italian flag. Futurists wanted Italians to give up dull, sombre colours. As early as 1914 they spoke out against neutral coloured clothing, and in 1933 they declared: 'We condemn the Nordic use of black and of neutral colors that give the wet, snowy, foggy streets of the city the appearance of a stagnant muddy melancholy . . . Colour! We need colour to compete with the Italian sun.' Ferragamo's shoes were often brightly coloured, and were especially popular for summer wear domestically as well as abroad. Without help from the Italian government, Ferragamo used his own contacts to arrange for the export of his shoes to important department stores throughout Europe and the Americas, until the escalation of the war made exports impossible.

German supplies of civilian footwear were already meagre when the war began. Germany was dependent on imports of leather. Sole leather, the heaviest and most durable grade, was the most difficult to obtain and the most important. In November 1939 leather shoes of a value less than 40 marks were the first to be rationed. To acquire a new pair, a declaration had to be made to a ration officer that the applicant had no more than two pairs of leather shoes and that one of those was beyond repair. Random checks were sometimes

Shoes by
Blachford
BUILT-IN QUALITY MAKES THEM LAST LONGER
ideal for
WAR WALKERS
ARE you on your feet for hours at a stretch—helping Canada win this war?
If you are, you can make those thousands of steps easier, more comfortable, in Blachford Shoes. They keep their shape longer—last longer. Even the smartest models are made on lasts which are planned for comfort.
Your Blachford dealer can show you a range of Blachford models—restricted, of course, because this is wartime.

Canadian advertisement for Blachford walking shoes, in *National Home Monthly*, November 1942.

made to ensure a claimant was telling the truth: if more than two pairs were found, all extra pairs were confiscated and the owner fined. However, wealthy Germans were not affected by this rationing, as luxury footwear that sold for more than 40 marks (and often closer to 130 marks), usually imported from Italy or Switzerland, did not require ration coupons, although it was heavily taxed.

Before the war, France manufactured about 70 million pairs of leather shoes per year, but within months after the occupation, shortages of leather and linen thread were already a problem. In both Germany and France cobblers had a backlog of shoes in need of resoling: with sole leather scarce, many women were sacrificing their leather handbags to repair their shoes. Many cobblers salvaged tires to make rubber soles, and a brisk business was made of adding metal top lifts and plates to heels and toes of walking shoes still in good condition, in an attempt to preserve their leather soles.

In January 1941 civilian rationing of shoes started in France: a voucher to acquire one pair of leather shoes was issued, with no guarantee when the next voucher would appear. The lack of winter footwear had already brought ski boots and golf shoes, with cleats removed, into the streets of Paris. In June 1942, the shoe trade's *Journal de la Chaussure* reported that 'the scarcity of leather only makes it possible to produce one pair of leather shoes at the most for every four or five inhabitants, or 9 million pairs of leather shoes. The difference is made good by wood. Twenty million pairs of shoes with wooden soles will be produced, plus 5 million pairs of clogs and wooden pattens for resoling' (meaning, presumably, that an old pair of shoes could be attached to these when leather was not available).

RIGHT, ABOVE **American rubber clump soles, designed to protect leather soles from wear, c. 1942–45.**

RIGHT **Italian sling-back pumps with leather soles and woven straw uppers, c. 1938–40. The precedent for making shoes from substitute materials was set by Ferragamo.**

VEZMĚTE S SEBOU DŘEVÁČKY

na dovolenou

K 65.-

K 55.-

K 73.-

K 65.-

Hledáte-li na dovolenou praktickou a příjemnou obuv, volte dřeváčky. Jsou vzdušné a proto příjemné v horku. Přijďte si k nám pro ně.

Baťa

In Germany, regulations to keep the war machine moving specified that footwear issued in the workplace could not be worn outside the workplace. By April 1941 shortages were so dire that Goebbels admitted the country was almost completely out of shoes. For uppers, patched leather and man-made leather substitutes of vegetable fibre were experimented with. Exotic leathers, when they could be found, including snake, lizard, and crocodile, were used – as well as tanned fish skin and ox stomach, with less success. For soles, alder and copper beech were introduced in summer 1941 so that leather-soled shoes could be saved for winter. Even wooden-soled shoes were rationed by late 1941. Wooden soles ranged in quality from rough to polished wood. Experiments were also tried with soles of Lucite (made up of scraps from aircraft windshield factories), linoleum, and aluminium, none with any great success.

One-piece wooden soles were stiff and uncomfortable, and hard to move in quickly – a distinct disadvantage when you were required to run for an air-raid shelter. Two- and three-piece wooden soles offered better flexibility but less resistance to damp. Experiments in Germany and France to make wooden soles more flexible and comfortable included using lamination – thin layers of wood set crosswise alternately, like plywood. The French shoe designer André Perugia patented a version of an articulated sole made of slats of wood glued to a flexible pressed fibre insole. Perugia designed clogs with twisted paper net uppers that could be painted to match a summer outfit, although cotton or oilcloth uppers were more popular choices. Magazines tried to point out the supposed beauty of clogs, suggesting they added height and made legs appear taller, thinner, and

OPPOSITE **Czech advertisement for wooden-soled shoes by Bata, *c.* 1942.**

RIGHT **German cotton, oilcloth and wood sandals, acquired as a souvenir by an American GI, dated January 1945.**

BELOW *Marie Claire* magazine in June 1941 showed a variety of shoes for summer with soles and uppers made of substitute materials.

BOTTOM French shoes with soles of wood covered with jute, and uppers of plaited straw, acquired as a souvenir by an American GI in Paris, summer 1944.

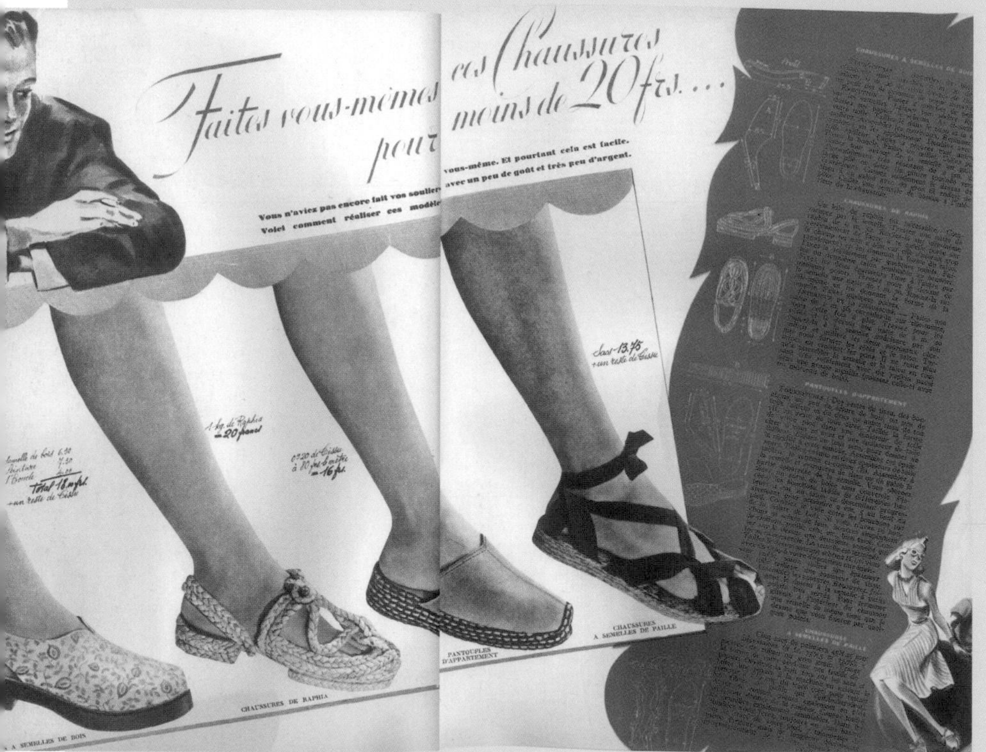

daintier, but few women were convinced. Alternatively, light-weight espadrilles with soles made of plaited raffia or straw were popular summer choices.

In Paris, the click-clacking sounds of wooden-soled shoes hitting the pavements could be heard by the spring of 1941. In March of that year the French shoe manufacturer Heyraud created a line of wooden-soled shoes, and some couturiers, including Maggy Rouff and Alix (see p. 33), featured clogs as novelties for their spring collections. Maurice Chevalier even sang about the new fashion in 'La Symphonie des Semelles de Bois' (The symphony of wooden soles). Many rural communities returned to wearing traditional *sabots* in France, or *klompen* in Holland, which had only fallen from use shortly after the end of the Great War. Until the 1920s, textile mill workers and children in northern England commonly wore Northumberland (aka Lancashire) clogs – wooden-soled shoes with leather uppers attached by brass tacks. When rationing was introduced, clogs were offered coupon-free to encourage their adoption, but those who had grown up wearing them had been enjoying a boom in earnings and had no interest in putting back the clock. In January 1943 fashionable variations on wooden-soled shoes were offered for English women. To encourage their sale, *Good Housekeeping* offered advice on how to walk in them:

> When you first put on a pair of these shoes, you'll feel at once how solid and comfortable they are – but you may have to adjust yourself by a little practice to the rolling tread of the rigid wooden sole. Experts tell us that the right way to

RIGHT French or Swiss felt and wood shoes, *c.* 1944–45.

BELOW French leather and wood shoes, dated September 1945.

RIGHT Wooden soles with pyrographic pattern, *c.* 1943–44. They are probably Italian.

do the 'Wooden-Sole-Walk' is this. From the moment the heel touches the ground, the shoe should be allowed to 'roll forward till the tip of the toe is reached'.

Shoes with hinged wooden soles were also offered, but they never became popular because they could not exclude moisture.

Soon after Paris was liberated in August 1944, newsreels of Parisian fashions focused on the towering headdresses and platform shoes. The higher French platform shoes renewed interest in the style in the United States; before 1944, most American platform soles were well under an inch (2.5 centimetres) in height, whereas some French ones towered more than 2 inches, with heels twice that height. By 1947, in France platforms had become symbols of occupation and rationing – the antithesis of post-war rebirth. In America, however, the style was at the height of its popularity, and in England it was only beginning to catch on after Princess Elizabeth wore a pair for her wedding in 1947.

Leather was more readily available in Britain than on the Continent during the war, and British leather shoes were made to a high standard for durability. Under Utility guidelines introduced in 1942, boot and shoe manufacturers were required to produce 50 per cent of all shoes to Utility standards. Utility grade footwear was built of the sturdiest leathers available, often with leather linings, double soles, and stitching. They may have looked heavy compared to fine dress shoes, but the point was that they should last for several years without needing substantial repair. Austerity restrictions in 1942 required all British leather shoes, whether they were made to Utility standards or not, to have neither open toes nor heels higher than 2 inches (5 centimetres).

English black suede, leather and painted wood shoes, c. 1941–44.

RIGHT English brown suede and leather shoes with crepe rubber soles, marked 'CC41' (see p. 43), c. 1944–45.

BELOW English beige suede platform shoes, 1947.

Sorry—
L Not Available
R $3.29
P $3.29
N $3.29
M $3.49
Top-fashion Platform Wedgies for ease-afoot . . . RATION-FREE
Gleaming nail-heads to step up your costume sparkle
Shoes on this page are available after August 15th

OPPOSITE **American ration-free shoes, from a Sears, Roebuck & Co. catalogue, Fall–Winter 1945–46.**

BELOW **American ration-free red cotton canvas shoes with brass studs, *c.* 1943–45.**

BOTTOM **American khaki canvas and brown leather shoes, *c.* 1943–45.**

Open-toed leather shoes were popular in North America, but in the British climate they made it difficult to keep your feet dry, especially after rubber galoshes disappeared from the marketplace.

With the fall of Malaya to Japan early in 1942, Britain's main source of rubber was gone. Rubber footwear and garments could now be made only for the services or for essential industrial and agricultural uses. Although rubber footwear for civilian use was banned and would remain so until 1947, some footwear with synthetic rubber soles for civilians started to appear on the market in 1944. Despite the shortages, the Board of Trade set aside rubber and steel for corset production. Social convention widely dictated the wearing of a foundation garment; the girdle or corset slimmed the waist, supported the breasts, reduced jiggling, and smoothed bulges, creating flatter hips and buttocks; and the bottom edge provided a location for garters to fasten the tops of stockings. Without a proper foundation garment one's existing dresses might be too tight, resulting in stressed seams and tears.

In the United States, leather footwear was the only article of clothing rationed under the Wartime Price Board subsidiary Office of Price Administration (OPA). When that rationing was introduced, in February 1943, department stores were invaded by panic buyers anxious to secure every kind of clothing. *Time* magazine related the problem on 1 March 1943:

> a what-will-come-next buying wave skyrocketed department-store sales to 45% above 1942 in the first week after OPA's shoe-rationing order. Despite Government assurances that rationing of other clothing was not in the cards, customers bought up retail clothing stocks as if they were the last they would ever see. The U.S. public has not yet learned that the best way to avoid rationing is to avoid overbuying in the first place.

Beginning on 9 February 1943 and lasting until 30 October 1945, leather shoes were limited to a maximum of 3 pairs per person per year, slightly less than the average pre-war purchase of 3.2 pairs per person per year. Before the war, American women owned an average of about 8 pairs of shoes each. With rationing, that amount would be reduced; however, the ration did not include leather-soled textile shoes (such as bedroom slippers), or any type of rope-, wood-, or cork-soled shoes, usually sold as novelty summer styles. Shoe leather colours were restricted by the Civilian Production Administration under Limitation order L-217: some dyes were difficult to procure during wartime, and – more importantly – limiting colours made shoes less desirable and reduced sales. For two years, American shops and catalogues offered a dreary array of leather shoes in black, white, navy blue, and three shades of brown. Two colours could be used in one pair of shoes, but only if the sole was made of non-rationed material. In Canada, similar restrictions were put on leather footwear, and the use of brass for nailheads and eyelets was forbidden.

In Britain, to avoid issuing higher coupon rations the Board of Trade launched a campaign in the summer of 1942 entitled 'Mend and Make-Do to avoid Buying New'. 'When you are tired of your old clothes, remember that by making them do you are contributing some part of an aeroplane, a gun or a tank', said Hugh Dalton, president of the Board. A follow-up report in December showed the campaign had not been well received: Britain's women felt they were already being asked to do more with less time and sleep and fewer ingredients, and were already mending and making do as best they could.

Hoping for a better response from the public in 1943, the Board of Trade recruited the Women's Voluntary Service (WVS) to help promote the more succinctly titled *Make Do and Mend* booklet, which introduced 'Mrs Sew and Sew' as a mascot for the campaign. The WVS had acquired a good reputation in the public's eye for their help in evacuating

Wood wedge shoes with scenes of fighter planes on fire, made in the Philippines as mementos for American soldiers returning home at the end of the war.

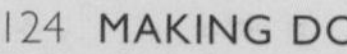

Straw platform shoes with matching bag, made in Honduras for the American market, c. 1944–46.

OPPOSITE

ABOVE LEFT **American *Make it Do Until Victory!* booklet, 1943.**

ABOVE RIGHT **American *Make and Mend* booklet, 1944.**

BELOW **French ideas for what to make from bandanna print handkerchiefs, in *Marie Claire* magazine, June 1941.**

children from major cities, staffing 'British Restaurants' (a nationalized service that supplied non-rationed meals), and operating clothing depots where good quality used children's clothes could be exchanged for larger sizes at no cost. The *Make Do and Mend* booklet gave helpful hints on cleaning and maintaining clothing and linens, avoiding moths, recycling woollen sweaters, and patching and making over older, worn clothes. Hugh Dalton wrote in the foreword: 'The Board of Trade Make Do and Mend campaign is intended to help you to get the last possible ounce of wear out of all your clothes.'

The slogans 'Aus Alt mach Neu' (From old make new) and 'Aus Zwei mach Eins' (From two make one) were Germany's version of 'Make Do and Mend'; but a lack of needles and particularly of sewing thread stymied German women from undertaking many of the projects suggested in articles and booklets, including ideas for disguising worn areas such as necklines and cuffs and altering linens and men's clothing into women's and children's garments.

Articles in popular British women's magazines helped with the cause of making do. Scarlet O'Hara, the Civil War heroine of *Gone With the Wind* – released in Britain in 1940 – made a dress from faded green curtains; now a Lux soap flakes advertisement exclaimed: 'The best parts of worn out lace curtains make lovely brassieres.' Articles appeared on making underwear from substandard parachutes; belts and hat trimmings from parachute cords; winter coats from blankets; evening dresses from lace curtains; and novelty projects such as jewelry from bottle caps, buttons, spools or wine corks. All this creative re-use

ABOVE **'The Cabinet Sewing Circle': a cartoon ridiculing the 'Make Do and Mend' scheme, by Leslie Gilbert Illingworth, from the *Daily Mail*, 13 March 1943. Among the Conservatives, in the foreground, are Churchill, with his cigar, and Anthony Eden; among the Labour members, on the far side of the table, are Ernest Bevin, far left, and Clement Attlee, far right.**

MAKE IT DO!
Until Victory!
Your WARTIME HANDBOOK
for SHOPPING
CONSERVATION
HOUSEHOLD CARE
by Maxine Garrison
MAKE and MEND
FOR VICTORY ★ BOOK NO. S-10 ★ PRICE 15 CENTS
15 Cts.
ALTERATIONS
MAKE OVER
ACCESSORIES
MENDING AND DARNING
RIEN QU'AVEC DES MOUCHOIRS
UNE GARDE-ROBE DE VACANCES SANS TICKETS

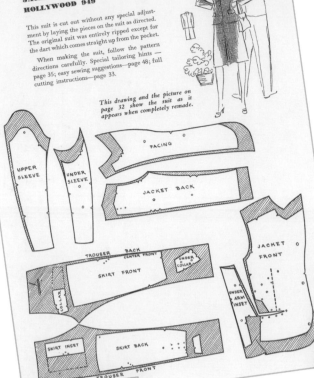

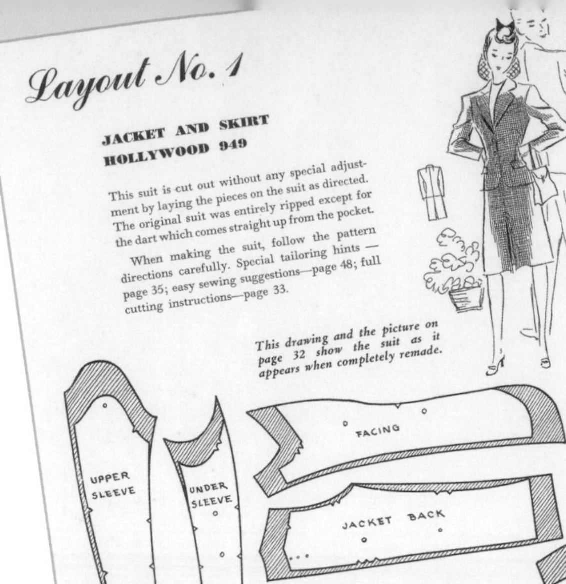

Layout No. 1

JACKET AND SKIRT
HOLLYWOOD 949

This suit is cut out without any special adjustment by laying the pieces on the suit as directed. The original suit was entirely ripped except for the dart which comes straight up from the pocket.

When making the suit, follow the pattern directions carefully. Special tailoring hints — page 35; easy sewing suggestions—page 48; full cutting instructions—page 33.

This drawing and the picture on page 32 show the suit as it appears when completely remade.

LEFT German ideas for how to add warmth to winter coats by adding appliqués of old material, from the journal *Deutsche Moden-Zeitung*, 1944.

BELOW English hat made of crocheted garden string, *c.* 1944–46.

OPPOSITE

ABOVE How to make a woman's suit from a man's suit, from the American *Make and Mend* booklet, 1944.

NEAR LEFT Canadian blue wool pinstripe woman's suit made from a man's suit, *c.* 1944.

FAR LEFT Advertisement for clothes made from blends including Aralac, the American name for an imitation wool fibre based on casein (see pp. 18–19), 1943.

How to make a skirt from a quilt: an idea published by the Canadian Wartime Prices and Trade Board (WPTB), 1943.

was not a uniquely British experience: similar suggestions were published in every country at war. During the Depression, not being fashionable had been a source of shame: now every sacrifice of a new garment was a patriotic gesture. The *Home Companion* magazine pointed out in July 1943: 'Nowadays, every re-made garment becomes a uniform of honour and every darn a "decoration."'

Before
After
Old discards are going into active service. A castoff curtain and some bits from the scrap bag snap to attention here in an outfit that any girl would love to wear. The best parts of an old curtain have gone to make the blouse. A tidbit of bias binding finished off neckline and sleeves. For the gay dirndl skirt, scraps were put together in patch-quilt fashion . . . triangles sewn into squares . . . squares into the required yardage. Here is patriotism with a purpose.
Re-made
From Butterick Patterns 2075-2482
WITHOUT RUFFLE
Front 1 Cut Two
Back 2
Cut One
3 Sleeve Cut Two
5 Front
2 Back
Fold

The shortage of heating fuel made knitted waistcoats and jumpers popular. Resourceful knitters short of yarn unravelled out-of-date and moth-eaten items for re-use. In England, the government provided wool and knitting needles to schools, where programmes were set up to teach children how to knit khaki, brown and navy blue gloves, scarves, and balaclava helmets for the forces. In France in 1941, skeins of wool were rationed, to be used exclusively for knitting babies' and children's garments. The customer was not allowed to choose the colour. The actress Simone Signoret recalled in her autobiography the occasion when she was allocated khaki wool. She protested, 'I do not know if I am going to have a boy or a girl . . . Whatever the case, I do not want to dress it as a soldier already.' A government communiqué put an end to irate complaints from expectant mothers by affirming that due to the present circumstances, dressing children for warmth was more important than elegance.

Home sewing was becoming increasingly popular, especially in North America. The *New York Times* reported on 8 June 1943 that the pattern industry projected sales in the United States by the end of the year to be a third higher than in 1939. One cause of the sales peak was that the American Wartime Prices Board had not included the pattern manufacturers in the 1942 Limitation orders of maximum allowable yardages for manufactured garments. However, the rules were extended to include patterns in February 1943.

Under Limitation order L-98, American sewing-machine manufacturers were requisitioned for war production. Nothing new could be made after 1 May 1942, other than parts to complete existing stock. After 16 June 1942, no new manufacturing could be done at all, although manufacturers were allowed to replace parts in machines brought in for repair. Sewing machines were not made for civilian use again until the end of 1945. To compensate, the Singer Sewing Machine Company offered rental machines, giving priority to women who enrolled in Singer sewing classes.

The end of the war did not end the trend in home sewing. The length of New Look-inspired clothing required women to find clever ways to alter existing garments to meet the new hemline, which by 1948 was hovering just above the ankle. Utilitarian patterns decreased in popularity, and the demand for high fashion patterns increased. In 1949 Vogue Patterns introduced its 'Paris Original Model' line by couturiers including Balmain, Fath, and Piguet.

American cotton patchwork skirt, *c.* 1943–45. The look of patched and remade styles was imitated in manufactured garments. This skirt is ready-made, but imitates a home-made make-do project similar to the pattern opposite.

PACIFIC FRONTS

Japan, Australia, New Zealand, and Canada

The manufacture and export of goods to Europe and North America made Japan a wealthy nation during the First World War. In the country's move towards modernization, the Japanese court and military forces had been wearing European-style clothing and uniforms since the middle of the nineteenth century, but rural, nationalist and conservative Japanese still wore the kimono. Traditional Japanese dress was clearly unsuitable attire for defending the homeland in the age of modern warfare: Western-style dress was more practical, and already prevalent in urban centres. However, in the 1930s modernization without Westernization was the goal of Imperial Japan. A national civilian uniform for men, suitable for wartime conditions, was proposed in 1937.

In June 1939 non-essential Western things were banned from Japanese life, including neon lights and permanent-wave machines; cosmetics and high-heeled shoes were shunned. The government worried about shortages and claimed extravagance was the enemy. Citizens were requested to refrain from making unnecessary purchases. On 7 July 1940 regulations were introduced that prohibited the manufacture or sale of luxuries, including fine jewelry, silk kimonos embroidered with gold or silver thread, and extravagant Western-style clothes; aimed at concentrating labour and materials for war production, they came into effect three months later.

An artificial silk *haregi* printed with images of war, late 1930s. Patriotic and militaristic images were used on printed textiles intended for coat linings and informal kimonos worn at home.

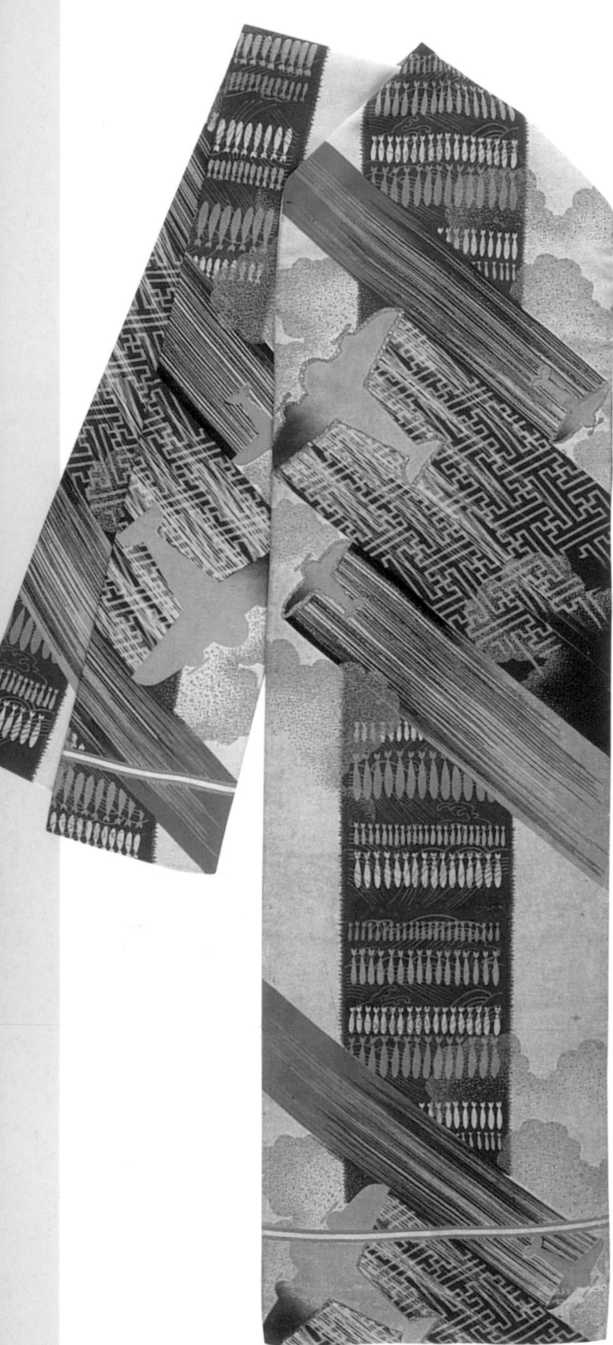

A *nagoya obi* of woven silk with metallic threads, with the theme of 'warplanes in action', 1930s. War was seen as a man's occupation, so patriotic themed textiles appeared mostly on men's and boy's garments, and rarely on women's garments, such as *obis*.

The uniform for male civilians first proposed in 1937 was introduced in November 1940. The *kokuminfuku* was a military-style suit, worn with an open-necked shirt, and produced only in khaki, the official colour of national defense. Within months of its launch, a committee was set up to design standard attire for women. Suggestions were solicited in an open competition, and the winners were chosen by the Welfare Ministry in February 1942. Three basic styles were decreed: Western-style one- or two-piece dresses that were functional and necessary for urban working women; a narrow-skirted kimono style with tight sleeves that saved more than 4½ yards (4 metres) of fabric per garment; and a jacket with trousers in a Japanese style called *monpe*. Although not considered flattering, *monpe* were practical for pulling on in case of air raids – the first of which took place over Tokyo on 18 April 1942, two months after the new fashions were unveiled.

In Japan, as early as 1939 shortages of cotton had led to regulations for the manufacture and supply of textiles, and in 1941 articles appeared in magazines here as elsewhere that gave instructions on how to re-use existing clothing, including how to alter kimonos into *monpe*-style trousers. The government instituted clothes rationing on 1 February 1942. City residents received 100 coupons a year, and country-dwellers 80; 50 coupons were needed to purchase a man's suit, coat or jacket, 12 were required for a shirt or blouse, and 3 for a hand towel. In September 1943 Japanese Commerce and Industry Minister Kichi Nobusuke chastised Japanese women for owning twice as many dresses as American women. He urged them to make do with what they already had, since one bolt of cloth for every woman in Japan would mean 500 fewer airplanes, or more than 5,000 fewer tanks. Even dyeing thread cost the war effort tons of coal. In 1944, the number of coupons was reduced by half as supplies became scarcer.

Japan's production of rayon decreased as the war progressed, due to the difficulty and expense of importing the necessary raw materials. In its place a very poor quality rayon was created, known as *sufu*. The fibre was made of bark, wood pulp, and small amounts of wool and/or cotton, if available. *Sufu* didn't launder or hold dyes well and tore easily, and it had such a poor reputation with

A woman's silk *haori* with the theme 'The Thrill of Flight', early 1930s.

色々の残布をはぎ合せて仕立た着物です。
無地や模様を色調を美しくはぎ合せて下さい。
前の胸の切替の中に三色の美しい色の布を小さく
あしらひました。
近頃の布地は色が良くないので、こうして美しい
色調で全体を引立たせませう。
淳一絵

LEFT AND ABOVE Japanese designs for acceptable modern dress in wartime: a narrow kimono, and a Western-style dress for urban wear, *c.* 1942.

OPPOSITE, ABOVE, AND THIS PAGE **Postcard images of rural and urban Japanese women wearing *monpe* (trousers) instead of the traditional kimono, *c*. 1943.**

the public that the name became synonymous with anything of poor quality: a '*sufu*-head' was a dolt. Nevertheless, *sufu* was all that was available by 1944: all other textiles were required for military use.

The American Lend-Lease Act of March 1941 allowed for aid to be provided to Britain and Russia, to be paid for once peace had been won. When the United States became involved in the war, a reverse lend-lease from British Commonwealth countries brought products to the United States, and American troops stationed in the Pacific relied heavily on Australia and New Zealand for supplies of food and clothing. American demands for military clothing, combined with the rapid expansion of Australian and New Zealand domestic forces, strained supplies and production capabilities. There was a serious labour shortage: women had been extensively employed in the clothing industries of both countries, but were moving to better-paid wartime occupations. Rationing of civilian clothing was introduced to compensate for the lack of production.

Rationing was first contemplated in Australia in mid-1941, not so much because of shortages but rather as a means to free up labour by reducing consumer goods, and restrict consumer spending to counter inflation. When the war moved to the Pacific in December 1941 the possibility of a Japanese invasion loomed, which seemed more likely after Darwin and other cities were bombed in early 1942. Rationing became inevitable when shipping was sharply curtailed, and existing stocks of some goods were only weeks away from depletion.

A Rationing Commission was created that studied the British coupon scheme as a model for Australia's civilian clothing problem. The Commission wanted to reduce men's clothing purchases by half, women's by a third, and children's by a fifth. Essential garments for industrial work would be only minimally rationed. The paper for the coupon books was cut to the same size as bank passbooks so as not to raise suspicion before the plan was launched.

Austerity measures imposed on Australian clothing in 1942 had a chain effect that included the closure of some shops. In September of that year, Mr Langsford, a Melbourne tailor, sought to draw attention to this after one of his own shops closed: he created an 'austerity suit' for himself costing less than £2, made from sugar bags, with the original markings left on as evidence of the fabric's origin. Pictured with Mr Langsford is one of his assistants, modelling a wool suit made from left-over suit lengths.

Word did get out through the printers, however, and some panic buying followed before rationing was introduced. The annual allotment was set at 112 coupons; of those, 56 would be available for the first six months, and any leftovers could be combined with the balance for the following six months.

Coupon rationing came into effect on 15 June 1942. A woman's coat was valued at 27 coupons, a suit at 23, a dress at 13, and a pair of shoes at 8. For men, a three-piece suit required 38 coupons in all, with each component assessed separately to encourage the abandonment of waistcoats; a non-wool overcoat required 40 coupons, a wool overcoat 38, and shirts and footwear each required 12 coupons. (That wool required fewer coupons than cotton or rayon was the opposite of the situation in Britain; but Australia was a great wool producer, and wool might hardly have been rationed at all had it not been needed for contracts for American uniforms, and shipments still going to the U.K.) Hats for men and women were also rationed, which was not the case in most other schemes. The first year proved to be the most difficult, when special coupons had to be issued for expectant mothers and outsize children, overlooked in the initial scheme. A lack of manufacturing capacity for men's and children's footwear caused a temporary shortage, and a desperate lack of cotton in 1942 was only remedied by an emergency supply purchased from India. By the middle of 1943, however, American Lend-Lease supplies came through, leading to a surplus of cotton for Australian civilian clothing needs.

In Australia, austerity restrictions accompanied rationing. Puffy sleeves and hem lengths were restricted, along with unnecessary buttons. The manufacture of evening and dinner gowns and evening coats and cloaks was prohibited, and dry-cleaning establishments were forbidden to clean long evening garments. The Minister for War Organization of Industry, John Dedman, introduced 'Victory' garments, including a man's single-breasted suit with no sleeve buttons, vest, or turn-ups/cuffs: this proved unpopular, and became known as the 'Dedman suit'. As elsewhere, women were encouraged to make do and mend, restyle old clothes, and use what materials were available for home sewing projects. Cotton feed and flour bags were popular materials for underwear and aprons as well as summer skirts, blouses and dresses.

An Australian rayon blouse printed with patriotic RAAF and British Commonwealth Forces motifs, 1940s.

In 1945, when the war ended, tons of bolts of wool intended for servicemen's uniforms lay in warehouses (most of it in military colours): wool was now available for civilian use, and when the new ration books came into effect on 15 November 1945, wool garments were assessed at even less than they had been before. An Australian woman's wool jacket was assessed at 11 coupons and a wool dress at 7 coupons, while a rayon or cotton jacket or dress each required 13 coupons. Many items were now removed from the ration books, including hats, gloves, ties, swimsuits, socks, handkerchiefs, pullovers and cardigans, all footwear, and men's shirts and underwear (except for woven cotton underwear, which was reduced to 3 coupons). Rationing continued in Australia until June 1948.

New Zealand's labour force was already stretched almost to the limit to supply their own needs before the entry of Japan and the United States into the war in December 1941, and the increased demand of military clothing contracts for American servicemen made the production of civilian clothing even more difficult. Temporary shortages – from children's footwear to women's underwear – were frequent, due to a lack of labour rather than material. New Zealand's clothing austerity and rationing system, introduced in May 1942, worked similarly to Australia's but with fewer coupons. The annual allotment was 52 coupons, as opposed to Australia's 112; a woman's coat required 12 coupons in New Zealand, 27 in Australia. Rationing ended in 1947, earlier than in Australia.

A lack of labour was a problem in Canada as well, where natural resources were plentiful but able bodies limited. The Wartime Prices and Trade Board (WPTB) was created on 3 September 1939 to deal with shortages and curtail inflation. By 1942 the WPTB had successfully reduced inflation to the lowest of all Allied nations, by setting basic prices and controlling wages. The WPTB maintained a close scrutiny of public opinion and even recruited citizens to monitor prices and point out any rise in costs or deterioration in quality.

As the Allies made headway in 1943, Canadian civilians felt that any extra suffering on their part would not speed victory. The wage ceiling, combined with forced savings (up to 10 per cent, repayable after the war), increased taxation, and lack of consumer goods led to outspoken criticism. Public disatisfaction led to a sizeable black market, hoarding, and food coupon exchanges. The WPTB's approach to coupon crimes was to indict only when offences were serious and conviction almost guaranteed, as the cost of enforcement was likely to exceed funds collected through fines.

As in every country involved in the war, there were reduced supplies and shortages of material for Canadian civilian clothing. The WPTB asked manufacturers to emphasize work clothes, winter underwear, and children's apparel. To save material and obtain maximum output, styles were simplified and maximum yardages defined. Conservation of wool, cotton, and rayon, in that order of importance, was the WPTB's main concern. Clothing firms were required to submit the designs and specifications of new styles to the WPTB for approval before manufacturing could begin. The resulting trimmer silhouette of Canadian clothing was in line with British and U.S. wartime fashions. Canadian yardage restrictions for bridal and evening garments and negligees were more stringent than those in the United States. A problem might arise when an American pattern for a wedding dress to be made at home was suddenly found to require more fabric than any store could supply. The covers

A Canadian handkerchief printed with the Union Jack, and a silk crepe handkerchief with images of Canadian soldiers, *c.* 1940.

HOLLYWOOD
Four Star
PATTERNS
25¢
1328
25¢
SIZE 16
THIS VERSION CONTRARY TO
CANADIAN WPTB REGULAT
HOLLYWOOD PATTERN

A paper pattern for a short and a long dress, made in the U.S.A., on sale in Canada. Because of the amount of fabric required for the long skirt, it is stamped 'THIS VERSION CONTRARY TO CANADIAN WPTB REGULATIONS'.

of most U.S. patterns that did not meet Canadian yardage standards were stamped to warn potential home seamstresses.

A standards branch was created in 1943 to deal with accusations of dull detailess clothing, but the WPTB admitted in its 1943 annual report that it was difficult to determine a fair relationship between price and quality. Like the United States, Canada managed to avoid clothing rationing, although the threat always loomed with the appearance of unassigned coupons at the back of each issue of food ration books.

By the end of the war, civilian wages and savings in Canada, Australia and New Zealand were high, and were viewed with concern as a possible cause of inflation in the post-war economy. Following the November 1918 Armistice, the lack of government controls had released a buying frenzy which produced a cycle of rapid inflation, overproduction, and a boom-and-bust economy that eventually led to the Great Depression. To avoid this cycle, rationing continued in all countries, for varying lengths of time, until production could meet demand. As items were removed from rationing, price controls remained, until the economy had become adjusted and stabilized. Nobody wanted to repeat the aftermath of World War I.

OCCUPATION COUTURE

Paris ignores the war

The spring 1941 French collections were the first produced entirely under German occupation. They were safe collections of useful easy-fitting clothes with lots of separates for versatility. This illustration appeared in *Modes et Travaux*, February 1941.

On the morning of 14 June 1940 the first German occupying forces entered a shuttered Paris, where there was little to occupy but empty buildings. Over the next few days the sandbags were removed from the monuments and German soldiers armed with cameras, looking more like tourists, strolled the avenues void of traffic but for military vehicles. Some shops reopened on 18 June, with an exchange rate fixed at 1 mark to 20 francs, even though the mark was worth only a little more than half that. Soldiers rushed the shops, buying everything that had been rationed or in short supply for eight months in Germany. Department stores were stripped bare of lingerie, stockings, cosmetics and perfume. Some shops adapted their prices to meet the exchange rate but risked penalization when inspections were carried out. By August, the Nazi authorities made it clear that any closed businesses in occupied France would be treated as abandoned, and confiscated unless reopened immediately.

Many of Paris's leading couturiers had already shut down before the occupation. Mainbocher had left for the United States shortly after war was declared. Creed and Molyneux returned to England; Molyneux escaped on one of the last vessels to leave before France fell. Jacques Heim went to work on the Riviera; many Jewish garment workers had gathered in Cannes and Nice, and there survived the war under Italian occupation. In December 1940 Heim's Paris atelier was 'Aryanized' by a provisional administrator. Louis Boulanger and the influential Madeleine Vionnet closed up shop, as did Chanel, who had fled to the south of France when war was declared, driven by her chauffeur. She returned to Paris but refused to reopen her salon, although the company continued to manufacture perfume. Her decision to close was perhaps more related to her business losing an increasing number of clients to the more

Designs by Piguet, Worth, and Maggy Rouff, in *L'Officiel de la Couture et de la Mode de Paris*, July 1942.

influential designer of the moment, Schiaparelli. Although the house of Schiaparelli remained open for the duration of the war, Elsa Schiaparelli had left Paris shortly before the occupation on a speaking tour of the United States (see p. 63); she returned to Paris in January 1941 and left again in May for New York, remaining there for the duration of the war.

Filling vacant Parisian ateliers, new designers Marcelle Chaumont and Marcelle Dormoy, both former employees of Madeleine Vionnet, opened in 1940, and Jacques Griffe, also a former employee of Vionnet, opened in 1942. The young Jacques Fath reopened his salon in 1941, after an earlier unsuccessful attempt, and increased his business during the war, using skilled workers from the various Paris houses that had closed.

As president of the Chambre Syndicale de la Haute Couture, Lucien Lelong was concerned for the workers and industries employed in the couture industry. Textile mills, embroiderers, seamstresses, cutters, models, milliners, and more – all relied upon the survival of couture for their livelihood. Without employment, artisans could face conscription into factories that created goods for making war. Closing shops only emphasized the German victory: it was not good for the country financially, and it did not keep the spirit of Paris alive.

In July 1940 a visit from German authorities to the headquarters of the Chambre Syndicale at 102 rue du Faubourg St-Honoré ended in the removal of most of the files, especially those related to overseas business. The occupiers wanted to obtain an accurate picture of the economic advantages of keeping couture alive. The following month, Lucien Lelong was informed of the Reich's decision on the future of haute couture: Parisian designers and their specialized workforce would be headquartered in Berlin and Vienna, the new cultural centres of Europe. The French-language German paper *Signal* commented on the plan in March 1941: 'Until now Paris has been the focus of the world in the realm of fashion, but the creators of the Seine have been clouded in their judgment of what is really beautiful, good and appropriate . . . Parisian fashion must pass by way of Berlin before a woman of taste can wear it.'

While Lelong recognized that the victors could do as they wanted, he argued that the skills of the enormous workforce that supported the industry could not be transplanted to two different cities and be expected to perform in the same manner. Couture required thousands of 'little hands'. Besides, French clientele would not travel to Berlin, and they were likely to refuse to wear clothes originating there. Lelong reasoned that fashion was a cultural activity, and every country had the right to create its own style. It was up to Germany to prove it could succeed without destroying or usurping Parisian haute couture. 'If Paris fashion must die – let it die in France', he said. His argument was convincing, and the German response was to let Paris couture continue – at least for the time being. Germany wanted the world to see a flourishing French capital under occupation, where luxury continued and there was 'business as usual'. France was to become an important service country for the Third Reich, supplying many of its military and civil needs. Closing couture would not help the occupation, and might lead to massive unemployment and social disorder.

How long couture could survive without foreign buyers and the supplies on which it had relied before the war was the real problem. Overhead expenses were formerly defrayed by the volume of sales, but now they had to be met by a fraction of previous sales: a third of Paris's business before the war had been to American clients, and a further third was to other non-French buyers, many of whom were also now cut off. Spain, Sweden and Switzerland, all neutral countries, continued to purchase French couture for the duration. And fashionable events slowly resumed in occupied France. The racecourse at Auteuil reopened on 12 October 1940, followed by restaurants, cabarets, theatres, and the opera. Throughout 1941 charity galas for causes such as aiding prisoners of war or creating soup kitchens were especially well attended. Parisian society became more comfortable with their occupiers at Franco–German tea and cocktail parties. Little by little a restrained elegance, minus some of the pre-war coquetry, returned to fashion.

Fashion editors and journalists praised the spring 1941 collections. Lucien François summed them up for the April edition of *Votre Beauté* in an article entitled 'Smiles of Paris':

> It has been proved yet again that in France nothing really perfect is produced unless it has to overcome all the odds. . . . The couturiers have performed miracles of grace, of creation, of rejuvenation, of invention. . . . Despite the shortage and rationing of raw materials, despite the disappearance of the foreign clientele, despite the limitation on the number of models . . . Despite the gloomy times, the Parisian creators were expected to do as well as usual; they have done better.

But a threat of clothing rationing was looming. Lucien Lelong met with authorities in February 1941 to seek special status for haute couture under a clothing rationing scheme. Lelong reasoned that it relied on a minimum of materials and resources to employ a maximum workforce of thousands of artisans. The authorities agreed, and couture was subject to different rules when clothing rationing was introduced in July 1941. It could continue to be sold independently of coupons, but clients would be required to obtain permission in the form of a couture card from a German authority, and to pay a luxury tax on their purchases. People with a couture card would receive only half as many coupons as people who relied solely on rationed clothes, and they would not receive coupons with the letters A and B, with which one could exchange two older garments for one new one. Parisians jokingly referred to this system as the 'pink market', since it worked outside of regular rationed goods like the black market.

The Paris fashion houses eligible for couture status would have to be authorized by the Germans. The number was originally fixed at thirty; after negotiation it was increased to ninety-five, but the number was reduced later in the war. Authorization was accompanied by strict regulations regarding the composition and presentation of collections. For the autumn and winter

1941–42 couture collections, a maximum of one hundred designs from each designer was allowed. This number was gradually reduced to sixty by spring 1944. The composition of the collections was also affected: regulations for autumn and winter 1942–43 limited the use of wool fabric by length for a standard width of 1.4 metres (55 inches): a dress was limited to 3.25 metres (about 3½ yards), a suit to 3.75 metres (about 4 yards), and a coat to 4.25 metres (about 4½ yards). These fabric lengths had to include all facings, belts, and pockets unless made of a non-woollen fabric. (In comparison, the British Utility scheme allowed for little more than half these amounts.) The only justification couturiers could adduce for exceeding the limit was if the client was overweight or tall. In addition, it was decided in June 1942 that collections must include at least one lace and one tulle dress (non-essential fabrics), and that at least 10 per cent of garments should employ embroidery, of which two garments would use embroidery as the dominant design element. Also, all authorized couture houses were required to keep a register available for inspection that listed for each garment sold the design number, description, quantity of fabric used, and the customer's name.

Fabric for theatrical use was not as strictly rationed, and provided a creative outlet for couturiers to promote artistic ideas through the stage and screen. Historical films passed German censors with the least resistance and allowed couturiers to explore historical fashions, which in turn influenced fashion collections. Elements of medieval, First and Second Empire, and 'Belle Époque' styles were especially strong sources of inspiration for fashions throughout the war.

With so few overseas buyers, the clientele for haute couture during the occupation changed. In 1941 there were nearly 20,000 couture cards issued; by April 1944 that number had dropped by a third. Surprisingly, the total number

Black wool and velvet dress attributed to Madame Grès, spring 1942. The 'dress of a million pieces' was the fashion of spring 1942, designed to keep idle hands busy while using up every scrap of available material. This dress used eighty-four pattern pieces in the construction of its skirt.

of cards distributed to German nationals (usually the wives of German dignitaries posted to Paris) never surpassed 200 cards per year – not including visiting Nazi officials such as Hermann Göring, who reportedly ordered twenty gowns for his wife from Paquin.

Clients included the regular French customers, who resumed their pre-war routine – Parisian society matrons, and actresses of stage and screen, who could afford the gowns that inflation had caused to soar in price. There were also some foreign clients, mostly the relatives of embassy employees from neutral countries. And there were two new groups of clients. The first consisted of the wives, daughters and mistresses of collaborationist French industrialists, officials and journalists who needed the right clothes to attend Franco-German receptions. The other group consisted of the 'BOFs'. BOF stood for *beurre*, *oeufs*, *fromage* (butter, eggs and cheese), the products through which these *nouveaux riches* had traditionally made their fortune on the black market. They typically showed up at the ateliers with pockets full of cash, wiping their feet too rigorously on the doormat. Their awkwardness upon arrival was soon replaced by confidence when they realized their cash was welcome, even if their vulgarity was met with polite disdain from the *vendeuse*, who would help with choosing garments, fittings, and sales. Paris *vendeuses* were known for 'taking care' of any clients they did not like with glacial courtesy; but couturiers could not afford to be picky, as prices soared to compensate for inflation. Despite the absence of many pre-war foreign buyers, inflation, and the shortages and regulations governing cloth usage, couture did rather well. Sales rose sharply after the first year of occupation, from 67,036,600 francs in 1941 to 463,368,040 in 1943. People who had incomes derived from rents and land could not spend money on improving properties, travel, or luxuries such as automobiles and jewels, so there was little else to do but acquire couture, antiques, art, and black market luxuries.

A 1943 issue of the magazine *Album de Mode de Figaro*, produced in Monte Carlo, managed to find its way to London and New York. Fashion editors were desperate to see what had been happening in Paris since autumn 1941, the last time anything had been known. In its 16 August 1943 issue,

OPPOSITE **Silk dress by Jeanne Lanvin, with a label dated summer 1943. This is probably the only one of its design, as every seam has been unstitched and resewn to its maximum allowance for a larger woman than the dress was originally made for.**

Jeanne Lanvin
PARIS

PIERRE
PAGÈS

OPPOSITE **Spectacular hats, and lavish use of material: an illustration from *L'Officiel de la Couture et de la Mode de Paris*, December 1943.**

Life magazine compared the French creations to New York designs with unfavourable conclusions. The flamboyant hats, draped and full skirts were seen as vulgar and blamed on German influence; but Schiaparelli, who was living in the United States, tried to explain that the fashions were probably being created in opposition to the occupation – luxury thrown in the face of the Germans. Around this time, Schiaparelli had received two outrageous millinery concoctions from Paris via Buenos Aires from a diplomat friend, and had worn one of them, a concoction of veils with blue and yellow wings, to a New York nightclub. The extravagance of the hat had brought her undue attention and complaints from a millinery group, prompting a visit from the Federal Bureau of Investigation to inquire, in a roundabout manner, how and where she had acquired the hats, which were so obviously Paris-made.

Extravagant Paris fashions and the war turning in favour of the Allies caused Berlin to think again of closing down haute couture. The first signs of trouble occurred when evening entertainments were cancelled due to lack of power for lighting. Evening gowns were no longer allowed for their excessive use of material, and couturiers were forbidden to promote their own work in any manner. Lelong succeeded in negotiating an extension on the interim closure of forty-seven couture houses while awaiting a definitive ruling. A reprieve came when German authorities concluded that the export potential of Parisian couture to neutral countries would benefit the German economy. However, Lelong's luck was running out, and his negotiation skills were wearing thin. In January 1944 both Grès and Balenciaga were closed down for exceeding their cloth allocations. Grès had to cease making her draped creations, and Balenciaga was allowed to reopen only through the intervention of the Spanish embassy. Things worsened for Germany after D-Day on 6 June 1944, and the couture industry was told it was

ABOVE **Winter coats, featured in *Marie Claire*, December 1943.**

to be closed down the following month. Only the quickly advancing American army and the liberation of Paris saved the industry from final closure under German occupation.

After Paris was liberated, in late August 1944, American GIs found themselves paupers in the price-inflated city. Thoughts of a couture gown for a sweetheart back home seemed impossible, until it was realized that goods were worth far more than money. *Time* magazine on 2 October 1944 told of one soldier who swapped a 2-lb can of coffee for a bright scarlet dress in Schiaparelli's shop: 'Eyeing the coffee greedily, the Schiaparelli manager moaned: "Vous êtes dur, monsieur" (You are hard, mister).' Informal black markets sprang up around Paris, where soldiers could exchange goods for enough money to buy at Paris prices. Military police and French civil police would arrest buyers and sellers when caught; but the black market was recognized as an economic safety valve, and the glut of soldiers' trade goods actually helped to reduce prices for items that had been especially rare, like cigarettes and coffee. The real problem was that U.S. government property, including gasoline, was being traded, and the war was far from over.

In mid-October 1944 the Paris fall collections were shown, despite a shortage of clients (many of the best couture customers were collaborators and had been arrested). *Time* reported on 16 October:

> The spectators were almost as arresting as the mannequins. One Parisienne wore black lace bobby socks with matching lace earrings. Others in towering electric blue or mustard yellow hats racked shiny bicycles in the marble lobby of Maggy Rouff's salon. Past a dead elevator (no electricity) they clattered on

Summer dresses by Callot Soeurs, Madeleine Vramant and Marcelle Dormoy, in *L'Officiel de la Couture et de la Mode de Paris*, March–April 1945.

two-inch wooden soles up four flights of blue-carpeted stairs, sat down and glorified the gilt chairs in the long showroom. A sprinkling of WACs, a handful of beady-eyed U.S. officers lined the wall. Appraising eyes watched pretty, pert mannequins strut, simper, pirouette.

The trend was reported as too lavish for American or British clothing regulations: there were full, short skirts, small waists, wide shoulders, leg-of-mutton sleeves, and trimmings of rabbit and mole, tinted and trimmed to look like chinchilla and beaver. Wool was scarce and prices high. A coat or dress could cost upwards of a thousand American dollars – too expensive for legal export, where duties levied would almost double the purchase price. In spite of the dire situation, couturiers showed a sense of frou-frou and humour. The house of Schiaparelli showed a full peplum gathered in front, like a bustle worn backwards, and Lelong put miniature jeeps on charm bracelets. Many couturiers showered patriotic names on their dress models: Jeanne Lanvin called a backless evening dress 'Liberty' and a pale pink day dress 'Free France'.

For the duration of the occupation most designers had kept their heads down and were content to have minimal relations with the occupiers, while working under the regulations that limited their creativity and clientele. The largest thorn in the side of the Germans was Madame Grès. Born Germaine Emilie Krebs, she had operated as Alix in the 1930s but sold the business in 1942. Then, with money borrowed from her husband, the Russian painter Serg Czerefkov, she reopened in 1942 as Madame Grès ('Serg' backwards). From her first collection she exasperated the Germans by using patriotic red, white and blue and ignored prohibitions on lengths of fabrics, staying faithful to the draped designs she was famed for. In January 1944, the Germans ordered the house of Grès closed on the grounds that it did not respect the regulations; but she was allowed to reopen in March.

Madame Grès may have shown little regard for rules, but open disdain towards the occupiers was unwise. The estranged wife of Philippe de Rothschild, Elisabeth (Lili) Pelletier de Chambure, was from an old French

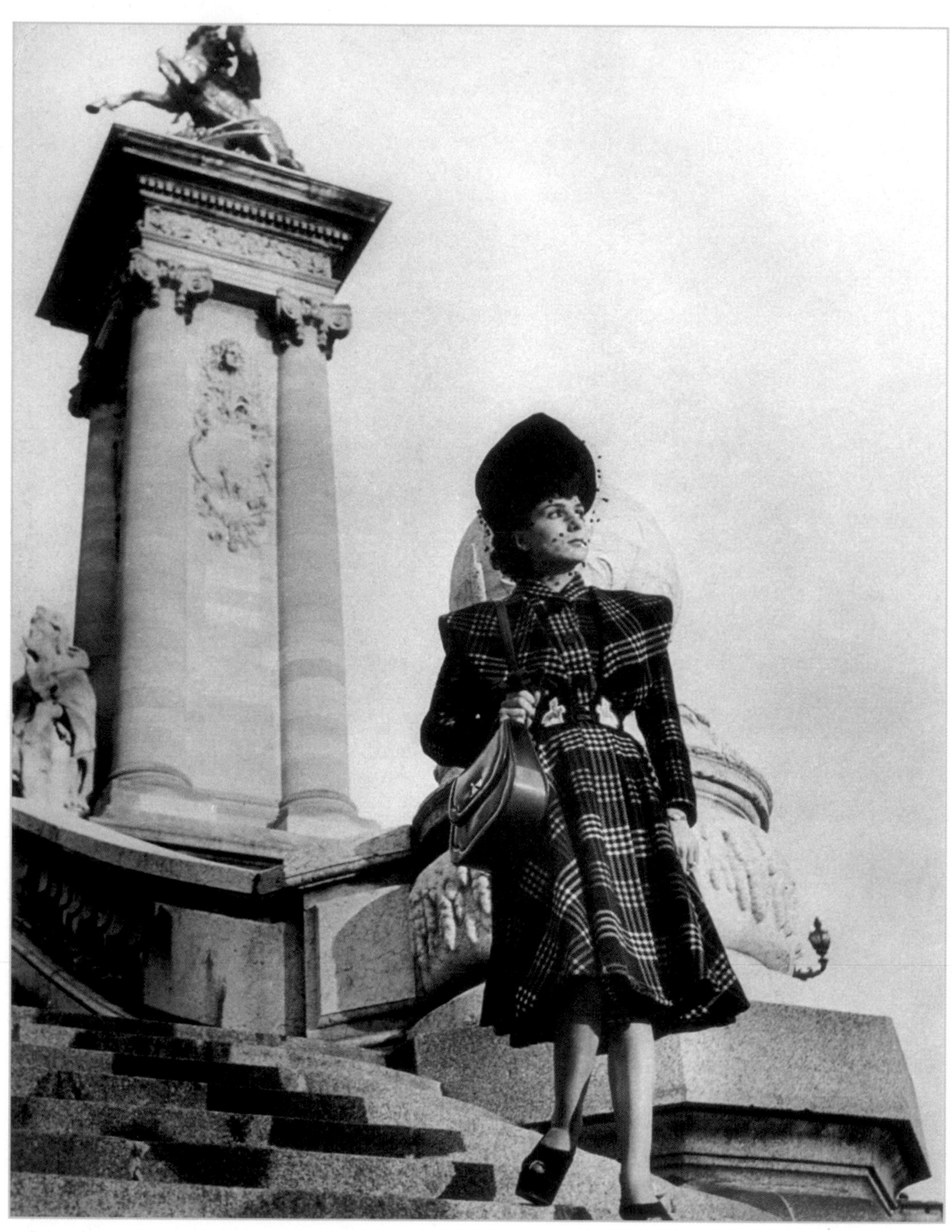

A model displaying a winter coat in August 1944.

Brown, cream and black houndstooth check coat by Nina Ricci, c. 1945. The cinnamon brown velvet turban was home-made – sewn to shape and stuffed with rags.

Catholic family, but her loud refusal to sit next to Frau Otto Abetz, wife of the German ambassador, at a showing of Schiaparelli's collection resulted in her arrest in July 1944. She was sent on the last transport to Ravensbrück, where she died, probably of typhoid, on 23 March 1945.

On the more collaborationist side was Jacques Fath: he and his wife Geneviève were notorious for attending German-hosted functions, and Fath did not care who bought his designs. Maggy Rouff and Marcel Rochas were often thought to be collaborators. Maggy Rouff's real name, Madame Besançon-Wagner, was well known, and her name's association with the great German composer Richard Wagner got her many invitations to German hosted functions that she couldn't constantly turn down without reprisal. Rochas was openly anti-Semitic, but although his prejudices were aligned with those of the Nazis he doesn't seem to have benefited from any fraternization with the occupiers. Chanel closed her atelier in the rue Cambon in the autumn of 1939, but her perfume and accessories boutique remained open for the duration of the war, with the Jewish Wertheimer brothers holding 70 per cent of the perfume business. She had worn patriotic colours in the months between the outbreak of war and the occupation, but in 1940 Chanel became involved with Hans Günther von Dincklage, a German officer who had ingratiated himself into Paris society in the 1930s while working as a spy. When laws in France were changed to eliminate Jews from economic life, Chanel tried to regain control of her company from the Wertheimer brothers; however, they had fled France for the United States in April 1940, giving power to their manager, who had negotiated a sale to the non-Jewish Félix Amiot.

When the war in Europe ended, on 8 May 1945, *l'Épuration*, or 'the purge', began. Lucien Lelong, as head of the Chambre Syndicale, was held accountable for his cooperation with German authorities, but because he had safeguarded the cultural heritage of French couture, by negotiating favourable conditions for the industry while offering minimal cooperation to the occupiers, and kept thousands of French men and women employed, the case was dismissed. Lelong had a more difficult time explaining to the Allies why Parisian fashion seemed to flourish under the occupation. His explanation, which had appeared

Outfits by Jeanne Lanvin, Jacques Fath and Marcelle Chaumont, in *L'Officiel de la Couture et de la Mode de Paris*, March–April 1945.

in the December 1944 issue of American *Vogue*, was that his only concern had been to keep everyone in the fashion industry employed and in France rather than in munitions factories, or transported to Berlin or Vienna. He and his fellow designers had no knowledge of what fashion was doing outside of France, nor of the regulations that limited production or styles anywhere but in France. He recognized that people were shocked by Paris fashions, but every yard wasted had been a yard less for the Third Reich. Lelong's statement proved his exceptional diplomatic skills, but some felt that his explanation was an 'after the fact' justification. The richest man in France, the cotton textile industrialist Marcel Boussac, had made cloth for German uniforms and linen linings for German firehoses. Was there any company still in business in France that had not cooperated to some extent with the occupiers? Non-cooperation would have resulted in loss of ownership of the business, arrest, and probable internment in a labour camp.

Lelong's business never fully recovered from innuendos of cooperation, and closed in 1948. But in the end it was the little people in the fashion industry who were charged with minor offences, such as shop clerks who had been too nice to German soldiers. Their crimes usually received minimal sentences or suspensions. In post-war France, it was imperative to rebuild the economy by rebuilding the luxury trades for export. Punishing anyone in those industries for indiscreet or possibly collaborative associations was not seen as beneficial to economic reconstruction.

Post-liberation French fashions seemed extraordinarily generous in their use of fabric compared to British Utility standards and American Limitation Orders. The spring 1945 collections were the first produced entirely after the occupation: they continued the trend for fuller, feminine cuts; but the clothes were not legally exportable, as they contravened L-85 regulations in the United States and Austerity measures in Britain. October 1945 saw the launch of the first big post-war collections, reported with more fanfare than the smaller show of 1944. Paris had scaled back its full skirts so that the collections were legally saleable outside France. In light of the fragile post-war economy and continuing shortages, Paris was still criticized for using too much fabric. However, it was noted that prices were far more reasonable than a year earlier: $350–$650 would buy most dresses and coats. The collections showed a mixture of tight and full skirts and a variety of hem lengths for different times of day. The most noteworthy feature was the rediscovery of the female form. Low necklines and an emphasized bust topped a more curvaceous figure. Lucien Lelong (whose lead designer was Christian Dior), Jacques Fath and Pierre Balmain were particularly noted for their feminine silhouettes. American designers scrutinized the images; *Time* on 29 October quoted one Manhattan designer as concluding, 'If this is the best Paris can do, we have nothing to worry about.'

However, American designers had a lot to worry about. Marcel Boussac had come to an arrangement with Christian Dior. He would bankroll the house, and, in turn, Dior guaranteed that he would design clothes that used extravagant amounts of fabric. The resulting collection, first shown in February 1947, became known as the New Look and was the catalyst for the rebirth of post-war Paris fashion (see pp. 191ff.).

Black wool evening dress by Jeanne Lafaurie, acquired by a soldier for his fiancée in early spring 1945.

PIECES OF RESISTANCE

New regimes and everyday apparel

Couturiers outside Paris did not benefit from Lucien Lelong's negotiations with the German occupiers. They received no special consideration, and for the duration of the occupation were subject to scant rations of material, austerity measures, and strict coupon regulations for the manufacture and sale of garments. Tailors and dressmakers outside the metropolis spent much of their time altering and making over old clothes, as long as the client supplied the materials. Some Parisian couturiers, cognizant of their privilege, designed outfits that could be copied for the benefit of average women: bicycling outfits, 'at home' trouser suits for unheated apartments, and sensibly styled suits and coats. But many Parisian couturiers created fashions with only their wealthy clients in mind. Most French women did not buy Parisian couture, and were limited in their wartime clothing purchases – having to cope with ration cards and shortages like everyone else in Europe.

Shoes decorated with the Cross of Lorraine, *c.* 1944–45. The Cross of Lorraine, part of the heraldic arms of Lorraine in eastern France, was associated with Joan of Arc, renowned for her perseverance against foreign invaders. The symbol was adopted by the Free French Forces under Charles de Gaulle, and frequently appeared as a symbol around the time of the liberation in 1944.

France was divided between the northern zone, occupied by the Germans, and the southern 'free' zone, which was administered by General Pétain from the town of Vichy. Set up in July 1940 after the fall of France, the Vichy Government was officially neutral but willingly cooperated with Nazi policies. Yet while it declared ideals similar to those of National Socialism, its glorification of French culture was sometimes a provocation to the Germans. In the autumn of 1940, the French textile manufacturer Colcombet produced a series of colour prints with patriotic phrases, including 'Vive la France' (Long live France) and 'Amour sacré de la patrie' (Holy love of one's country). The prints were illustrated in the same issue of *L'Officiel* as scarves commemorating Marshal Pétain. Whether in Vichy France or occupied France,

Advertisements for textiles and scarves with patriotic prints by Colcombet, from *L'Officiel de la Couture et de la Mode de Paris*, May 1941. The 'Écharpes du Maréchal' (scarves of Marshal Pétain) include the Marshal's portrait and other symbols of Vichy France. The advertisement for the typewriter print fabrics called 'Dactylo' (Typist), with the mottoes 'Amour sacré de la patrie' (Holy love of one's country) and 'Vive La France' (Long live France), appeared on the verso of the same page in the magazine.

patriotism tended to offend the Germans. The couturier Madame Grès tested the limits of German patience by promoting the *tricolore* of the French flag – *bleu, blanc, rouge*. The colours were unquestionably popular choices for fashion, and not just on Bastille Day, 14 July. French magazines repeatedly used them for cover illustrations.

The Vichy government saw fashion-conscious coquettes as partly responsible for the country's downfall. New France would honour women who embraced traditional values. Natural beauty was the new aesthetic, and the ideal figure was lean and athletic, helped by meagre food rations and increased physical activity through walking and cycling. The fashions of New France were often inspired by traditional regional dress. Summer fashions in both occupied and Free France often embraced elements of peasant dress, including gathered cotton skirts in tiny floral prints.

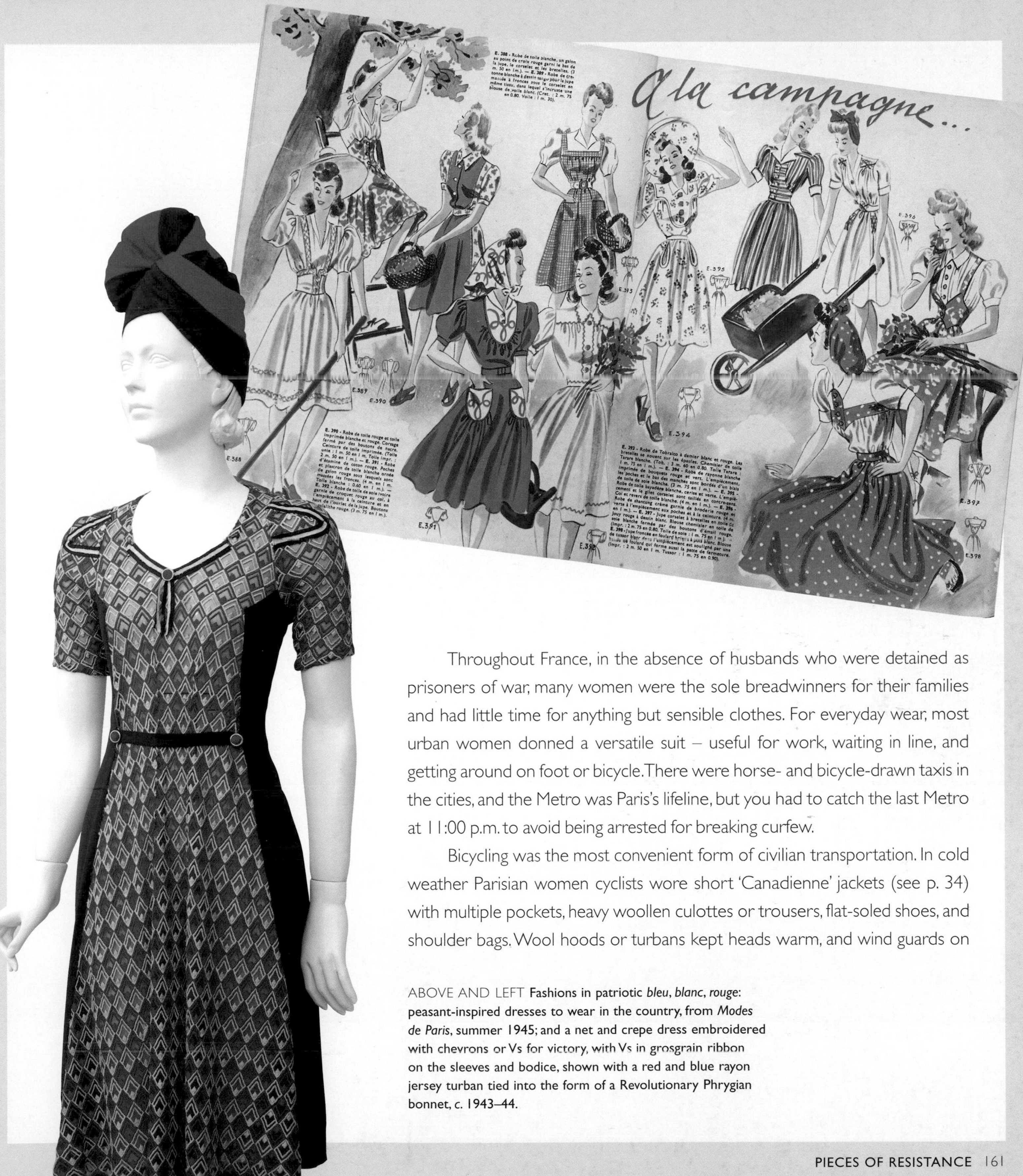

Throughout France, in the absence of husbands who were detained as prisoners of war, many women were the sole breadwinners for their families and had little time for anything but sensible clothes. For everyday wear, most urban women donned a versatile suit – useful for work, waiting in line, and getting around on foot or bicycle. There were horse- and bicycle-drawn taxis in the cities, and the Metro was Paris's lifeline, but you had to catch the last Metro at 11:00 p.m. to avoid being arrested for breaking curfew.

Bicycling was the most convenient form of civilian transportation. In cold weather Parisian women cyclists wore short 'Canadienne' jackets (see p. 34) with multiple pockets, heavy woollen culottes or trousers, flat-soled shoes, and shoulder bags. Wool hoods or turbans kept heads warm, and wind guards on

ABOVE AND LEFT **Fashions in patriotic *bleu, blanc, rouge*: peasant-inspired dresses to wear in the country, from *Modes de Paris*, summer 1945; and a net and crepe dress embroidered with chevrons or Vs for victory, with Vs in grosgrain ribbon on the sleeves and bodice, shown with a red and blue rayon jersey turban tied into the form of a Revolutionary Phrygian bonnet, *c.* 1943–44.**

bicycle handles made of cups of felt or oilcloth helped protect thinly gloved hands from icy winds. For fair weather cycling, shorts had been popular in the last summer before the war, but conservative Vichy France frowned on them. The government even banned women from wearing trousers on the Riviera unless they were accompanied by a bicycle. In Lyons, the magazine *Marie Claire* issued a ten-commandment list in their 24 June 1941 edition that stated: 'Only on a bicycle shalt thou wear culottes.'

The record cold winter of 1940–41 was made worse by the lack of heating fuel. Some joked that the way to stay warm was to wear everything you owned at once. Wool and fur garments were already in short supply, but designs for indoor winter clothing included quilted housecoats with matching trousers and velvet lounging pyjamas.

French civilians had little access to new furs, but those with old fur coats could take them for restyling. A shortage of thread and needles vexed the French fur industry, which was kept busy with German military clothing contracts for soldiers on the Eastern Front. So important were those contracts that French Jewish furriers were given special protection in 1942, and several hundred were released from camps to keep fur production on schedule in

ABOVE **Fashions for cyclists by leading couturiers, June 1942. Attempts by couturiers to make stylish cycling clothes failed to appeal to most women, who were limited in their purchases by rationing.**

ABOVE RIGHT **A cycling outfit, October 1941.**

1943. The supply of pelts quickly dwindled, since the largest fur sources were Allied nations: Russia was the main source of sable, ermine, and various types of lamb, and Canada and the United States were the main sources of mink, marten, weasel, seal, beaver, raccoon, skunk, squirrel, opossum, muskrat, and silver fox. Monkey and leopard could be traded for along the west coast of Africa, and nutria, chinchilla and ocelot were available from South America – but wartime conditions meant trade was too costly for Germany if shipments were lost. Marten, red fox, and mole were the only pelts found in German-controlled Central Europe other than domestically raised rabbit, which was plentiful and was commonly dyed and shaved to resemble a wide variety of more expensive furs. Perhaps most shocking was the use of domestic cat, which had a better quality fur than rabbit. There was also reindeer and fox from Scandinavia, but the finest Norwegian blue fox pelts found their way more often to furriers in the United States, via neutral Sweden and then Britain.

There had already been shortages of wool and fur garments and leather shoes before the occupation, so it was not surprising when footwear ration coupons were issued in January 1941, paving the way for clothing rationing. The shortage of leather led to the banning of large bags, which had been popular because they carried so much. Leather belts were also restricted in size: women's could not be wider than 4 centimetres (1½ inches) and men's could not exceed 2.5 centimetres (1 inch). Inventive belt alternatives included crocheted string, plaited straw or woven ribbons. Schiaparelli's small handbags comprising a basket with a lining of cotton chintz or chamois closing with a drawstring were popular alternatives to leather bags. Felt or oilcloth bags with drawstring closures were also popular. In February 1941 Lelong showed wooden bags, starting a fashion. The writer Colette in her wartime journals recalled making a handbag from her mother's Indian shawl.

A patriotic French handkerchief with the figure of Marianne – the embodiment of France – wearing a Phrygian bonnet and a *tricolore* sash, c. 1945.

One of André Girard's impressions of Paris fashions, reproduced in American *Vogue*, June 1944. In the accompanying interview, he praised popular styles such as skirts made from two shawls sewn together – the more dissimilar the shawls, the more amusing the skirts – and some hats were trimmed with cardboard in architectural renditions of little houses or even the Eiffel Tower.

A limitation on the sale of clothing was introduced on 14 February 1941; in April, while still awaiting a rationing system, consumers were allowed to acquire a new garment in exchange for two worn but still usable garments. On 1 July 1941 a book of 100 coupons was issued, but only the first 30 coupons could be used immediately. Not all clothing was rationed: garments made of lace, tulle, lamé or angora were not rationed, nor were hats or all ribbons up to 20 centimetres (8 inches) in width – but not rationed often meant not available. A pair of cotton stockings required 4 points, as did a short-sleeved blouse; a rayon skirt required 10 points; and a silk dress a high 18 points. In 1942, when 40 coupons were issued, a rayon skirt required 12 points, a rayon blouse 6 points, and a cotton sweater 9 points.

Shortly after the defeat of France in June 1940, German authorities directed French textile industries to increase their production and use of artificial fibres. Before the war, rayon production had made up only 7 per cent of the French textile industry, well behind most European countries. The magazine *Pour Elle* reported on 10 December 1941 that one tree trunk weighing 100 kilos (220 pounds) could make 265 shirts, 80 dresses, or 37 coats. These were promising results from a minimum of raw material. In November 1940, textile manufacturers were reorganized as subsidiaries of France-Rayonne, to which German interests contributed a third of the capital in the form of patent rights and technical advice. However, unsteady supplies of coniferous wood chips confounded production schedules. Other substitute materials were experimented with, including Spanish broom, reeds, beanstalks, sisal agave, and human hair. In March 1941, *Le Figaro* asked: 'How will we be dressed tomorrow? mulberry tree cloth? nettle cloth? glass fibre or hair-cloth? rabbit wool or horsehair? ... Where are the woolllen, cotton, silk and rayon industries?'

The textile firm Colcombet was charged with encouraging couturiers to increase their use of the new textiles. An exhibition in July 1941 at the Petit Palais in Paris featured the new fabrics in multiple applications, including couture suits and coats from Lelong, Piguet and Hermès. A novel addition to the exhibition was a rainwear exhibit made entirely of transparent vinyl.

Even with larger supplies of rayon, by April 1942 material shortages required austerity measures similar to those already in place in Germany, Britain, and the United States. Box pleat inserts on men's jackets, half belts on coats, pocket flaps, and turn-ups/cuffs on trousers were restricted, double-breasted waistcoats were banned for all but ceremonial occasions, and boys under the age of fifteen could not have long trousers.

To disseminate French fashion, numerous magazines continued to publish photographs and line drawings of couture and couture-inspired clothing. Many of the 'French' fashion magazines were really German- or Austrian-owned publications: they used 'France' or 'Paris' in their titles to suggest French fashion authority, but had offices across Europe and produced print runs for different language markets. Of the genuinely French magazines, *Femina* closed at the beginning of the war, but the influential *L'Art et la Mode* and *L'Officiel de la Couture et de la Mode de Paris* both still had a large readership. *Votre Beauté*, *Modes et Travaux*, *Le Petit Écho de la Mode* and *Marie Claire* (which had withdrawn to Lyons in the free zone in 1940) continued to publish. They were more like women's magazines, offering patterns, suggestions for remaking clothes, and even economical household tips. Practical content meant they were less likely to be shut down as non-essential publications.

A French painter named André Girard had ingratiated himself with the Paris couture scene when he had been appointed art director of the French Pavilion at the 1939 San Francisco Exposition, and his theme had been how the great Parisian artists had inspired couture. In early 1944 it became known that he worked as a radio operator for the underground, and he escaped from France to the United States. *Vogue* magazine was eager to interview him for news of Paris fashions. In the interview, which appeared in the June 1944 issue, he spoke not of couture but of the clothing of the little people – the *midinettes*

Another of André Girard's drawings reproduced in American *Vogue*, June 1944. Enormous collars, he said, concealed old-fashioned shoulder-lines and worn necklines, buttons sculpted of ceramic or wood became works of art, and patches became chic appliqués.

Accessories – bags, a scarf, shoes, gloves and umbrellas – illustrated in *Paris et l'Élégance féminine*, January–April 1945.

(young seamstresses in the fashion world) of Paris who defied Nazi occupation by donning fashions created out of necessity. 'Every month, each new German restriction was countered by some new hit of bravado, by some dodge so clever that the conqueror refrained from protesting . . . Thus, there was the battle of the hats, the battle of the buttons, and the battle of the belts . . . For example, multi coloured V's' (popularized by Churchill in 1941, the V had become a symbol of Allied victory). The most daring opposition to the German occupation occurred in 1943, when Parisians took to wearing black and yellow breast-pocket handkerchiefs to protest the 20 October order that French Jews had to wear yellow stars, outlined in black.

Carmel Snow, editor in chief of *Harper's Bazaar*, noticed upon her return to Paris in December 1944 how Parisian women in soaring headdresses click-clacked across the pavements in wooden-soled shoes and how they used enormous collars, ceramic buttons and fanciful patches to hide problems with older garments. Even when it was worn out, Paris still exuded style. The British designer Hardy Amies, who worked with the Belgian section of British Intelligence during the war, recalled his time in Brussels between September 1944 and April 1945:

> I was vastly impressed by the appearance of the women. Many of our hostesses . . . had made frequent visits to Paris during the war and were dressed in the very height of fashion – height is the right word – for there were many examples of those very tall, elaborately trimmed hats, mostly draped turbans. . . . The shape of clothes was still marked by very broad shoulders, narrow waists and skirts full and short so as only to cover the knee . . . 'bottomed' by a pair of platform-soled shoes, made of cork or wood. The costume was completed by an umbrella and often by a short, shaggy fur coat. It was flamboyant, sexy in an abandoned sort of way, and horribly inelegant, but it was provocative . . . To make it graceful it had to turn into the New Look.

FASHION AMONG THE RUINS

The German home front

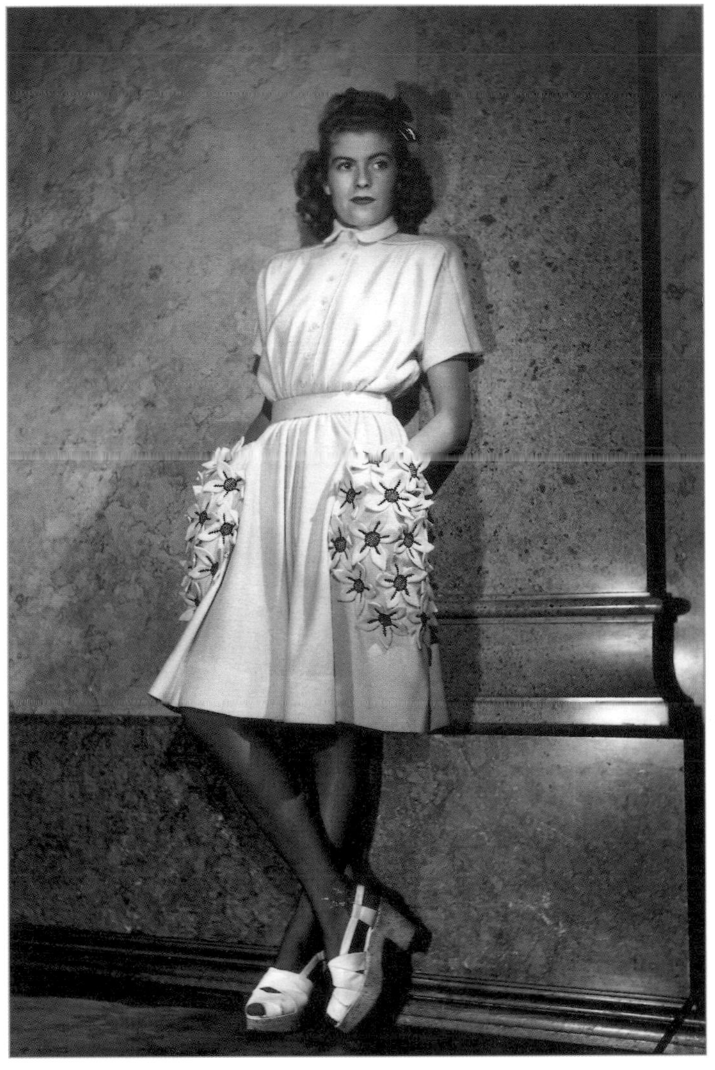

A fashion image by Rolf-Werner Nehrdich, Berlin, *c.* 1941–42. Most German high fashions appearing in German magazines were labelled as 'unavailable until after the war' and were made only for export to neutral, occupied, and aligned countries.

The largely Jewish-owned and operated German garment industry of 1933 had been completely Aryanized by the time Hitler invaded Poland on 1 September 1939. With less experience, and already suffering from shortages, the German fashion industry was struggling before war even began. The Deutsches Mode-Institut, which had come into being in 1933 to promote German fashion, had all but disappeared by 1941. The only 'voice' of German fashion came from the Berlin designer salons that were organized into the Berliner Modelle Gesellschaft (BMG) to lead German fashion design for export markets. The salons staged semi-annual shows and, at times, selected Viennese firms to participate from the Austrian version of the BMG, the Haus der Mode. These presentations were intended not for the German public but rather for buyers from neutral, occupied and aligned countries, to bring in much needed foreign currency for the war effort.

The French defeat in June 1940 was both worrisome and advantageous for the German fashion industry. Some worried that if Paris couture shut down, Germany would lose design ideas for ready-to-wear collections. Others, however, viewed the defeat of the competition as an opportunity to elevate the prestige of German fashions. Goebbels' Propaganda Ministry backed the creation of a new magazine to be the official voice of German fashion, *Die Mode*, which debuted in January 1941. Although Paris couture was in fact still healthy, German fashion magazines now had to rely entirely on German designs for content, since Goebbels no longer allowed them to publish images

OPPOSITE A fashion image by Rolf-Werner Nehrdich, Berlin, *c.* 1942–43.

RIGHT Two views of a black velvet dress labelled Modesalon, Berlin, *c.* 1944–47. In the mannequin's hair is a Dutch black suede and felt necklace, *c.* early–mid-1940s.

of French fashions. *Die Mode*, together with the longer-established fashion magazines *Die Dame* and *Elegante Welt*, presented clothes and products that were intended for export, apart from some sales to wives of top Nazi officials. From 1941 until 1943 the magazines slowly got thinner, the paper quality deteriorated, and colour photography disappeared. In the spring of 1943, as Allied bombings of German cities increased, non-essential periodicals, including fashion magazines, were stopped due to paper shortages, although some women's magazines with fashion content continued to be published in a limited format into 1944. For Germans struggling with clothing cards and shortages, women's magazines offered realistic views of German fashion. Articles and photo-essays focused on restyling older fashions, making clothes warmer, cooking meatless meals, making baby clothes, and generally economizing in the household. National-Socialist-approved publications usually portrayed a dirndl-clad maiden or mother on the cover, but within, the contents were almost completely free of politics – unlike American fashion and women's magazines, which were infused with propaganda on almost every page. In Germany, propaganda was a state-managed function, but in America corporations used propaganda and patriotism to sell products.

Rationing in the Third Reich started years before the war began. Butter had been rationed since the autumn of 1936. Days before Germany invaded Poland, fuel rationing

German hand-knitted dress, *c.* 1941–42. For the 'folk' pattern used in its ornament, see opposite.

was introduced, and general food rationing began two days before Poland capitulated on 27 September 1939. Government vouchers were at first required for some clothing, including leather shoes and wool coats, to ward off panic buying and hoarding before general clothes rationing began on 16 November. The first *Kleiderkarte* (clothing ration card) was confusing, but despite its deficiencies it became a model for the British ration card scheme. The system was based on 100 points; the points were usable in stages, and some rationed articles like leather shoes required the prospective purchaser to declare that they only owned one viable pair. Stockings and socks were limited to 4 pairs per ration card at 4 points: if any more were acquired, double points were charged. The number of coupons required for each type of clothing also varied according to material and size: larger clients were charged more coupons – the only rationing system to do so during the war. For winter overcoats and men's wool suits, old ones had to be turned in before new ones could be acquired. There were sometimes additional problems of quality with the new man-made textiles which Germany was producing in huge numbers: a wardrobe limited by coupons required the garments to wear and clean well, especially as the dry-cleaning process was largely unavailable during the war.

German knitting pattern called 'Peasants' Garden', c. 1941–42, showing a motif, and suggesting various ways in which it could be used to ornament garments. For a dress with similar patterns, see opposite.

'Our old summer clothes made new': a German version of 'Make Do and Mend', from the magazine *Neue Moden*, March 1940.

With war production the first priority, civilian clothing was not being manufactured at pre-war levels, and stores were quickly emptied of stock. The second clothing card, issued in the fall of 1940, was increased to 150 points, hinting that there would be an increase in stock – but that turned out to be an empty promise when points were increased on clothing items to match the increased value of the card.

1940–41 Reichskleiderkarte – total 150 coupons

Men's coupons

Overcoat	120
Sweater	21
Pullover	15
Trousers	28
Suit (not exceeding fabric use of 3 1/3 yards by 1 1/2 yards) [3.6 x 1.4 m]	80
Shirt (depending on size)	0 – 24
Pyjamas	29 – 45
Nightshirt	19 – 30
Bathing trunks	12 – 15
Socks	4 – 8
Handkerchief or tie	1

Womens's coupons

Gown	23 – 42
Suit (wool 56 – rayon 25 – other material 36)	25 – 56
Sweater	9–19
Winter coat	100
Apron	10 – 12
Scarf	4 – 8
Nightgown	16–22
Brassiere	10–14
Shirt or blouse	7 – 12
Girdle	8
Stockings	4

Each card issued after 1940 worsened, with fewer points and longer time periods between issues. The third card, of 120 points, released in fall 1941, was required to last until January 1943. The fourth card was then issued for 80 points, which was required to last until June 1944.

From the moment rationing began, non-rationed items were hoarded, and the black market appeared. Despite the risk of imprisonment and even execution, the market grew at a phenomenal rate. Forays into the country to trade for fresh fruit and vegetables became known as *Hamsterfahrten* – 'hamstering trips' – and were so routine that it was commonly believed farmers' wives were the only women in Germany not lacking for silk stockings. Ruth Ann Friedrich noted in her diary on 30 August 1943 that to peasants 'city dwellers are of no interest unless they barter goods . . . They trade bacon for dress goods, eggs for jewellery, butter for silk stockings.' Bartering was a common practice in town and country: a well-dressed butcher and a well-fed clothier usually knew each other.

As more men were ordered into military service, women were required to become heads of the household, and to seek work in

123875 *

LWA Dresden

Vierte Reichskleiderkarte

für Herrn

geboren am

Wohnort

Wohnung

(Mit Tinte auszufüllen)

Die Karte gilt bis 30. Juni 1944; sie ist nicht übertragbar. Die Karte darf nur zur Betriedigung des Bedarfs des Karteninhabers benutzt werden. Mißbräuchliche Benutzung wird bestraft. Aus dem Zusammenhang der Karte gelöste Kartenteile und Abschnitte sind ungültig.

Auf die Karte können die umstehend genannten Waren bezogen werden. Bei jeder Ware ist angegeben, wieviel Abschnitte von dem Verkäufer vor Aushändigung der Ware von der Karte abgetrennt werden. Beim Bezug von Socken und Strümpfen trennt der Verkäufer außer den Abschnitten den entsprechenden Bezugsnachweis von derselben Reichskleiderkarte ab. Der Bezug von Socken und Strümpfen ist auf 7 Paare beschränkt. Davon sind 5 Paare gegen Abtrennung der vorgesehenen Abschnitte erhältlich. Zwei weitere Paar Socken oder Strümpfe können nur gegen die 1½fache Anzahl von Abschnitten bezogen werden. Die Abschnitte a—e sind für den Bezug von Waren vorgesehen, die gegebenenfalls besonders bekanntgemacht werden.

Für bestimmte Stoffe und Fertigwaren sind Sonderregelungen ergangen. Sie können in den Geschäften erfragt werden.

M. 0605

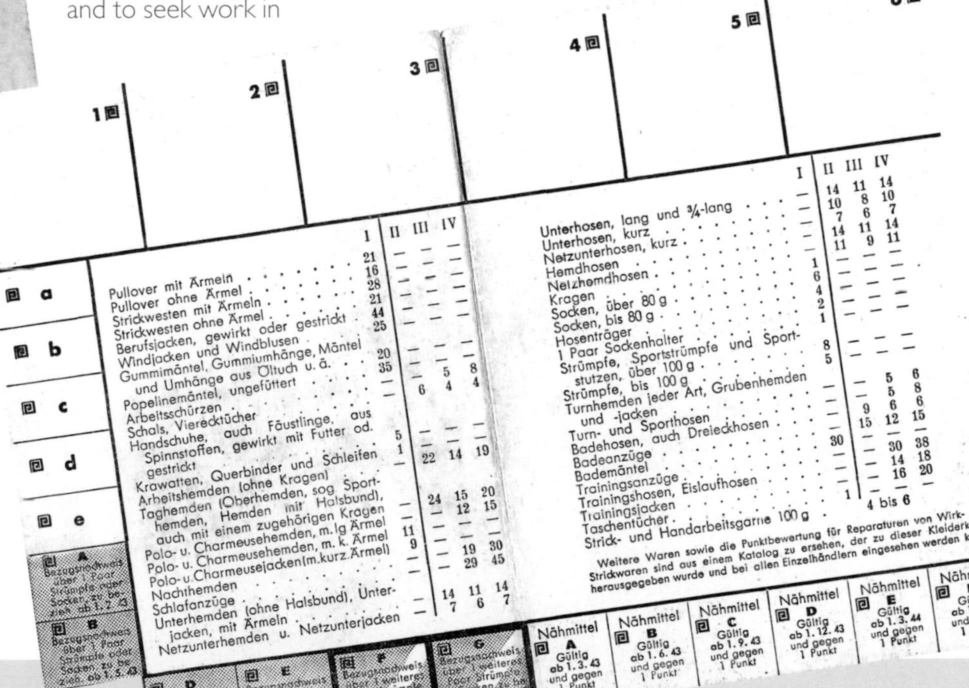

1 2 3 4 5 6

a b c d e

	I	II	III	IV
Pullover mit Ärmeln	21	—	—	—
Pullover ohne Ärmel	16	—	—	—
Strickwesten mit Ärmeln	28	—	—	—
Strickwesten ohne Ärmel	21	—	—	—
Berufsjacken, gewirkt oder gestrickt	44	—	—	—
Windjacken und Windblusen	25	—	—	—
Gummimäntel, Gummiumhänge, Mäntel und Umhänge aus Öltuch u. ä.	20	—	—	—
Popelinemäntel, ungefüttert	35	—	—	—
Arbeitsschürzen	—	—	5	8
Schals, Vierecktücher	—	6	4	4
Handschuhe, auch Fäustlinge, aus Spinnstoffen, gewirkt mit Futter od. gestrickt	5	—	—	—
Krawatten, Querbinder und Schleifen	1	—	—	—
Arbeitshemden (ohne Kragen)	—	22	14	19
Taghemden (Oberhemden, sog. Sporthemden, Hemden mit Halsbund), auch mit einem zugehörigen Kragen	—	24	15	20
Polo- u. Charmeusehemden, m. lg Ärmel	—	—	12	15
Polo- u. Charmeusehemden, m. k. Ärmel	11	—	—	—
Polo- u. Charmeusejacken (m. kurz. Ärmel)	9	—	—	—
Nachthemden	—	—	19	30
Schlafanzüge	—	—	29	45
Unterhemden (ohne Halsbund), Unterjacken, mit Ärmeln	—	14	11	14
Netzunterhemden u. Netzunterjacken	—	7	6	7

	I	II	III	IV
Unterhosen, lang und ¾-lang	—	14	11	14
Unterhosen, kurz	—	10	8	10
Netzunterhosen, kurz	—	7	6	7
Hemdhosen	—	14	11	14
Netzhemdhosen	—	11	9	11
Kragen	1	—	—	—
Socken, über 80 g	6	—	—	—
Socken, bis 80 g	4	—	—	—
Hosenträger	2	—	—	—
1 Paar Sockenhalter	1	—	—	—
Strümpfe, Sportstrümpfe und Sportstutzen, über 100 g	8	—	—	—
Strümpfe, bis 100 g	5	—	—	—
Turnhemden jeder Art, Grubenhemden und -jacken	—	—	5	6
Turn- und Sporthosen	—	—	5	8
Badehosen, auch Dreieckhosen	—	9	6	6
Badeanzüge	—	15	12	15
Bademäntel	30	—	—	—
Trainingsanzüge	—	—	30	38
Trainingshosen, Eislaufhosen	—	—	14	18
Trainingsjacken	—	—	16	20
Taschentücher	1	—	—	—
Strick- und Handarbeitsgarne 100 g		4 bis 6		

Weitere Waren sowie die Punktbewertung für Reparaturen von Wirk- und Strickwaren sind aus einem Katalog zu ersehen, der zu dieser Kleiderkarte herausgegeben wurde und bei allen Einzelhändlern eingesehen werden kann.

A Bezugsnachweis über 1 Paar Strümpfe oder Socken, zu bezieh. ab 1. 2. 43

B Bezugsnachweis über 1 Paar Strümpfe oder Socken, zu bezieh. ab 1. 5. 43

D Bezugsnachweis über 1 Paar Strümpfe oder Socken, zu bezieh. ab 1. 2. 44

E Bezugsnachweis über 1 Paar Strümpfe oder Socken, zu bezieh. ab 1. 5. 44

F Bezugsnachweis über 1 weiteres Paar Strümpfe od. Socken, zu bezieh. ab 15. 7. 43

G Bezugsnachweis über 1 weiteres Paar Strümpfe od. Socken, zu bezieh. ab 15. 12. 43

Nähmittel A Gültig ab 1. 3. 43 und gegen 1 Punkt

Nähmittel B Gültig ab 1. 6. 43 und gegen 1 Punkt

Nähmittel C Gültig ab 1. 9. 43 und gegen 1 Punkt

Nähmittel D Gültig ab 1. 12. 43 und gegen 1 Punkt

Nähmittel E Gültig ab 1. 3. 44 und gegen 1 Punkt

Nähmittel F Gültig ab 1. 6. 44 und gegen 1 Punkt

The fourth German clothing ration book, issued in January 1943, was supposed to last until June 1944, but its use was halted in August 1943 for lack of supplies. This one was issued to a man living in Leipzig.

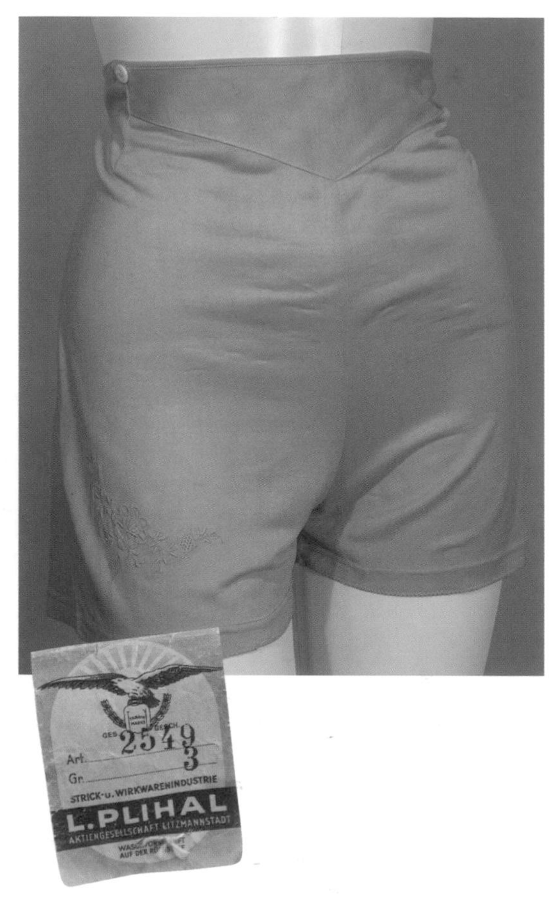

Pink jersey lingerie pants, with the original paper label of the manufacturer, L. Plihal, in Litzmannstadt – the German name for Lodz in Poland, occupied in September 1939.

war industry. Contrary to Nazi ideals of femininity and the danger of female liberation, overalls, jumpsuits, trousers and culottes were seen on the streets. Women were needed and accepted for wartime work – but only until they could return to their duties as wives and mothers. Germany differed from Allied countries, however: propaganda was not used to recruit women for active war-related duties until total war was declared in 1943.

Life on the home front worsened after the attack on the Soviet Union, in the summer of 1941. Germany was unprepared for the long battle on the Eastern Front, and inadequate food and clothing supplies prompted discontent from both soldiers on the front and civilians at home. Winter clothing shortages became so serious that on 23 December 1941 Hitler imposed the death penalty for anyone caught stealing donations intended for soldiers on the Eastern Front. On 1 January 1942, all wool and fur clothing belonging to Jews was to be surrendered. So that soldiers did not know who had owned the clothing, all labels revealing the maker and owner were to be removed, including yellow Stars of David that Jewish Germans had been required to wear on all outdoor clothing since 1 September 1941. The deportation of Jews and other 'undesirables' from all over the Reich had begun in October 1941, but the ghettos of Polish cities had already been used as labour camps for a year. The ghettos of Lodz and Warsaw were making clothing for German troops and civilians in exchange for food and coal. From black horsehide leather coats for the SS to felt millinery flowers and over a million pairs of wooden-soled clogs, the Reich profited from ghetto clothing production.

Improvements in supplies during the summer of 1942 gave hope to civilians for the acquisition of a couple of basic garments, but by autumn these supplies had again become scarce. Women were being asked to 'Aus Alt mach Neu' (From old make new) and 'Aus Zwei mach Eins' (From two make one), Germany's version of Britain's Make Do and Mend programme, but with shortages of thread and yarn making do presented difficulties. Even worse, sanitary napkins were no longer in production, and soap was a rare commodity (only about 60 grammes [2 ounces] of toilet soap were available per person per month). Most dry-cleaning establishments had closed, and the

German brown and green crepe dress made from two older dresses, *c.* 1941–46.

Green velvet one-piece dress made from curtain fabric, with a red and white paisley print rayon panel for the bodice front, *c.* 1941–46. Probably German, it is home-made and unlabelled, with signs of many alterations, including four different hem lengths.

few that remained were very slow as they waited for the necessary chemicals. Washing powder for clothes was rationed to 250 grammes (about 8 ounces) per month. When no laundry soap could be had, clothes were sometimes washed in the liquid of boiled ivy leaves, and baths were sometimes infused with water that was boiled with pine needles to help cut the dirt. Accounts of the time record that the smell in public trams and subway cars was overwhelming on hot summer days.

The second winter of the Russian offensive was even worse than the first, and by the spring of 1943 German cities were experiencing severe and regular bombing. How the war was going to end was now clear to the German people. After Goebbels' call for total war in February 1943, any attempts by the government to keep up appearances on the home front were being abandoned. Most sporting events, nightclubs, fancy restaurants, and confectionery shops were closed. 'Better to wear patched clothes for a few years than to run around in rags for a few centuries' was the slogan of Goebbels' campaign that threatened to close all beauty parlours, hairdressers and couturiers – an order that was rescinded when Goebbels was told by Hitler that war was not to be declared on Germany's women.

Increased concentration on production for war eliminated almost all civilian goods, including those destined for Germany's dwindling clothing export market. For most Germans, the clothes they owned in the summer of 1943 would be all they would have for the next two years, or more. In August 1943, clothing cards were discontinued until further notice. What supplies remained were reserved for war workers, children, pregnant women, and victims of bombing raids; private tailors and seamstresses were only allowed to repair existing garments. Women began donating their clothing ration cards to paper-recycling collections, registering their frustration while ironically pointing out to the authorities the cards' worthlessness. Crime was also on the rise. Purse snatchings and break-ins, especially during air raids, were common. Even thefts in air-raid shelters were on the rise, especially after women were advised to bring as much clothing as they could carry with them to the shelters to protect it from destruction.

At concentration camps new arrivals' possessions were confiscated, sorted and stored. Clothing items gathered here were redistributed to bombing victims and soldiers on the Eastern Front, or recycled into new textiles. SS female guards and the wives of officers would pick the best items for themselves. At Auschwitz clothing was stored in a barracks ironically nicknamed 'Kanada', after the perceived land of plenty (it was here that the infamous piles of shoes were photographed at the end of the war). The wife of Rudolf Höss, the commandant at Auschwitz, set up a studio where interned seamstresses restyled clothes from 'Kanada'. Frau Höss was known for the exceptionally stylish clothes she wore to social events, and avoided the jealousy of other SS official's wives by allowing them too to have 'schick' clothes made in her studio.

In the weeks that followed Germany's unconditional surrender on 7 May 1945, the press reported and photographed scenes of women wearing two different shoes, torn and dirty military jackets, and bits of rope and cord acting as belts on oversized trousers. The *Trümmerfrauen* (rubble women) who systematically piled up the remains of destroyed buildings and cleared the streets were found in every destroyed city of the former Third Reich. Fashion was not their concern – nor had it been for most German women for a very long time.

New clothes would come, but food and shelter were the first priorities. The first post-war fashion show in Berlin, on 8 September 1945, featured the *Flickenkleid* (patch dress), made from dozens of small scraps of material salvaged from bits of blankets, curtains, uniforms, and tablecloths. Gloves crocheted from the threads of unravelled sugar sacks and a handbag woven from gas mask straps served as its accessories. The immediate post-war years were even more difficult in some ways than the war years had been, but in 1948 the currency of the Western sectors of occupied Germany was reformed, boosting the country's reconstruction, and speeding its way to recovery.

An army jacket with all insignia removed, dyed brown: this was worn by a woman in Berlin as her only jacket from 1945 until 1948.

NEW LOOKS

Rebuilding fashion in the post-war world

Blouse made from a military surplus silk map. Often called 'escape maps', these were made for airmen in case they were shot down over enemy territory. Silk was warm, durable, resisted creasing, and could be concealed under clothing. Pectin added to the ink kept the dyes from running or washing out when immersed in water, even sea water. After the war the maps were applied to various uses, including blouses and headscarves.

DuPont promised American women there would be 'nylons' for Christmas 1945, but technical problems of switching back to peacetime production delayed their return until February 1946. Patience was important in the post-war world, which still looked very much like the wartime world.

In Britain and the United States, shortages, government regulations, and wartime priorities had brought progress in fashionable styles to a near standstill from 1942 until 1946. Britain tried to jump-start its post-war fashion business with an exhibition held at the Victoria and Albert Museum in London in 1946 entitled 'Britain Can Make It' that featured fashions from London designers. In France, couture had shown some development in style, but Paris had been cut off from much of its pre-war client base, and in the first post-war collections had to cut back on the material used to meet legal requirements for export. In Germany, buying any clothing had been nearly impossible since 1943; the post-war economy would only noticeably improve after currency reform was introduced in 1948 for the newly divided Western part of the country. The Eastern third of Germany, together with Poland, Czechoslovakia, and the rest of Eastern Europe, had fallen under the control of the Soviet Union, and their post-war redevelopment would not contribute directly to Western cultural progress, as their presence became obscured behind the 'Iron Curtain' – a phrase made popular by Winston Churchill in 1946.

French women sporting dyed hair for the first time since the war began, 1945.

Wartime debt and post-war inflation were of great concern. With every country facing shortages of housing, fuel and consumer goods, rationing and price controls continued until a cautious deregulation of the wartime economy could commence. The largest problem was convincing civilians to accept rationing for several more years. Even once it was ended, price controls remained, and taxes still went towards war debt repayment for years, even decades, after the end of the war. Britain's final repayment to the United States for Lend-Lease aid during World War II was made in November 2006.

ABOVE Floral print dresses by Worth and Schiaparelli, April 1946.

LEFT French navy blue crepe wedding dress with white crepe appliqués, *c.* 1946–47.

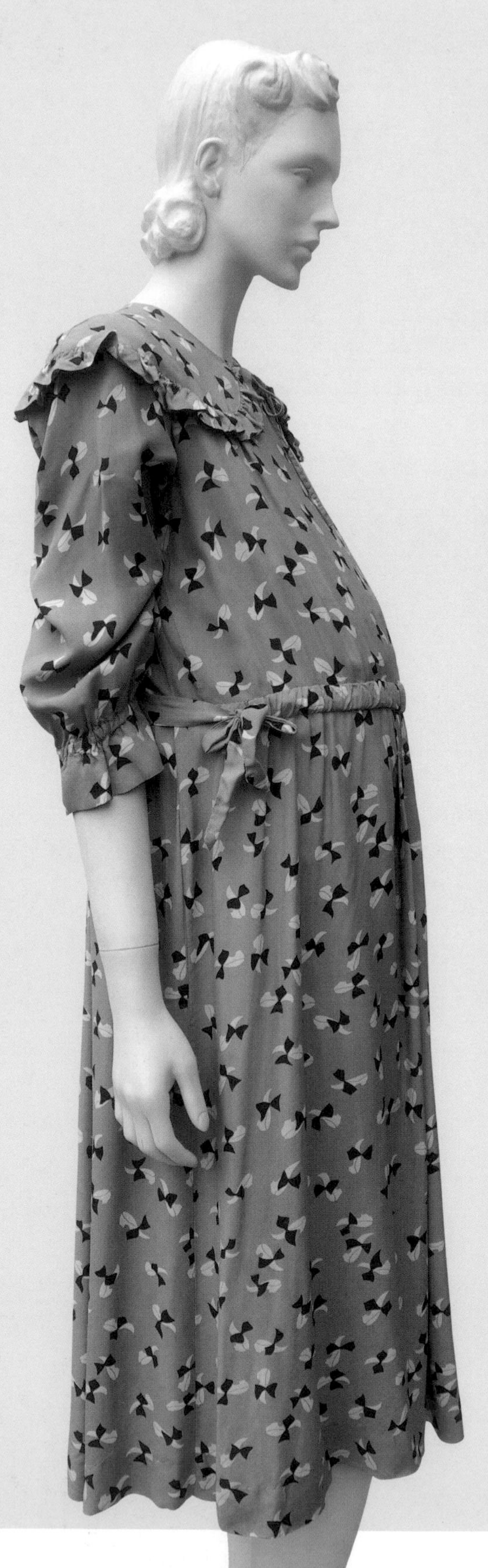

American print rayon maternity dress, *c.* 1946–47.

As wartime industries in the former Allied countries were readjusted to produce civilian goods, war workers returned to their pre-war lives. Many women had taken up war work out of patriotic duty or to make ends meet. Equal pay was decades away, but many women enjoyed the money and independence work brought them. However, industries and businesses reserved most available positions for returning veterans, leaving few opportunities for women outside the home.

Advertisers, particularly in the United States, appealed to the demographic of returning veterans and their brides. A new house in the suburbs, a new car in the garage, new appliances in the kitchen, a new television in the living room – the American dream overflowed with consumer goods, appealing to a generation that had done without luxuries for so long. Couples settled into family life, and maternity clothing sales skyrocketed in 1946, as the largest birthrate in history took off in the lands of the former Allies.

The American clothing industry was now larger and more independent than it had been before the war, and American designers were regularly featured in fashion magazines. In 1939 California had been the fourth largest centre for clothing production in the United States, after New York, Chicago and St Louis, and it grew larger during the war. The area's climate popularized outdoor living and encouraged the creation of comfortable, casual clothes for indoors and outdoors. Sportswear and bathing suits made up the bulk of the California apparel industry, but dressier clothes were becoming increasingly influential. The film costumier Gilbert Adrian had come to fame in 1932 when he created a fluffy full-sleeved dress for Joan Crawford for the film *Letty Lynton*. The dress inspired copies that sold in the thousands across the country, and was influential in setting the fashion for a broad-shouldered silhouette that became the hallmark of 1940s fashions. In 1942 Adrian turned his attention to fashion design – both custom work from his salon in Los Angeles and ready-to-wear suits and dresses made available through high-end department stores across the United States. In 1945 he was turning out over $2 million worth of clothes, and New York fashion critics gave him the Coty Award for being the most influential designer in the country.

Yellow cotton poolside ensemble by Marjorie Montgomery, California, *c.* 1944–46. Marjorie Montgomery was famous for making playsuits that could be dressed up – a hit for weekend travellers.

Before the war, California designers were gaining a reputation for quality and style but none had enough money to advertise nationally. *Vogue* spoke encouragingly of California's attributes in its 15 July 1940 issue: on the west coast, it wrote, 'all sorts of experiments in designing are constantly being made. The clothes are young, spirited, well-made, with a dashing, what do I care if it's never been done before attitude . . . The whole tone of this group of alive, gay, excited, young designers is refreshing.' In 1942 the Southern California Apparel Cutters (SCAC) were thought up as an association to promote California as a style Mecca. Military contracts boosted the apparel industry, and in April 1944 the SCAC was promoting a 'Made in California' label. In 1946 the SCAC changed their name to California Apparel Creators (CAC), to be more inclusive of all manufacturers in the state. Evidence of California's mushrooming clothing industry could be seen in the thousand names in the first roster of the CAC. *Time* reported on 23 September 1946 that fifty new apparel manufacturers had moved in to Los Angeles alone during 1945. The article went on to point out:

> Last year the industry did a business of $320,000,000, up almost 500% over 1939. This year it expects to gross $400,000,000, making it even with Chicago as the nation's second biggest fashion center. Some sunny Californians predict that California's dress business will zoom in a few years to a round billion, not far behind New York's, biggest in the world.

California found its success through capturing the sportswear industry and promoting it as casual wear. For women, casual wear included a variety of wrap-around or shirtwaist cotton dresses, collarless unstructured coats, slacks, poolside ensembles, and pedal-pushers – invented by California designer Lynn Eccleston in 1944. The first order of business of the CAC as an association, in 1946, was to file an injunction to restrain non-Californians from using the word 'California-styled' on labels.

Purple cotton print dress, labelled 'Fay Foster, California', *c.* 1947–48

In the autumn of 1947, the Manufacturers' and Wholesalers' Association of San Francisco went to Paris to show their creations to buyers from around the world. The idea was the brainchild of Adolph Schuman, who had founded Lilli Ann Co. in 1933 and built it into a clothier known for women's smart suit styles. *Time* magazine reported on 27 October 1947:

> In the red-draped, colonnaded ballroom of Paris' decorous Hotel George V . . . had come manufacturers and models to show Paris the spring styles of San Francisco's up-&-coming clothing industry . . . as the beauteous California models paraded in their bathing suits and dresses before buyers and fashion writers . . . Georges Berheim, manager of Paris' huge Galeries Lafayette department store, cried: 'Sensational! I would like to buy the whole collection.'

Even though Parisian designers snubbed the show, buyers from Cairo to Stockholm contracted for thousands of dollars' worth of California fashions.

Ultimately, Schuman hoped to combine French fabrics and notions with the manufacturing techniques of San Francisco's mass producers. Schuman did develop contracts with French and Italian textile manufacturers, and for his work in helping to revitalize those industries, he was made a *chevalier* of the French Legion of Honour, and was awarded the Italian Order of the Legion of Merit.

OPPOSITE

Cheong Sam with pants, labelled 'Queen Kamehameha', *c.* 1947–51.

Bathing suit with overskirt, labelled 'King Kamehameha', *c.* 1948–50.

Kamehameha, the largest commercial manufacturer of Hawaiian garments, began using tropical floral cotton prints from the United States in 1937 instead of importing Japanese textiles. After the war, when tourists flocked to the islands, the Hawaiian garment industry flourished.

Back draped coat, illustrated in *L'Officiel de la Couture et de la Mode de Paris*, March 1945.

Although California led the way for the post-war recovery of the American garment industry, labour costs became prohibitive for some types of clothing manufacture. In the shoe industry, this meant that only large-volume mass-produced styles were profitable in the U.S.; and in the years that followed the end of the war, Italy quickly rose up to become the centre of high fashion footwear. Many American importers and retailers turned to Italy, contributing to the country's economic recovery and making it one of the major exporters in post-war Europe.

The Italian textile industry had survived the war relatively unscathed and was in place to provide yardage to the country's post-war clothing industry. After Italy capitulated in September 1943 the southern half of the country, not under German control, began reconstruction. Alongside the shoe industry, the clothing industry expanded rapidly. Separates, which had been sensible solutions for wartime dressing, became the foundation of the post-war sportswear and knitwear industries. Some of Italy's best designers rose to fame in the late 1940s, including Biki, Marucelli, the Fontana sisters, Simonetta, Schubert, Antonelli, Veneziani, Enzo, and Pucci. Printed canvas handbags, devised in the absence of leather, brought fame to Gucci in the postwar years.

France's economic salvation came through the rebuilding of luxury trades, especially wine and fashion. Shortly after the liberation of Paris in August 1944, plans were underway by French designers to re-establish its supremacy as the centre of the fashion world. Borrowing an idea from the eighteenth-century French tradition of dressing dolls in the latest fashions to promote designs, dressed dolls were created for an exhibition entitled 'Théâtre de la Mode' (The theatre of fashion), which was shown in Paris in the Pavillon de Marsan in March 1945 and was still on display in May when the war ended in Europe. Miniature sets designed by prestigious artists provided backgrounds for 170 wire mannequin figures 70 centimetres (27½ inches) in height with plaster mask faces. Dressed and coiffed by thirty-five couturiers and twenty-five milliners, the dolls were displayed in various real and imaginary locales, ranging from the Place Vendôme to a bombed house. After Paris, the exhibition was shown in its entirety in London in the autumn of 1945, and parts of it travelled

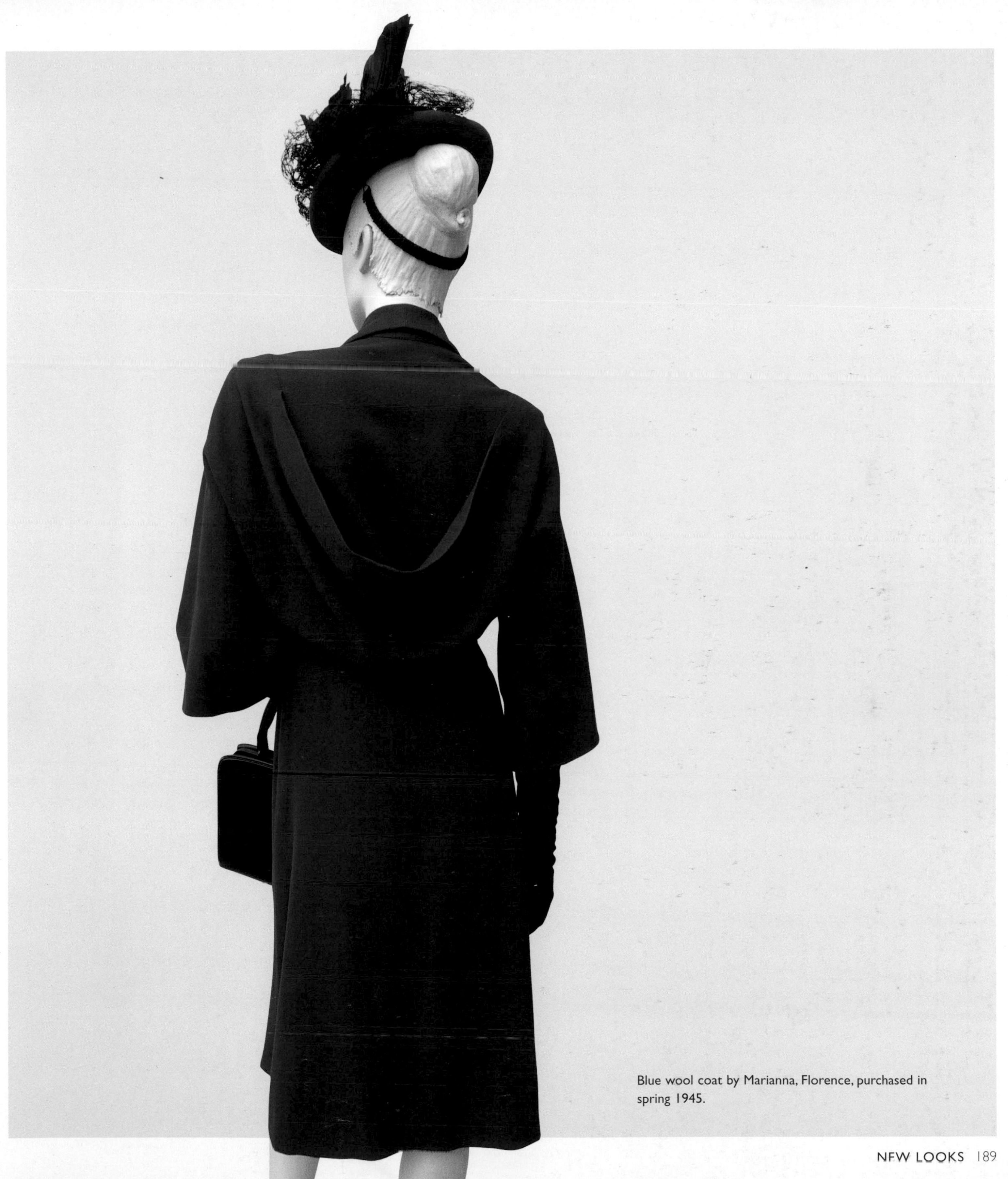

Blue wool coat by Marianna, Florence, purchased in spring 1945.

BELOW Coral raw silk dress by Jacques Fath, with straw and red silk velvet hat by Madame Suzy, *c.* 1947.

RIGHT Black and cream silk cocktail dress with beaded bodice, unlabelled but attributed to Balmain, *c.* 1946.

JACQUES FATH
PARIS

Figures from the Théâtre de la Mode, 1946. One wears a black dress by Balenciaga, the other a green and white suit by Marcelle Dormoy.

to Barcelona, Copenhagen, Stockholm, Vienna and Leeds. In the spring of 1946 the dolls were updated and the number of models increased, and they were sent to New York for a show in May and June. They were supposed to demonstrate that the war had not stifled couture, and Paris was open for business. However, there were clearly different silhouettes coming from different designers, as fashion was in a state of flux. The full crinoline skirt dress with nipped waist and soft shoulder had appeared in fall 1939 and was back again in evening clothes by January 1945. Designers played with two silhouettes over the next few years, offering both full and narrow skirts. The dolls' clothes included a variety of skirt lengths and fullnesses, throwbacks to pre-war fashions, a few samples of the French styles that had shocked the Allies in 1943, and some suits that imitated British and American government-restricted fashions. France was not going to recapture its spirit or pre-war clientele through a doll show.

On 12 February 1947 Carmel Snow, of *Harper's Bazaar*, sat down to view the debut collection of a new Paris fashion house, Christian Dior. All the fashion editors were expecting Dior's first collection to be promising, especially Bettina Ballard of American *Vogue*: when he was still at Lelong in 1946, she had noticed how Dior had given a 'fresh and tempting look to clothes in the lethargic post-war fashion atmosphere'. Ernestine Carter reported in British *Harper's Bazaar* that the models entered the showroom

> arrogantly swinging their vast skirts, the soft shoulders, the tight bodices, the wasp-waists, the tiny hats bound on by veils under the chin. They swirled on, contemptuously bowling over the ashtray stands like ninepins. This new softness and soundness was positively voluptuous.

Part of the collection's appeal was in its abundance – the excessive use of luxurious fabrics and time-intensive labour. The overtly female form that he presented was created through the use of padded hips and bust lines. (Dior's tiny models, made thinner from years of scant wartime rations, were far from the voluptuous figures they portrayed in his clothes.) The response was overwhelmingly positive. Carmel Snow had quipped that the clothes had 'such a new look'. This phrase was widely repeated, and before the year was out Christian Dior's collection became known as the 'New Look' – capturing world attention in the fashion and news presses.

Christian Dior had been a designer from 1941 to 1946 in the atelier of Lucien Lelong, where he had worked alongside Pierre Balmain. Balmain left shortly after the liberation to start his own atelier. In 1945 Dior was approached about taking over as designer of the fashion house known as Gaston (it had been established in 1925 as Phillipe et Gaston). He met with the owner, the cotton magnate Marcel Boussac, who was also the head of the Comptoir de l'Industrie Cotonnière. Dior wasn't really interested in taking over an existing atelier that had an established history of doing things its own way. He explained to Boussac that he wanted to make clothes like those he remembered from his youth, when his mother wore long skirts and petticoats. Boussac realized that longer, fuller skirts and petticoats meant more fabric would be used, helping to re-establish the French textile industry. Before accepting an offer of ten million francs from Boussac to found his own company, Dior sought the advice of psychics. They assured him that this was the right time to make the move, and that his clothes would revolutionize fashion. Dior had liked working at Lelong, and amicably agreed to complete the 1946 collections before striking out on his own.

Dior had always been a superstitious man, and his favourite number, 8, was the inspiration for the hourglass silhouette he was keen on promoting. Dior called his first collection 'Corolla' – the inner whorl of petals in a flower. This blossoming collection based on the figure 8 was the epitome of what the fashion media would dub the 'New Look'. In reality, Dior's silhouette was far from new. The style was heavily influenced by fashions of the mid-1910s and before. The basic elements of a tiny waist, soft shoulders, full, long skirt, and prominent bosom had also been introduced, mostly for evening dresses, just before the start of hostilities in 1939. In 1943 and 1944, Parisian couturiers had tried making fuller skirts and tighter waists, to the extent that their fabric allowances would allow; but they met with disapproval from the German

OPPOSITE **A 1945 advertisement for B. Altman & Co. of New York shows features of the New Look more than a year before Dior's February 1947 fashion show.**

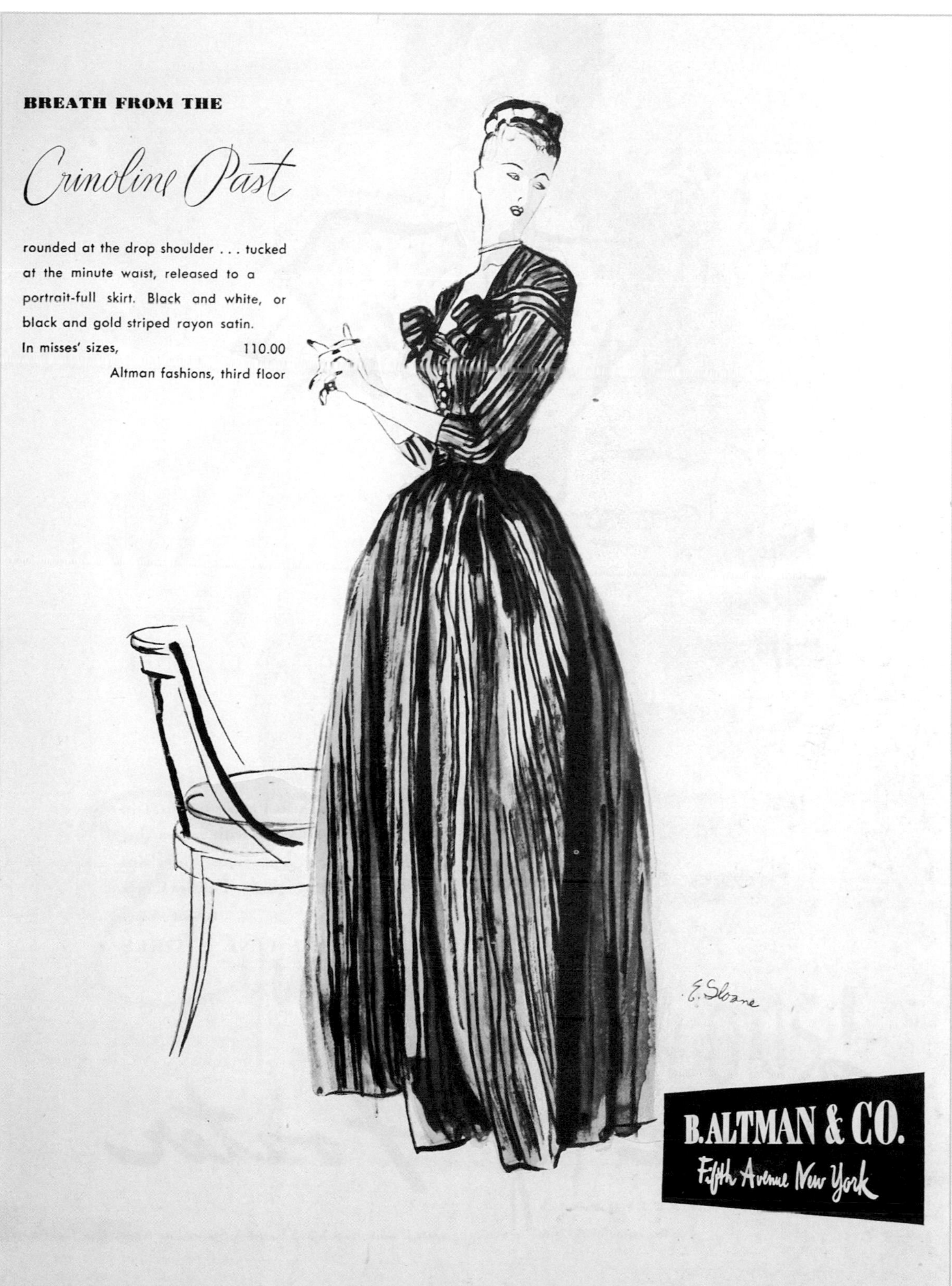
BREATH FROM THE
Crinoline Past
rounded at the drop shoulder . . . tucked at the minute waist, released to a portrait-full skirt. Black and white, or black and gold striped rayon satin.
In misses' sizes, 110.00
Altman fashions, third floor
E. Sloane
B. ALTMAN & CO.
Fifth Avenue New York

Designers showed both full and narrow silhouettes in the first few years following the war.

ABOVE LEFT Strapless evening dress with full skirt by Nina Ricci, drawn by Christian Bérard, from *Paris et l'Élégance féminine*, January–April 1945.

ABOVE Illustration from *La Femme chic*, October 1945.

LEFT Illustration from *L'Officiel de la Couture et de la Mode de Paris*, October 1946.

authorities and, when the news got out, with shock from Allied countries who saw the excess as an unnecessary frivolity in a time of crisis. Many designers had shown the 'New Look' silhouette in evening wear in 1945 and 1946 collections. But Dior transformed evening elegance into day and afternoon clothes more boundlessly than other designers had dared, and also promoted the semi-formal evening dress that came into its own as the cocktail dress. *Vogue* editor Bettina Ballard recalled buying a Dior-designed dress in 1946, when he was still working for Lucien Lelong:

> In my enthusiasm, I ordered an evening costume, a very new conception with a calf-length black satin skirt, a pale mauve chiffon off-the-shoulder bodice, and a covered-up jacket. In London two weeks later I wore this costume with terrific pride to the 400 Club, only to be turned away at the door as not being in evening dress. Englishwomen swept by me in their trailing pre-war chiffons, shedding beads as they walked, but in my new Paris creation for the evening I was considered underdressed.

Dior was only one of many designers continuing the pre-war style, but his version of the feminine silhouette was known for being the nth degree of fashion. *Leader* magazine on 16 April 1949 carried an article by the British designer Victor Stiebel entitled 'Rise and Fall of the New Look'. Stiebel noted that Jacques Fath, Pierre Balmain, and Jean Dessès were all moving in the same direction as Dior:

> the fact that for his opening he . . . produced superlative clothes that were a couple of jumps ahead of anything seen since the war – and the fact that the whole thing was timed with the precision of a military operation – meant that Dior grabbed the credit and today is known as the couturier responsible for the New Look. He wasn't. The New Look was inevitable.

American green and grey wool suit with peplum by Fred Block, *c.* autumn 1947, remodelled *c.* 1948 to lengthen the skirt, by inserting a yoke which would have been concealed by the long jacket.

Suits by Balenciaga of 1939 (RIGHT) and Dior of 1947 (BELOW). The full skirt, rounded hip, narrow-waisted silhouette had appeared in fall 1939 in many designer collections and was back in 1945. In 1947 Dior softened the shoulder more than most designers, and overly accentuated the figure by padding the hips and bust, winning the approval of fashion reporters.

American cowboy and Indian print rayon crepe afternoon dress, *c.* 1947.

Dior also didn't make every dress excessive: some of the lesser known of the 125 garments in his first collection in February 1947 included narrow skirts and simpler suits, to please all buyers.

As word spread about the New Look, the fashion met some negative responses. There were objections to the cost, and to the extravagant use of materials, which would render existing knee-length wardrobes unfashionable within months. At a photo shoot in Montmartre in March 1947 the models were attacked by some Parisians, to whom they virtually appeared as French royalty slumming in the streets of Paris in 1789. British critics included members of the Labour Government like Bessie Braddock, who commented upon the New Look as 'the ridiculous whim of idle people ... who ... might do something more useful with their lives'. The unapologetically feminine style was seen by some as relying on antiquated social conventions to be successful – the antithesis of the liberated women who had fought as hard on the home front as men had fought on the front lines. Some American women in Dallas formed the Little Below the Knee Club, and at an event in Chicago where Dior was present the Chicago chapter of the club brandished placards with 'Down with the New Look', and 'Christian Dior, Go Home'. The shy and unassuming-looking designer passed unnoticed. Dior's name was famous, his face was not: when he arrived in New York in September 1947, Dior wrote in his autobiography, he went unrecognized until the customs agent saw the name 'Dior' in his passport and commented with a wink, 'Well, so you're the designer – What about the skirt length?' All this controversy drew more attention to him, and as is often the case any publicity is good publicity. Dior's fashions were being reported so enthusiastically by the fashion media that he seemed to be saving the Paris couture industry single-handedly.

Dior had picked the right moment for his unveiling. The post-war period had grown weary, Europeans were tired of cleaning up debris: they wanted to set off fireworks! The summer of 1947 saw the initial signs of a return to normalcy in the French capital, including grand parties and the first tourists since 1939. The Americans had just had their L-85 wartime clothing regulations lifted the previous November, and American designers were coincidentally showing

Two views of an American pink floral on navy blue print rayon afternoon dress, *c.* 1947. Despite the New Look's popularity with the fashion press, a modified version of a feminine silhouette that retained shoulder padding found more favour with American women into the late 1940s.

longer skirts in spring 1947. The square shoulder was still the most popular style for its ability to balance wide hips in straight skirts, although some American designers, like Claire McCardell, had been pushing for natural shoulder lines since 1942. Americans were also flush with cash. In 1948 Dior's clothes accounted for 75 per cent of all Parisian haute couture sales, most of it exported to North and South America.

The initial buyers of the 'New Look' found the style cumbersome for daily use. In the United States, many women craved post-war luxury but still required clothing suitable for life at home and work. In Britain, fabric allowances were still heavily controlled by government intervention. Modification was necessary to make the silhouette useful to the masses. Dior's full skirts, which had contained some 18 metres (20 yards) or more of pleated and gathered material, were reinterpreted by British and American designers as A-line skirts, providing the same silhouette but without excessive yardage. Princess Elizabeth wore British versions of the New Look, which used A-line skirts with longer hemlines.

The long-line corset made a comeback to help create the hourglass waist of the New Look silhouette for women who, unlike Parisian waifs, did not need padding above and below. In Sophie Gimbel's fall 1947 collection for the Salon Moderne at Saks Fifth Avenue in New York, the New Look was seen in a more evolutionary manner. *Time* magazine reported on the show in their 15 September issue:

> Nowhere was there a sign of fantastic extremes that had given the New Look its painful expression. Sophie had simply gone her own, independent way and created a New Look that was an easily recognizable alteration of the Old. Shoulders were padded slightly less than before and waists were narrower, but few were corseted, and daytime hemlines, only slightly lower, were still a long way from the ankles.

Sophie Gimbel freely offered her opinion on the New Look when asked by the reporter from *Time:*

> Everyone knows that dresses were too short [but] our girls have beautiful figures. Do you think they'll want to spoil them in padded hips? Even if they do like this tight waistline, how many are willing to go through the agony to get it? I put on one of those new corsets . . . I've never been so uncomfortable in my life.

The New Look was to become the mainstream silhouette of the 1950s, but the style attributed to Dior did not triumph overnight. Most clothes did not follow the excessive lengths, sweeps and curves of the New Look silhouette until autumn 1948, a full year and a half after Dior's first show. Instead of padded hips and busts, which had been necessary for the overtly feminine shape on miniscule Parisian models, many American women preferred a modified New Look, even if it meant retaining padded shoulders to create the illusion of an hourglass shape by exaggerating the topmost part of the figure. The 24 September 1947 edition of the *San Mateo News* reported on the U.S. versions of Dior's New Look: 'Adapting the styles for American taste [the manufacturer] has avoided the completely rounded shoulders of the French originals, and has used modified shoulder pads just enough to flatter the average American figure.' The silhouette could be imitated in two-piece wool suits as easily as in rayon or silk gowns for dressier occasions and cotton for housedresses. With the rescinding of American Limitation Orders in November 1946, American clothes for spring 1947 had already showed longer skirts. By 1948 most dresses and suits had hems hovering from mid-calf to just above the anklebone. Women who had invested in new clothes shortly after the war looked to ways of adapting their existing clothing for the longer hem lengths. For suits with longer jackets, dropping the skirt on a yoke could add four or more inches (some 10 centimetres) to the hem length. The modified New Look was a strong seller across the United States and also found success in Britain, which was still restricted by rationing until 1949 and Utility styles until 1952.

Dior received news in the summer of 1947 that he was to be the recipient of an award for contribution to excellence in fashion design from the Neiman Marcus department store in Dallas, Texas, along with Italian shoemaker

VENEZIANI

OPPOSITE Italian evening gowns by Veneziani, 1948.

RIGHT American tartan patio or summer evening dress by Claire McCardell, *c.* 1949–50.

Salvatore Ferragamo, American designer Irene, and British designer Norman Hartnell. Dior recalled he was told he would be the first French couturier to receive the honour. This was not strictly true, as Schiaparelli had received the award in 1940, but perhaps her Italian birth had outweighed her French career. Dior was delighted to accept, and wanted to travel to the United States to see American women in their own surroundings – after all, they had been the source of 60 per cent of all sales from his first collection. And here he came into contact with the small but vocal group of women from the Little Below the Knee Club. The loud minority did not deter Dior: he continued the New Look silhouette in his second collection for autumn 1947

With each collection after 1947 Dior altered hemline lengths, and by 1954 he was abandoning the New Look silhouette entirely. He continued to seek revolution over evolution in fashion – but getting it right the first time did not mean he would repeat his success, as some of his later less well received collections showed. Fortunately for Dior, he listened to sound business and financial advice, and diversified his fashion empire to include perfume, stockings, hats, and shoes, as well as lines of prêt-a-porter garments for specific markets in London, New York, Canada, Mexico, and elsewhere. This proved to be a lucrative sideline for the couturier until his death in 1957.

The New Look became the dominant silhouette of the 1950s; its extravagant use of material was a reaction to wartime deprivation. The war constrained fashion from its usual path of progression, but necessity was almost literally the mother of invention. Synthetic materials were used to make the minimal clothing styles that liberal wartime mores considered appropriate dress. Fashion had never before used so little fabric; short sleeves and knee-length skirts in close-fitting styles accentuated the female silhouette. Bare midriffs, introduced for beach wear in the late 1930s, found success in sportswear, and in the absence of stockings, the leg was not merely exposed, but bare.

The movement towards minimalism continued after the war when Parisian designer Jacques Heim took the bare midriff a step further by exposing the belly button in a two-piece bathing suit he called 'L'Atome', after what he

thought was the smallest thing in the world. Its unveiling on 5 July 1946 occurred only a few days after the American atom bomb test on Bikini Atoll in the Marshall Islands. Less than two weeks later, on 18 July, something even skimpier made its debut. Working at his mother's lingerie shop, Louis Réard designed a two-piece bathing suit made from less than a square foot (30 x 30 centimetres) of material, and called it the Bikini. When he hired the showgirl Michèle Bernardini from the Casino de Paris to model his creation for the Paris fashion press, the nearly nude model bared not only her belly button but also her buttocks: what Réard had really designed was a string bikini, twenty-five years before its time. Although Heim had been first, the navel-exposing two-piece bathing suit became known as the Bikini, rather than the Atom. However, it was Heim's more modest bikini styling that caught on with sun-bathers – although most public beaches banned their wear for several years.

War was the dominant influence on fashion in the early 1940s. The elegance and excess of the late 1940s were a reaction to the spare, liberating styles that it inspired, but minimalism and comfort were not entirely abandoned in favour of the New Look. Alternatives to the stringencies of high fashion could be found in sportswear, and in the 1950s and early 1960s fashion became an evolutionary story of the marriage between freedom and constraint, a balance between the extremes of extravagance and minimalism – between more and less.

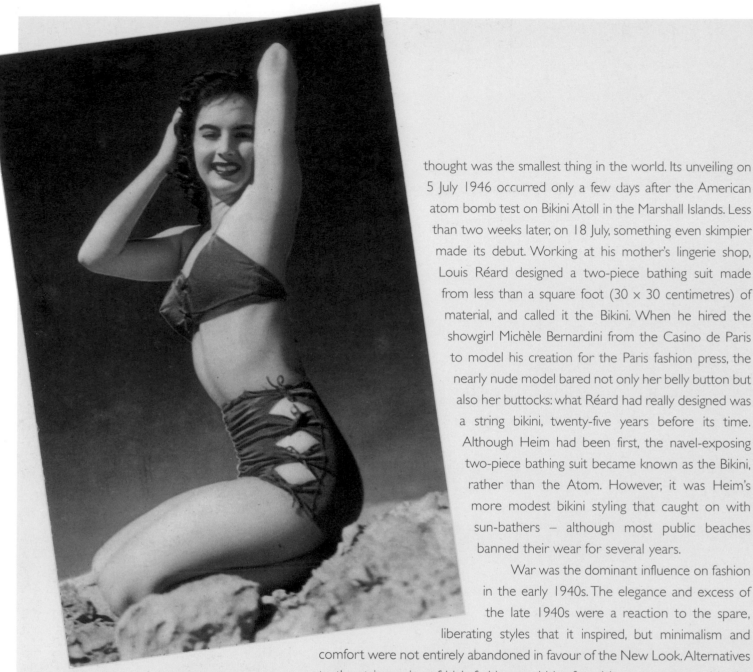

ABOVE AND OPPOSITE **Italian postcards of bathing beauties, showing the transition from bare midriff to fully exposed belly button, *c.* 1947. Shortages of rubber during the war limited the use of Lastex, a stretch fabric used for girdles and swimwear. The two-piece bare midriff bathing suit was introduced as a novelty just prior to the war, and favoured in wartime since it required less fabric for construction.**

ACKNOWLEDGMENTS

I would like to thank a long list of individuals and institutions who helped make this book possible. First, I have to thank those who gave me their own clothing from the era for this publication, especially Hana Pelnar and Binty Mustard. I am also grateful to the many dealers and Vintage Fashion Guild members, including Susan Robbins and Bonnie Barber, who took an interest in my research and kept an eye out for items or information I was searching for. The talented hands of Chris Stoeckle, who sculpted the mannequins' 1940s look, and the patience and keen eyes of Kenn Norman, for reading and rereading the draft chapters, are also appreciated. I also need to thank my editor, Emily Lane, and my book designer, Karolina Prymaka, at Thames & Hudson, as well as all the staff who have been so helpful.

I am deeply indebted to the collectors and museums who generously allowed pieces from their collections to be photographed for this book, gratis. I would never have been able to purchase all the images from Jacqueline M. and Edward G. Atkins, Jefferson, New York (p. 133, photo Bruce White); Bonnie Barber (p. 130); Bret Fowler, Main Off 5th, Stroudsburg, Pennsylvania (pp. 25, 94); Katy and Frank Goebel, Germany (pp. 11, 12 left, 99, 112 bottom); Claus Jahnke, Vancouver (pp. 13, 22, 23, 112 top, 117, 172, 173, 175, 176); Margaret Lyons, Toronto (p. 10 right); Susan McCullough-Stacy, Siren Vintage (p. 45); Minoru, Akemi, and Atsushi Narita, Yokohama (p. 135, photo Bruce White); Ivan Sayers, Vancouver (pp. 1, 44, 47, 53, 54, 55 left, 57 right, 78, 80 left, 104 (photo courtesy Vancouver Museum), 106, 147, 177 left, 179); The Seneca College Fashion Resource Centre, Toronto, (p. 40); and Tanaka Yoku, Tokyo (p. 134, photo Nakagawa Tadaaki/Artec Studio).

A search that circled the globe for images resulted in an international list of sources that also include The Allentown Art Museum collection, Allentown, Pennsylvania (Gift of Kate Fowler Merle-Smith 1978.26.519) (p. 139, photo Robert Walch/Allentown Art Museum); Archives Balenciaga, Paris. Photo Dorvyne (p. 196 right); Australian War Memorial, Canberra (p. 138); Bata Shoe Museum, Toronto (p. 118); Bundesarchiv (Federal Archives of Germany) (pp. 20, 21); Condé Nast Publishing (American *Vogue*) (p. 30 lower right, 60 right, 63, 66, 164, 165, 196); Getty Images (pp. 37, 86, 87 top, 88, 89, 154, 162, 182); Imperial War Museum, London (pp. 46 [4700–27], 55 right [EPH6395]); Photograph by Keystone–France, Camera Press, London (p. 7); Maryhill Museum of Art, Goldendale, Washington (p. 191); Marymc Auctions (p. 62); Museum of Decorative Arts, Prague (pp. 14, 15, 116); *National Geographic* (p. 109); Solo Syndication/Associated Newspapers and National Library of Wales (p. 126); U.C.L.A. Special Collections library, Los Angeles (p. 87 bottom); and Underwood Archives (p. 30 top).

Any artefacts or images not acknowledged above are from the author's collection, and all photographs are by the author unless credit is otherwise given.

BIBLIOGRAPHY

Books and articles

Hardy Amies, *Just So Far*, London, 1954
Jacqueline Atkins, ed., *Wearing Propaganda: Textiles on the Home Front in Japan, Britain, and the United States*, New Haven/London, 2005
Bettina Ballard, *In My Fashion*, New York, 1960
Asa Briggs, *Go To It – Working for Victory on the Home-Front 1939–1945*, London, 2000
Mike Brown, *The 1940s Look*, Dunton Green, Kent, 2006
Sandra Stansbery Buckland and Gwendolyn S. O'Neal, 'We Publish Fashion Because They are News', in *Dress, The Annual Journal of the Costume Society of America*, vol. 25, 1998
CC41 Utility Furniture and Fashion 1941–1951, Geffrye Museum Trust, London, 1974
Angus Calder, *The People's War*, London, 1969
Edmonde Charles-Roux et al., *Théâtre de la Mode – Fashion Dolls: The Survival of Haute Couture*, Maryhill Museum of Art, Goldendale, Wash., 2002
Terry Charman, *The German Home Front*, New York, 1989
C. Willet Cunningham, *Looking Over My Shoulder*, London, 1961
Edwina Ehrman, *The London Look – Broken Traditions 1930–1955*, London, 2004
John Esten, *Why Don't You? Diana Vreeland Bazaar Years*, New York, 2001
Madeleine Ginsburg, *The Hat – Trends and Traditions*, London, 1990
Irene Guenther, *Nazi Chic? Fashioning Women in the Third Reich*, Berg, 2004
Carol Harris, *Women at War*, Stroud, Glos., 2000
Norman Hartnell, *Silver and Gold*, London, 1955
L. G. Holliday, *Wartime Controls and Restrictions on Domestic Trading in the United Kingdom*, January 1942
Nancy Koplin Jack and Betty Schiffer, 'The Limits of Fashion Control', *American Sociological Review*, vol. 13, no. 6, Dec. 1948, pp. 730–38
Jeff Keshen, 'One for all or all for one: government controls, black marketing and the limits of patriotism, 1939–1947', in *Journal of Canadian Studies*, 1994
Roberta S. Kremer, ed., *Broken Threads: The Destruction of the Jewish Fashion Industry in Germany and Austria*, Berg, 2007
Barbara Ladouceur and Phyllis Spence, *Blackouts to Bright Lights: Canadian War Bride Stories*, Vancouver, 1995
Peter McNeil, 'Put Your Best Face Forward: The Impact of the Second World War on British Dress', in *Journal of Design History*, vol. 6, 1993
Arthur Marwick, *The Home-Front – The British and the Second World War*, London, 1976
Official Year Book of the Commonwealth of Australia, 1944–1945
Berndt Ostendorf, *Liberating modernism, degenerate art, or subversive reeducation? – The impact of jazz on European culture*, Amerika Institut, Munich http://ejournal.thing.at/Essay/impact.html
Eugenia Paulicelli, *Fashion Under Fascism: Beyond the Black Shirt*, Berg, 2004
Penelope Rowlands, *A Dash of Daring – Carmel Snow and her life in Fashion, Art and Letters*, New York, 2005
Susan Samek, 'Uniformly Feminine – The Working Chic of Mainbocher', in *Dress, The Annual Journal of the Costume Society of America*, vol. 20, 1993
Jon Savage, *Teenage: The Creation of Youth Culture*, London, 2007
Elsa Schiaparelli, *Shocking Life*, London, 1954, repr. 2007

Christopher Sladen, *The Conscription of Fashion*, Aldershot, Hants, 1995
Valerie Steele, *Fifty Years of Fashion – New Look to Now*, New Haven/London, 1997
Lou Taylor, 'Paris Couture 1940–1944', in *Chic Thrills: A Fashion Reader*, ed. Juliet Ash and Elizabeth Wilson, London, 1992
Dominique Veillon, *Fashion Under the Occupation*, Berg, 2002
Gavin Waddell, 'The Incorporated Society of London Fashion Designers: Its Impact of Post-War British Fashion', in *Costume, The Journal of the Costume Society*, no. 35, 2001
Maureen Waller, *London 1945*, New York, 2005
Palmer White, *Elsa Schiaparelli: Empress of Paris Fashion*, New York, 1986
Ralph Willett, 'Hot Swing and the Dissolute Life: Youth, Style and Popular Music in Europe 1939–49', in *Popular Music*, vol. 8, no. 2, May 1989, pp. 157–63
Elizabeth Wilson and Lou Taylor, *Through the Looking Glass – Rationed Fashion 1939–1950*, London, 1989
Ina Zweiniger-Bargielowska, *Austerity in Britain: Rationing, Controls, and Consumption 1939–1955*, Oxford University Press, 2000

Period magazines and news articles

Life magazine
1939: 4 Sept. Tight corseting – 18 Sept. Postillion hat – 9 Oct. Bunchy necklaces and bustles – 23 Oct. War's effects on fashions – 30 Oct. Britain mobilized 1,500,000 women for war – 13 Nov. Dorothy Lamour's sarong; London adapts fashions for blackouts – 18 Dec. Knitting for Britain.
1940: 15 Jan. WPA starts measures 100,000 women to get standard dress sizes – 25 March New types of plastics – 5 April Some Scenes from the Economic War Front of Parisian Fashions – 6 May Bare knees – 20 May Fashion swings to simplicity as Paris concentrates on war – 10 June Nylon: women hope new yarn will halve their stocking bill – 26 Aug. Paris weaned designers test their ingenuity in U.S.A. – 9 Sept. Vinylite shoes – 28 Oct. Fashion designers find new style ideas in navy – 18 Nov. NY stores start fad for Navy styles; All American fashions – 9 Dec. Turban wave – 23 Dec. Sweaters.
1941: 17 Feb. Shoe styles inspired by cowboys and the navy – 26 April Red in fashion – 16 June British models take styles to South America – 4 Aug. British women at war – 11 Aug. Last silk shipment from Japan; Dutch man parades nude in Amsterdam to demonstrate against Nazi clothes rationing – 22 Sept. French manikins in Paris show latest in hats – 15 Dec. Zipperless dresses.
1942: 19 Jan. Churchill's zipper suit – 23 March Homemade hats – 30 March Wartime junk jewelry – 13 April Patches are popular – 20 April Slacks in style; Women lose pockets and frills to save fabrics – 4 May Home front organized war against destructive clothes moth – 25 May Cotton dresses get top fashion rating – 22 June Wartime weddings – 29 June Salvage fashion fair shows how to make wearables from scraps – 13 July Painted legs are summer solution of stocking problem – 24 Aug. Fatigue hats – 21 Sept. WPB orders end of production of zoot suits – 26 Oct. Laced corsets return as zippers and elastic go out.
1943: 11 Jan. Uniforms copy military styles – 1 March Bow ties and mannish suits for women – 8 March Veronica Lake puts up hair at government request – 5 April Montgomery beret – 17 May Safe but attractive wardrobe for workers becomes fashion fad – 24 May War taps Brazil's wild rubber – 31 May Cotton stockings offer novelty; War restrictions on rayon – 14 June Bareback dresses – 21 June Zoot suit riots – 5 July Bare leg makeup – 16 Aug. Paris and NY styles – 13 Sept. Leotards – 18 Oct. Europe's clothes – 13 Dec. Rationing and price control.
1944: 8 May American designers – 15 May High school fads – 5 June Brief bathing suits – 12 June Western styles – 28 Aug. Pedal pushers – 11 Sept. Paris is free – 2 Oct. Paris fall creations – 20 Nov. Paris fashions – 4 Dec. Aralac – skim milk textile.
1945: 26 Feb. Californian wins fashion award – 5 March Wraparounds – 12 March Eisenhower jacket – 19 March Dache makes surplus WAC hats chic – 2 April Old clothing collection for war victims begins – 16 April New Paris trends – 7 May Novelties for fashion – 4 June Parisian stylists show fashions on dolls – 10 Sept. Lilly Dache packs for Paris – 24 Sept. New Fall silhouette – 8 Oct. Texas raises first US silk – 22 Oct. Victory lingerie, Californian way of life – 12 Nov. Hattie Carnegie.
1946: 18 Feb. War brides – 1 April Paris makes fashion comeback – 29 April Dipping hemlines – 30 Sept. Fashion showings bring back high style.
1947: 24 March The house of Dior – 14 April Whirling dresses – 12 May Skirts up or down – 16 June Fashion turmoil – 7 July Play clothes – 1 Sept. Waist pinching fashions – 15 Sept. The New look for old dresses – 27 Oct. French model loses New Look; New Look for $100.00.
1948: 1 March Dior close-up – 8 March Eisenhower models civilian suit – 7 June T-shirts – 28 June The clothing workers' union – 4 Oct. Lauren Bacall designs own maternity clothes.
1949: 25 April Paris fashions – 25 July Young designers – 5 Sept. Does your skirt have the Parisian length?
L'Officiel de la Couture et de la Mode de Paris, September 1939–December 1949 (some months not printed during the war)
American *Vogue*, September 1939–December 1949
Other period fashion and women's magazines, including *Die Mode*, *Album du Figaro*, *La Femme chic*, *Modes et Travaux*, *Marie Claire*, *Good Housekeeping*, *National Home Monthly*, and British *Vogue*
New York Times online www.times.com
Time magazine online www.time.com

INDEX

Page numbers in *italic* refer to illustrations and captions.

Adebe 21
Adefa 21–23, *22, 23*
Adrian, Gilbert *64, 65*, 67, 184
air-raid clothing *30*, 31–32, *31*, 134
Album de Mode de Figaro (magazine) 148–51
Alix *33*, 118, 153
Alpine style 13
Altman, B., & Co. (New York) *193*
Amies, Hardy 45, *47*, 53, 161, 167
Amiot, Félix 155
anti-Semitism 19–23, 176
Aralac 18, *128*
Arbeitsgemeinschaft deutscher–arischer Fabrikanten der Bekleidungsindustrie (Adebe) 21–23, *22, 23*
Arbeitsgemeinschaft deutscher Unternehmer der Spinnstoff-, Bekleidungs- and Lederwirtschaft (Adefa) 21
Arden, Elizabeth 95, 113, *113*
L'Art et la Mode (magazine) 165
Auschwitz, 'Kanada' 179
austerity restrictions: Australia 40, 137–39; Britain 49, 54–57, 120, 157; France 165; New Zealand 139. *See also* United States, Limitation Orders
Australia 40, 137–39, *138, 139*; supplies to U.S. forces 137, 138

bags *30*, 31, *35, 44, 57*, 163, *166*
Bakelite *74*, 111
Balenciaga *28*, 151, *191, 196*
Ballard, Bettina 191, 195
Balmain, Pierre 131, 157, *190*, 192, 195
Bata shoes *116*
bathing suits 202, *202, 203*
'Bavarian' costume 12, *13*
Beaton, Cecil 103
Benenson, Fira 61
Bérard, Christian *196*
Bergdorf Goodman (New York) 61, 63
Berheim, Georges 186
Berlin designer salons 169–72. *See also* Germany
Bernardini, Michèle, Bikini model 202
Bikini bathing suit 202
black markets 148, 152, 175
blackout cloth 28, *51*
Block, Fred *195*
Bonwit Teller (New York) 61
Boulanger, Louis 143
Boussac, Marcel 156, 157, 192
Boy Scout movement 11
Braddock, Bessie 197
Braun, Eva 12, 95
Britain: air-raid clothing *30*, 31–32; Austerity restrictions 49, 54–57, 120, 157; casualness in dress 103; fashion exports 35, 45, *47*, 53; knitted garments *51*, 130; Lend-Lease debt 45, 182; London fashion designers come together 45; make-do and mend campaign 124–26, 126–30; post-war fashion 181, 198; rationing 37–42, *37–39*; rubber shortages 123; shoes 118–23; Utility clothing 42–53, 120, 199; women's factory clothes 91–92; women's services uniforms 92, 94; wool exports *40, 41, 42*
'Britain Can Make It' exhibition 53, 181
brooches *57, 74–75, 80, 92*
'Bundles for Britain' *57*
buttons *79*, 161, *165*, 167

California: clothing and fashion 62, 67, 184–88
California Apparel Creators (CAC) 185
Callot Soeurs *152*
Calloway, Cab 85, 89
Canada *26, 29, 91, 114*, 124, *128*, 140–41; imported British fashion goods *40, 41, 42, 47*
Canadian Women's Army Corps (CWAC) 95
'Canadienne' jackets 34, 161
Carbide and Carbon Chemicals Corp. 111
Carnegie, Hattie 67, 83
CC41 label 43, *48*, 49, *49, 50*, 53, *121*
cellophane 17, *109*
celluloid 111
Chambre Syndicale de la Haute Couture 100, 144, 155–56
Champcommunal, Elspeth 45
Chanel 28, 143, 155
Chase, Edna Woolman 61
Chaumont, Marcelle 144, *156*
Chevalier, Maurice 118
Chicago Tribune design prize 62
children's clothing 42, 54
Churchill, Sir Winston 81, *126*, 181
Civilian Production Administration (CPA) 67, 78–79, 124
Colcombet 17, 159, *160*, 165
colours, restrictions on, in U.S.A. 68
Comptoir de l'Industrie Cotonnière 192
concentration camps 179
corsets 23, 25, 54, 123; New Look and 198–99. *See also* foundation garments
cosmetics 91, 92, 94–97, *96*
cotton garments *26, 51, 52, 185, 186–87*; stockings 111–12
Coty awards 62
Creed, Charles 45, 143
culottes *79*, 162, 176
Cunnington, Charles 31–32
Curie, Eve 34
cycling clothes 25, 161–62, *162*
Czechoslovakia *14–15*, 15, *116*
Czerefkov, Serg 153

Dacron 111
Dalton, Hugh 41, 49, 124
Die Dame (magazine) 172
Davis, Sammy Junior *88*
Dedman, John 138
Delanghe, Angele 53
demob suits 89
Desmarias, Madame (Montreal) *29*
Dessès, Jean 195
Deutsche Moden-Zeitung (magazine) *129*
Deutsches Modeamt 17
Deutsches Mode-Institut 17, 21, 169
Dietrich, Marlene 13–15
Dincklage, Hans Günther von 155
Dior, Christian 157, 191–98, *196*, 201
dirndl skirts and dresses *11*, 12, 13, 15, *78, 83*, 172
dolls (Théâtre de la Mode) 188–91, *191*
Dormoy, Marcelle 144, *152, 191*
'Double Eleven' label *50, 52*, 53
dressmaking *see* home-sewn garments
DuPont: nylons 109, 181; 'Wonder World of Chemistry' exhibition 111

Eaton's (Canada) 46
Eccleston, Lynn: casual wear 185
Eden, Anthony 86, *126*
Eisenhower ('Ike') jackets *77*
Elegante Welt (magazine) *16, 19*, 172
Elizabeth, Princess (later Queen Elizabeth II) 120, 198
Elizabeth, Queen (later Queen Mother) 25, 29
Ente nazionale artigianato e piccole industrie 13, 17
l'Épuration 155
evening wear (America) *60*, 71, *71, 84–85, 201*, (Australia) 138, (Britain) *29, 45, 47*, (France) 25, *28*, 151, *157, 194*, 195, *200*, (Italy) *200*

Fair Labor Standards Act 59
Fashion Digest (magazine) 69
fashion magazines: Germany 169–72; occupied France 165. *See also* individual magazines by name
Fath, Jacques 131, 144, 155, *156*, 157, *190*, 195
Femina (magazine) 165
La Femme chic (magazine) *194*
Fercioni of Milan *16*
Ferragamo, Salvatore 114, *115*, 201
Ferretti, Antonio 18
Le Figaro (newspaper) 164
'folk' costume 11–15, *11–15*
Folmar, Wilson 61
Forrestal, Mrs James 92
Fortuny, Mariano 15
Foster, Fay *186*
foundation garments *66*, 123. *See also* corsets
Fourrures (magazine) 34
France: air-raid clothing *31*; clothing rationing and regulation 146–47, 163–65; competition with Italy 15, 18, 19; couture exports 34–35, 61, 145, 198, 201; Fascist influence on haute couture 13; fashion influence of in Germany and Italy 15–17; fashion

outside Paris 159–67; flight from Paris 28, 35; footwear and leather shortages 115, 117–18, *119*, 163; fur industry shortages 162–63; historical film and theatre 147; home-knitted garments 130; luxury trades rebuilt post-war 188; 'make do' campaign *127*; man-made fibres 164–65; 'New France' ideal of beauty 160–61; Théâtre de la Mode 188–91; traditional regional dress 160–61; Vichy government 159–64; Victorian and Belle Époque influences 25, *28*, 147; Zazous 85. *See also* Paris
France-Rayonne 164
François, Lucien 34, 146
Frankau, Ethel 61
Frauen-Warte (magazine) *11*
fur garments 162–63
Futurists 114

Galeries Lafayette (Paris) 186
Gallenga, Monaci 15
Garland, Judy 83
gas masks *30*, 31, 33
Gaston (formerly Philippe et Gaston) 192
Gaulle, General Charles de *159*
George VI, King 29
Germany: beauty aids in wartime 95; black market 175; clothing from concentration camps 179; clothing from ghettos 176; deteriorating social conditions 177–78; effect of allied bombing 172, 178; fashion magazines 169–72; footwear and leather shortages 114–15, 117, 173; 'make do' campaign 126, *129*, 172, *174*, 176, *177*; man-made textiles 18, 19, 173; Nazi attitudes to and influence on fashion 11–13, *11*, 17, 18, 19–23, *20–21*, 85–87, 169, 172, 176; post-war (division) 181, (reconstruction) 179; rationing and shortages 33, 38, 169, 172–79, *175*; recycled clothing 179; stocking supplies 112, 173; Swing Kids 85–87; women's work clothes 91, *93*
Gimbel, Adam 63
Gimbel, Sophie 61, 63, 198–99
Girard, André *164*, *165*, 165–67
Goebbels, Joseph 12, 17, 95, 117, 169–72, 178
Goebbels, Magda 12–13, 17, 23
Good Housekeeping (magazine) 118–20
Göring, Emma 12–13, 148
Göring, Hermann 148

Greer, Howard 63
Grès, Madame *147*, 151, 153, 160; as Alix *33*, 118, 153
Griffe, Jacques 144
Guardian newspaper (Montreal) 89
Guatemalan woven patterns 15
Gucci 188

hairstyles 31, 87, 94, 95–97, 120, *182*
handbags *see* bags
Harper's Bazaar (magazine): American 33, 61, 67, 161, 167, 191; British 191
Hartnell, Norman 29, 45, *46*, 201
hats: American *64*, *76–77*, *92*, *98*; berets *51*, *52*; British *49*, *51*, *52*, 100–103, *129*; French 25, 97, *97*, 100, *100–103*, *150*, 151, *155*, 161, 164, 167, *190*; German 97, 99; turbans *81*, 91, *92–93*, 97–100, *102–3*, *155*, 161, *161*
Haus der Mode (Austria) 169
Hawaii 15, *187*
Heim, Jacques 83, 143, 202
Hepcats 84, *87*
Hermès 165
Heyraud shoes 118
Hitler, Adolf 11, 95, 176, 178
Hockanum Woolens *70*
Hollywood and fashion 62, 86
Home Companion (magazine) 130
home-sewn garments 38–39, 70, 131; wedding dresses 106, *106*, *107*
Höss, Rudolf, and Frau Höss 179

I. G. Farben 18, 19
Incorporated Society of London Fashion Designers (Inc. Soc.) 45–53
Irene (U.S. designer) 201
Italy: competition with France 15, 18, 19; Fascist influence on fashion 11, 12, 13, 17, 114; influence in Germany *16*; knitwear 188; League of Nations sanctions 18; and man-made fibres 17–19; post-war fashion 188, *189*, *200*; Renaissance influence 15, 114; shoes 114, *115*; silk 18; traditional costume encouraged 13

Jacqmar 45, *54–55*
Japan 19, 133–37, *133–37*
Jeunesse Populaire 85
jitterbugging *84–85*
Josef *110*
Journal de la Chaussure (magazine) 115
jumpsuits *30*, *93*, 176

Kamekameha *187*
kangaroo pockets *32*, *34*
kimono 133, 134, *136*

Kline's Inc. (St Louis) 83
knitting and knitwear *51*, *56*, 130, *172*, *173*, 188
Krebs, Germaine *33*, 153

Lafaurie, Jeanne *157*
LaGuardia, Fiorello 61
Lambert, Eleanor 62
Lanital 18
Lanvin, Jeanne 33, *149*, 153, *156*
Lanz, Josef 13, *13*, *14*
Latham, Natalie Wales 57
Lavelay, Victor de 81
Leader (magazine) 195
leather shortages 109, 114–17, 120, 123, 163, 173
leg paint *112*, 113, *113*
Lelong, Lucien 100, 144–46, 151, 153, 155–56, 157, 163, 165, 192
Lend-Lease Agreement 45, 182
Ley, Dr Robert 23
Life (magazine) 67, *86*, 151, 202
Lilli Ann Co. 186
Limitation Orders (U.S.A.) *66*, 67–70, 78–79, 124, 131, 157, 197–98; list of restrictions 71–73
lisle stockings *see* stockings, cotton
Little Below the Knee Club 197, 201
Lodz 176, *176*
'The London Ten' 53
L'Oréal 113
Los Angeles 62, 67
Lucite *92*, 111, *111*, 117

McCardell, Claire *64*, 67, 198, *201*
Mademoiselle (magazine) 83
Mainbocher 68, 92, 143
Maizels, Alfred 38
'make do' 124–31, *126–30*, 138
man-made materials 17–19, *109*, *110*, 111, 117, 164–65, 173. *See also* textile manufacturers
maps on silk *181*
Marcus, Stanley 62, 67, 68
Marianna (Florence) *189*
Marianne (magazine) 25, 32
Marie Claire (magazine) *102*, *118*, *127*, *151*, 162, 165
Martin, Will, Trio *88*
Mass Observation 40, 100
maternity clothing 41–42, 71, 184, *184*
Mattli, Jo 53
Max Factor 113
men's clothing: austerity restrictions (Britain) 54–57, (France) 165; post-war 89, *89*; zoot suits 84–89
Metropolitan Museum of Art Costume Institute 62
Mexican prints and embroidery 15, *17*

Milgrim 63
military/patriotic influences 28, 33, 34, *35*, *60*, *73–81*, 133–34, *139*, *140*, 159–61, *163*
Millinery Stabilization Commission 59
Miranda, Carmen 100
Die Mode (magazine) 169–72
Modesalon (Berlin) *171*
Modes de Paris (magazine) *161*
Modes et Travaux (magazine) *143*, 165
Molyneux, Edward 32, 33, 45, 53, 143
Monteil, Germaine 61
Montgomery, Marjorie *185*
Montgomery, General Bernard: makes beret fashionable 51, *51*
Morton, Digby 45
Mosca, Bianca 45
Museum of Costume Art (New York) 62
Mussolini, Benito 11, 12, 17, 19

National Coat and Suit Industry Recovery Board 59
National Home Monthly (magazine) *107*, *110*, *114*
National Recovery Act 59
Nehrdich, Rolf-Werner *169*, *170*
Neiman Marcus (Dallas) 62, 63, 201
neoprene 111
Neue Moden (magazine) *93*, *174*
Neuer Modenspiegel (magazine) *12*
New Look 157, 191–97; home sewing and 131; modified to A-line and other adaptations *195*, 198–99; negative responses 195, 197
New York and fashion 59, 61–62, 67, 68, 83, 84, *109*, *193*; Lanz store in 13, *14*
New York Dress Institute *61*, 62
New York Times 59, 61, 62, 131
New York World's Fair 59, 109
New Yorker (magazine) 84
New Zealand 112, 139
Nobusuke, Kichi 134
nylon 109, *109*, 111, 181. *See also* parachute 'silk'

L'Officiel de la Couture et de la Mode de Paris (magazine) *144*, *150*, *156*, 159, *160*, 165, *188*, *194*
overalls 32

Pachuco culture 87, *87*
Panorama de la Mode (magazine) *12*
Paquin *101*, 148
parachute 'silk', wedding dresses 106
Paris: black markets 148, 152; collaboration 155–56; hairstyles

(1944) 120; *midinettes* defy Nazis 165–67; and New York 61; occupation couture 143–52, 153–56; post-occupation couture 152–53, 157; post-war fashions 157, 181, *183*, 188–98; pre-war fashions 23, 25–28, 32; silk stockings story 112; threat to Paris couture 144–45; Zazous 85. *See also* France
Paris et l'Élégance féminine (magazine) *166*, *194*
Pelletier de Chambure, Elisabeth (Lili) 153–55
Perlon 19
Perspex 111
Perugia, André 117
Pétain, Marshal Philippe 159, *160*
Le Petit Écho de la Mode (magazine) 165
Pickford, Mary *91*
Piguet, Robert *31*, 33, *101*, 131, *144*, 165
plastic *79*, *109*, *110*
Plexiglas 111
Plihal, L. *176*
polyester fibres 111
Pope, Virginia 62
Pour Elle (magazine) 164
prêt-à-porter 17, 83, 201
propaganda: American *69*, *70*, 172; German 172, 176
propaganda prints: housecoat *55*; Jacqmar *54–55*
pyjamas 32, 33

quality control, in Britain 42–53

rayon *14*, 17–18, *19*, *45*, *51*, 111; in America *75*, *109*, *184*, *197–99*; in Australia *139*; in Canada 92, *161*, *177*, *184*, *197–99*; in France *161*, 164–65; in Japan 134–37; stockings 111, 112
ready-to-wear (prêt-à-porter) 17, 83, 201
Réard, Louis 202
recycling 19. *See also* 'make do'
regional (folk) costume 12, 13–15
rhodophane 17
Ricci, Nina *155*, *194*
Riegel, Georg 21
Rochas, Marcel 155
Rooney, Mickey 83
Roosevelt, Eleanor 107
Roosevelt, Franklin D. 11, 15, 73, 95
Rosenstein, Nettie 61
'Rosie the Riveter' 92
Rouff, Maggy 32, 118, *144*, 155
rubber: shortages 67–68, 123, *202*
Rubinstein, Helena 95, 113, *113*
Russell, Peter 45
Saks Fifth Avenue (New York) 61–62
San Francisco Manufacturers' and Wholesalers' Association 186
Sarfatti, Margarita 17
scarves *54–55*, 159, *160*
Schiaparelli, Elsa 17–18, 25, 32, *32*, 34, *35*, 144, 152–53, 155, 163, *183*, 201; in America *62*, 63, *63*, 144, 151
Schuman, Adolph 186
Sears, Roebuck & Co. *122*
Settle, Alison 45
Seventeen (magazine) 83
Sherard, Michael 53
Shipp, Reginald 43
shoes: children's 42; with Cross of Lorraine motif *159*; espadrilles 118; by Ferragamo 114, *115*, 201; leather shortages and substitutes 109, 114–24, (in France) 163, (in Germany) 114–15, 117, (plastic) 111; (platform-soled) 114, 120, *121*, *122*, *125*; (wooden-soled) 115, *116–20*, 117–20, *124*, 161, 167
Signal (magazine) 144
Signoret, Simone 130
silk: in America 67, 109; in France *149*, *190*; in Germany 19; in Italy 18; in Japan *134–35*; military surplus *181*; parachute 'silk' 106; stockings 112
silk, artificial 106, *133*
Singer Sewing Machine Company 131
siren suits *30*, 31
slacks *see* trousers
snoods 97
Snow, Carmel 33, 61, 161, 167, 191, 192
Sorger, Irving 83
Southern California Apparel Cutters (SCAC) 185
Speer, Albert 95
sports and casual wear *26*, 62, 185, 188, 202, *203*, *203*
Stiebel, Victor 45, 53, 195
stockings: Aristoc 32; cotton 111–12; liquid 112–13; nylon 181; shortages 112; silk 112; synthetic materials 111
Suzy, Madame (millinery) *190*
Svéraz (magazine) *15*
swimwear 202, *203*, *203*
Swing, influence on youth styles 83–87
Swing Kids 85–87

teenage fashion *83*
Terylene 111
textile manufacturers *69*, *70*, *73*, 164. *See also* man-made materials
Textron *69*
Théâtre de la Mode 188–91, *191*
Thorpe, Jay 61, 63
Time (magazine): on fashion and clothing in America 61, 63, 78, 123, 185, 186, 198–99; on Paris fashions 59, 157
Todtenhaupt, casein-based fibre 18
Trachtenkleidung 12, 15
trousers: men's 84, 85, *86–89*, 89, 174; women's (slacks) 31–32, 72, 86, *92*, 112, 134, *136*, *137*, 176, 179, 185
turbans *see* hats
Trümmerfrauen (rubble women) 179
Turin 15

uniforms: couture industry and 33; Fascist youth movements 11; Japanese civilians 133–34; women's services 92, 94, *95*
United States: 'Bundles for Britain' *57*; garment/fashion industry (post-war) 184, *195*, 197–99; garment/fashion industry (wartime) 59–81; home sewing patterns 131; Lend-Lease 45, 137, 182; Limitation Orders 67–73, 78–79, 103, 124, 131, 157, 197–98; Make It Do campaign *127–28*, 131; and 'New Look' (adapted) *195*, 198–99, (opposition to) 197; platform-sole shoes 120, *124–25*; pre-war fashions 13, 15, *17*, *25*, *27*, *30*; shoe rationing 123–24; shortages of raw materials 109–11
Utility clothing 42–53, *48–50*, *52*, *53*, 120, 199

V for Victory *78*, *79–81*, *161*, 167
Valois, Rose *97*, *102*, *103*
Veneziani 188, *200*
'Victory' garments, Australia 138
vinyl rainwear 165
Vinylite *110*, 111
Vionnet, Madame 143, 144
Vogue (magazine): American *30*, *60*, 61, *63*, *66*, 67, 78, 92, 97, 156, *164*, 165, *165*, 185, 191, 195; British 32, 45, 49, 94, 103; French 13
Vogue Patterns 131
Votre Beauté (magazine) 165
Vramant, Madeleine *152*

War Production Board (WPB) 67, 87, 95, 111
War Resources Board *73*
weddings and wedding dresses 103–6, *104*, *105*, 107, *107*, *183*
Wertheimer brothers 155
Whalen, Grover 62
Windsor, Duke and Duchess of 15
Woman's Own (magazine) 94
Women's Voluntary Service (WVS) 37, 42, 124
woollen garments *50*, *195*
Woolworth's 42
Worth 45, *144*, *183*

youth subcultures 83–89

Zazous 85
zippers 17
zoot suits 84–89